W9-BXO-847

UP AGAINST THE FOURTH WALL

BOOKS BY JOHN LAHR

NOTES ON A COWARDLY LION

SHOWCASE 1: PLAYS FROM THE

EUGENE O'NEILL FOUNDATION (EDITOR)

UP AGAINST

THE
FOURTH WALL

ESSAYS ON
MODERN THEATER
BY JOHN LAHR
GROVE PRESS, INC.
NEW YORK

© 1970

The essays in this book originally appeared in *Evergreen Review*. "The Theater's Voluptuary Itch" is the expanded version of an article which first appeared in *London Magazine* under the title "Getting Laid on Broadway."

To
John Watts, Sam Edwards
and Fred Jordan
the editors who gave me a chance
And for Mildred, Jane and Anthea
the women who kept the faith

Fourth wall. Concept of the naturalistic theater, according to which the proscenium arch represents the fourth wall of the room in which the action takes place, removed for the benefit of the audience but without any of the performers taking cognizance of the fact.

Contents

ACKNOWLEDGMENTS

A critic will always have his enemies; but thank goodness for his friends. I am grateful to Susan Bloch and Helen Brown, assistant editors of *Evergreen Review,* for their careful readings of my essays; and to Alice Furland who typed this manuscript.

To my wife, Anthea, I owe the greatest debt. Enduring stage gunshots and late nights, she has shared the thrill and the boredom of nearly five hundred productions in the last three years. Many of the arguments in these essays have been crystallized through our conversations. Cheerleader, editor, indexer, confidante—she has believed in my approach to criticism and kept me at it.

J. L.
New York City
April 1970

UP AGAINST THE FOURTH WALL

1

The Theater's
Voluptuary Itch

*T*he body, so long the brunt of the Church's bad joke and society's damp palms, is being discovered on stage. And with it, sex has been ushered back with a realistic vigor, frothing from years of stilted asides and tightly trussed corsets. At a time when the Broadway spectacular has lost its tactile appeal, the exposed body—that most ancient and

impoverished prop—may bring yelps from the middle-class
audience, but it never sends them to sleep. Flesh is in the
air; and the voluptuary itch has seized the theatrical imagination. As one correspondent, sniffing the winds of change,
recently observed with galling feminine intuition:

> Lately, the Off-Off Broadway actors' involvement
> with the spectators has so intensified that one fully
> expects to get laid during the next evening at the
> theatre . . .[1]

The use of nudity on the American stage has always been
more interesting for its impulses than its erotic effect. The
American commercial theater continually evokes a nostalgia
for the flesh, cashing in on Eros while at the same time
avoiding it. The body on stage has become an image of
overwhelming repression, where good spirits gloss the ambivalent amalgam of sex, Puritan impulse, capitalism, and
potency in a unique American daydream. Even in Elizabethan society Ben Jonson chronicled the sexual energy with
which the masses took to the new materialism—a gargantuan image of lust, very similar to the ideal Florenz Ziegfeld would cater to in America, when we, like Elizabeth's
England, were finding an affluence and an energy new to our
history.

Sir Epicure Mammon's dream in Ben Jonson's *The Al-
chemist* has a lushness which paralleled Ziegfeld's:

> I will have all my beds blown up, not stuft:
> Down is too hard: and then, mine oval room
> Fill'd with such pictures as Tiberius took
> From Elephantis, and dull Aretine
> But coldly imitated. Then, my glasses
> Cut in more subtle angles, to disperse
> And multiply the figures, as I walk

> Naked between my succubae. My mists
> I'll have of perfume, vapour'd 'bout the room,
> To lose ourselves in: and my baths, like pits
> To fall into: from whence we will come forth,
> And roll us dry in gossamer and roses . . .

This is Ziegfeld's dream as well as Mammon's; and in the sexual imagery, and the velveteen vocabulary we see man's potency equated with material goods. Mammon, in fact, admits as much when he plans a seduction, saying, "Nay, we will *concubere* gold: I will be *puissant.*"

Flesh on stage not only threatens the society's sense of decorum but brings it back to the primal guilt of Adam and Eve which the Church has misconstrued from the teachings of Jesus. The flesh is always ensconced in artifice; the fig leaf never far from the mind's eye. As William Cole has pointed out in *Sex in Christianity and Psychoanalysis*:

> . . . The preponderance of theological opinion, in
> both Jewish and Christian circles, has interpreted
> the original sin as pride and rebellion against God.
> The Church's negative attitude toward sex has
> misled many into the belief that the Bible portrays
> man's fall as erotic in origin. Neither the Bible
> itself nor the history of Christian thought sub-
> stantiates such a belief. If there were any truth in
> it, Hebrew life would have been dominated by
> asceticism which it clearly was not. The evidence
> shows that the Old Testament is throughout
> naturalistic and positive in its attitudes toward
> sex, as in its view of the material world and man.
> It is this heritage which underlies the entire mes-
> sage of Jesus . . .[2]

No matter how voluptuous Ziegfeld's famous stable of women, their presentation was always larger than life. The

Ziegfeld spectaculars fed on a physical longing for the flesh and a Puritan fear of it. His women walked across the stage or stood still—alabaster statues to an ideal of Platonic purity. Ziegfeld, called "the Great Glorifier," paraded his women in money—feathers, sequins, pearls—and publicized the costs of the costumes. This profusion was his trademark—the lavish mixture of beauty and wealth kept sex at a distance from the audience's imagination while inspiring a voluptuary wonder. Ziegfeld catered to the masturbatory ideal the society condoned:

> They [women] must attract men. You cannot define that quality. In one word, I would say it was a promise: a promise of romance and excitement— all the things a man dreams about when he thinks of the word girl. "A pretty girl is like a melody that haunts you night and day"; that's it, that haunting quality . . .[3]

This "haunting quality" is a dream, not actuality—something in which man never moves from wish-fulfillment to reality or, indeed, acknowledges the fact of Eros, sexuality, in his *actual* life. The theater is playing to the audience's repressed libidinal instincts in the most outrageously cynical manner. Sex is exposed as fundamentally negative—titillating, but out of reach. As Norman O. Brown has pointed out in his important book, *Life Against Death:*

> . . . Negation is the primal act of repression; but it at the same time liberates the mind to think about the repressed under the general condition that it is denied and thus remains essentially repressed.[4]

The tactic is still making Broadway audiences salivate. *Golden Rainbow* (1968), starring Steve Lawrence and

Eydie Gormé, epitomizes this "meat-ball" mentality. The producers realized cynically that nightclub bravado and a good, almost-clean fun are not enough. As a result, the show boasts a second act production number as artless as a Keane painting—the most decadent, perverse, essentially humorless spectacle in Broadway's recent history. "Fall of Babylon" is a camp take-off on the Las Vegas lavishness intended to gild the eyes of the audience. It is a parody which turns in on itself, a mockery of the show's ambivalent intentions. Muscular Babylonians, oiled and dressed in gold, pole-vault on their spears; nudes are paraded (with pasties, of course) on stakes; a Steve Reeves surrogate enters with one leather pants leg and a whip. As a nude gyrates in front of him, the lash beats against the floor. There is a hothouse ballet, an interlude from the old Broadway revue formula, and finally Babylon burns, but not before the dancers are raised above the holocaust in a Botticelli seashell. The body, as an object, becomes the focus of an alluring evil. The women flaunt their dugs with artistic hauteur—wooden, artificial, and vaguely absurd.

The question of the body is raised not only in musical entertainment, but on Broadway's legitimate comedy stage. Robert Anderson's *You Know I Can't Hear You When the Water's Running* includes a one-act vignette in which an author tries to convince a producer and actor to play his scene in the raw. The play within a play, titled "Shock of Recognition," operates on the same dynamic of Puritan titillation, toying with the flesh but never actually believing in it. The language betrays the lie:

JACK: You're so damned prudish, you won't even call it by
      the right name . . . all these euphemisms . . . Equip-
      ment . . . Thing . . .
HERB: What would you like me to call it?
JACK: The technical word . . . the correct word . . . is penis.[5]

So that's what one calls it! Mr. Anderson's prissiness denies the life of the body as well as the vitality of the language. His situation, focusing on whether the actor will appear naked on stage, affirms a vision of the body in keeping with Anderson's puritanical impulse. The actor, Pawling, tries to sell himself and his physique for the role. When he drops his trousers, he admits:

> Well, I . . . It's embarrassing discussing this sort of thing, but . . . girls have sometimes . . . uh . . . laughed or giggled . . . at first. Of course, it's not the look that counts . . . Well I've been turned down for parts because I was too short or too tall . . . too fat or too thin . . . too young or too old. . . . But I never did or didn't get a part because of . . .

The final words of the play are the actor's, who calls back to the producer after exiting from the room:

PAWLING (*his voice is heard*): Hey, Mr. Miller, Look! (. . . HERB *dully motions* PAWLING *to go away, and barely gives a glance. Then suddenly he realizes what he's seen. His head jerks up, straight in front; then he does a slow turn to check out what he's seen.*)
PAWLING (*his voice*): I told you. . . Ridiculous!

The flesh is made pathetic; and in Anderson's facile, self-conscious manipulation of his characters, sex on stage loses not only its humor but its honesty. Emotion is as stifled as language; real life never finds its rhythm in the situation because neither the author nor his language are probing for truth.

Language which does not acknowledge the body cannot acknowledge life. Valéry once described human speech as

"the beautiful chains which entangle the distracted god in
the flesh . . ." Lenny Bruce's rebellion was not only against
societal conventions, but against an emasculated language
which hid Eros in its syntax. The linguistic hypocrisy has
its emotional correlative. Bruce slips into a mental monologue in his autobiography which illustrates his satiric obsession—one which Anderson and the middle-class society
have fed, yet rarely understood.

> (With drum and cymbal accompaniment)
> To is a preposition.
> To is a preposition.
> Come is a verb.
> To is a preposition.
> Come is a verb, the verb intransitive.
> To come.
> To come.[6]

In *You Know I Can't Hear You When the Water's Running,* the playwright justifies his decision for nudity by
exclaiming, "Damn it, Herb, it's about time the theater grew
up . . . We got to let some air in here someplace . . ." Anderson's playwright (like himself) is not interested in changing
the form, but in painting it over with fresher pigment. The
playwright is speaking from a "grown-up" position, nervous
about tampering with civilized sentiment. This is exactly the
reverse of what has been happening in America's experimental theater. The instincts for ritual, the demand to
move away from the text and approach content through
improvisation, are attempts to define a special territory for
the stage which no other medium can provide. The emphasis
on stage "magic" and the physical transformation of the
body focus on an intentional "childishness," a "playfulness"
which brings the stage back to its primitive, mythic origins.
Esthetically, the justification for such an approach is not,

as Anderson's playwright maintains, to "let the audiences recognize their own lives," but to free the actor and audience from the repressive decorum of the stage. Theater, then, becomes a liberator. As Norman O. Brown has maintained:

> Art, if its object is to undo repressions, and if civilization is essentially repressive, is in a sense subversive of civilization. Some of Freud's formulations on the role of the indispensable third person suggest that the function of art is to form a subversive group, the opposite of that authoritarian group the structure of which Freud analyzed in *Group Psychology and the Analysis of the Ego.* The indispensable third person must be suffering from the same repression as the creative artist. The relation between the artist and the third person is one of identification and identification is the relation which, according to *Group Psychology,* binds together the members of an authoritarian group. In contrast with the repressive structure of the authoritarian group, the aim of the partnership between the artist and the audience is instinctual liberation . . .[7]

Many Off-Broadway playwrights are trying to face this repression, understanding where they must go, yet curiously unable to get beyond the middle-class inhibitions behind their rebellion. In an interesting adaptation by the Performance Group of Euripides' *The Bacchae* entitled *Dionysus in 69,* men from the audience are coaxed into the festival. They smile nervously at the anticipation of being felt up in a flesh pile. They are smothered in touch; but the performers judiciously avoid their genitalia, giving each a rubdown which never comes to the point. *Dionysus in 69,* which wants to examine the politics of ecstasy, must first conjure it before going beyond it. This never quite happens. The men, at first nervous, strain finally to watch what is happening behind their prone bodies, and are less interested in a dry run than the drama.

One of Leonard Melfi's one-act plays, *Jack and Jill*, puts adult bodies (and a Puritan self-consciousness) in a child's playground and has his two characters talking about "dumb, stupid orgies" and later comparing their genitalia: "I'm scared, Jack. Doesn't your thing have to be in the air? (Oh, God, I'm so embarrassed.)"[8] The artificiality and smallness of the play comes from the author's inability to control his own self hatred. Even in Rochelle Owens's *Istanboul,* containing a passionate love scene in which a man's pants are gradually pulled to his ankles and the woman is nude beside him, the play cannot be honest to the lusty ideal it wants to convey. The actress nervously reaches for more sheet to cover herself as soon as the spotlight is off her.

Liberation of the body is not merely a reflex of the times: it has its responsibilities. Badly used, it can become a servitude. The theater wants to get back to the kind of intense, libidinal pleasure of childhood play; but often lacks that spontaneity. If Melfi's play evokes a physical guilt, *Gizmo: A Play to Evoke Your Suicide* by Daffi shows sex turned to puerile aggression. In this irrelevant theater piece, the main performers (the male dressed in posing jock; the woman in a loin cloth) go through a series of clumsy but carefully culled positions from the *Kama Sutra*. The momentum of sexual energy is intended to reach out to the audience. The actor moved to the attractive girl sitting next to me and pulled her arm, hoping that the incantations and thrust of the play would suck her into the vortex of the flesh pile. She resisted vociferously. Anguished, the actor whispered, "C'mon, I've only got three minutes." The synthetic orgy took place without her, reinforcing in its careful choreography the very concepts it ostensibly wanted to liberate.

Christmas Turkey, by Ed Wode, wove a story of tribal cultishness around an actress who sat fully exposed on the stage for the evening. The "success" of the piece (it even received coverage in English papers) was its exhibitionist's impulse; the body became the brunt of a bad joke. Ultimately, the body—no matter in what shape or condition— contains a primal curiosity. Stripped of its outer cover, the human form may lose its erotic overtones or may seem essentially unattractive. Nevertheless, it can fill a stage when acting or intelligence fail. That is its visceral appeal; and the most obvious area of misuse. In *Scuba Duba,* the hollowness and fundamental lackluster of Bruce Jay Friedman's intention is glossed by an attempt at outrageousness, food for fodder instead of insight. At one point, a Cockney tart walks down a staircase with her large breasts, like cow pies, lopped over her corset. Not ugly, not pornographic, not even shocking. An image which, like the play, is the urgent, sloppy, rather sad gesture of a comic writer at a loss for words.

In experimenting with the body, many of the writers and actors interested in its potential have forgotten the dimension of humor certainly necessary for an environment of acceptance. As Norman O. Brown observes:

> Art gives us this positive pleasure in so far as it attains that goal which must always remain the goal of humanity—conscious play. Freud has seen that the category of conscious play gives the final distinction between dreams and neurosis and art; the dream is always a wish, but wit is actualized play . . .[9]

Without showing the body, Harold Pinter has created not only the atmosphere of repression which keeps it cloaked, but the unexpressed desires which filter through a screen of language. He has captured with humor the *game* of sexual struggle. When Lenny tries to overwhelm Ruth with fantasies of sexual strength in *The Homecoming,* she beats him at his own rhetoric. A glass of water takes on phallic proportions and immensely erotic (but not titillating) force:

RUTH: Have a sip. Go on. Have a sip from my glass. *(He is still.)* Sit on my lap. Take a long cool sip. *(She pats her lap. Pause. She stands, moves to him with the glass.)*
LENNY: Take that glass away from me.
RUTH: Lie on the floor. Go on. I'll pour it down your throat.[10]

Pinter's characters languish in a primordial vulnerability —violent and fearful, lusting and impotent. The body is an alien object to be toyed with, remembered, and furtively embraced. On the other hand, Michael McClure's *The Beard* attempted to gorge a new, more physical consciousness, a Platonic tidbit. In McClure's heaven, the body becomes a sweaty feast, not a denial. His attitude is at the other end of the sexual spectrum from Pinter's. He brings to it, not Frank Harris's black bag, but rather a saving wit which breaks down repression:

> . . . (the theater) should bring an audience either a thought or feeling, or a sense of beauty, or stimulate the imagination and remind them of their essential quality as mammals, or awaken the realization of Blake that "the body is the descent of soul into matter," or simply invoke a sense of wonder at being alive . . .[11]

In *The Beard,* Jean Harlow and Billy the Kid sniff around each other in an elaborate ballet of lust. In heaven as on earth, these folk heroes disport themselves like sailors on leave. Combined, they have the speaking vocabulary of a parakeet. This is not Dante's Christian heaven, but a meatier one. At the end of the play, Harlow mimes ecstasy as Billy moves his head beneath her skirt. The galaxies spin around her. A woman near me mumbled in disbelief—"He's getting down on her. Look, George!" The celestial seduction ends with Handel's "Hallelujah Chorus" and McClure makes his point about the body and soul with a theological guffaw. Sexual freedom is played against the Christian Muzak, the same ideology which forced Saint Augustine to speak of marriage as "medicine for immorality." McClure's description of the play ("I see [it] as a poem in meat on a shelf in space.") may seem preposterous or mystical; but it is not without its pertinence to those who would demand of art that it embody a life-style, struggling against societal repression, bringing man in maturity to an acceptance of the libidinal peace of childhood.

Dionysus in 69 is the first American theater event to take as its theme the new self-consciousness toward the body and the unshackling of the sexual instinct. The actors in *Dionysus* are trained to a heightened, acrobatic concept of performance. The males stripped to a jock strap; the females in brief body tunics (sometimes nude) move through a series of carefully disciplined images. The theater, conceived by the controversial former editor of *The Drama Review*, Richard Schechner, is best when it is vivid and simple. Men lie prone on the floor while the women straddle them, fixing their legs tight between groins. Bodies pass under legs and bare backs squirm in a tortuous rebirth. At the conclusion of the event, the men are slaughtered, lying like flayed beef, in textures of flesh. The audience, too, is conditioned to new emotions by an environmental stage, a series of three-tiered constructions allowing the audience to watch the performance from a variety of perspectives. They can climb, or hide, or walk about. It creates a unique *childlike* feeling, a jungle-gym of challenge and adventure which is enhanced by the fact that each member of the audience must enter the theater alone, summoning both courage and trust in an alien environment, moving like Alice through a wonderland of new gestures and sounds. By making the theatrical experience a physical adventure, Schechner's Performance Group wants to expand the audience's understanding of liberty. Schechner has maintained:

> Liberty can be swiftly transformed into its opposite, and not only by those who have a stake in reactionary government. Ritualized experience without the built-in control of a strong social system—an Asmat society or an Orokolo society —can pump itself up into a destructive fury . . . Are we ready for the liberty we have grasped? Can we cope with Dionysus's dance and not end up—as Agave did—with our sons' heads on our dancing sticks?[12]

Schechner's theater piece raises the question but does not answer it. His contemporary Dionysus is carried literally out of the theater by his followers, campaigning for allegiance under the banner of emotional totality: "I promise you nothing except joy, violence, blood, all the feelings in you," says Dionysus. Schechner's theater piece points out the paradox that experimental theater has yet to solve: the analytic impulse of adulthood may seek solace in childishness but cannot recover the innocence of pure response.

A most successful integration of the body and the stage was Paul Foster's *Tom Paine,* brilliantly directed by Tom O'Horgan. This improvisational play set out to expand the boundaries of the stage, providing not only a variety of

dense stage images but also demanding a wider range of
emotional responses from the audience. In a dream se-
quence, Paine is overwhelmed by sexual reverie. The La
Mama Troupe swirls around him, nude behind chiffon nets.
The effect is lyric and sensual; the body brings a sense of
variety to the audience without bludgeoning it into recognition. O'Horgan uses the flesh as a forceful pigment on a
large canvas. In Rochelle Owens's *Futz,* he conveys incest
and innocence by having a man suckled at the breast of an
actress. The naturalness of both effects attests to the success of the productions in which the mind expands with the
stage experience, instead of contracting into self-consciousness. The La Mama Troupe, like the Open Theater, is
evolving a stage experience which is also a life-style. Stage
movement approaches a more organic, total sense of the
actor—trusting, tactile, interdependent—where bodies
move together, combining and subtracting ideas which are
beyond speech. The acceptance of the body, the demand to
make it felt and touched is a communal ideal and obviously
a political one. This is not only a radical break with stage
traditions, but also a break with traditional patterns of
societal relationships. In *The Concept,* a play improvised by
ex-drug addicts, the addict-actors come out to the audience
at the finale asking to be embraced. People leave their seats
and hug these outcasts who have screamed their anguish
and their hopes in this psychodrama. At the moment of
embrace, the play ceases to become artifice and merges into
life, breaking through stereotypes and bigotry. All these
productions aspire to a new style which acknowledges the
salvation of the body. As Camus has pointed out in *The
Rebel:*

> . . . stylization . . . supposes the simultaneous
> existence of reality and of the mind that gives

reality its form. Through style, the creative effort
reconstructs the world, and always with the same
slight distortion that is the mark of both art and
protest . . .[13]

The "group grope" not only wants to affirm the body,
but relax the performer (and audience) into a fuller sense of
identity in which the senses are activated by new use, instead of dulled by conventional response. The experiments
at the Esalen Institute at Big Sur, discussed at length in
William C. Schutz's provocative *Joy*,[14] parallel the instincts
and ideas of these seminal theater experiments. The effect
of free-form theatrical experience is to change the dimension
of the theater from what was once public and popular to
something private and individual. The theater, no longer
the art form of the masses, can set about developing its one
incontrovertible asset—immediacy.

At a benefit in 1968 for the Open Theater, their rendition
of "Wild Mountain Thyme" brought the audience from their
seats on to the stage. They danced with the actors in a
genuine euphoria—simple, easy, but undeniably moving.
What these theatrical experiments must tread is the difficult
bridge between group therapy and artistic statement. They
run the risk of becoming too insular, of creating an experience where the audience combines with performers in a
precious womb of passive acceptance, where the body never
confronts a fresh and difficult reality. If it becomes too literal,
this experimentation could bear out Camus's dictum that
"when stylization is exaggerated and obvious the work becomes nothing but pure nostalgia."[15] At the same time, unleashing the body to find new rhythms and a new sense of
itself could make the theater viewers part of an important
quest in which the stage art and its audience reestablish a
primeval bond long lost, a fellowship moving toward in-
stinctual liberation.

2

The Adaptable
Mr. Albee

*Well, perhaps we had better
examine the differences between
good and bad writers. Good writers define reality; bad ones merely
restate it. A good writer turns
fact into truth; a bad writer, more
often than not, accomplishes the
opposite. A good writer writes
what he believes to be true; a bad
writer puts down what be believes
his readers believe to be true. The
good writer believes the intellectual and moral responsibility of
his audience to be equal to his
own; the bad writer considers the
opposite posture proper . . .*[1]

—Edward Albee

*I*s it possible for intellectual dishonesty to masquerade as the creative act? The spectacle of Edward Albee's
dilapidated Muse is an interesting case in point. Having
been crowned early in his career with the poet's laurels,
Albee is constrained to speak with a significance that eludes
his talent. He sees evil but cannot fathom it; he speaks out

for honesty in plays which are dishonest at their core. Albee's adaptations, for which he claims much more credit than the critics allow, are indicative of the playwright in transition, groping for a point of view and, sadly, an easy acceptance.

Adaptation is a difficult art, and no one could fault Albee for turning his hand to it. He has produced three adaptations: *The Ballad of the Sad Café* (1963), from the novella by Carson McCullers; *Malcolm* (1966), from the novel by James Purdy; and *Everything in the Garden* (1967), from the play by Giles Cooper. Albee has defended adaptations from his catbird seat as America's Working Playwright:

> . . . I would agree that the majority of adaptations which arrive on our stages, be they adaptations of novels or European plays, are worthless, either through ineptitude or distortion, but it would be negligent to forget that much of the work of such pretty fair playwrights as Sophocles, Shakespeare, Racine, Giraudoux, and Anouilh has been adaptation.
>
> No, the trouble with most of the stage adaptations we get in New York these years is that they are works either of professionals who are hacks or learned men who are not theater professionals . . .
>
> Adaptation can be a perfectly respectable occupation and more important, a valid artistic act. And naturally, no self-respecting playwright would, unless the roof were falling in on him and his, set about to adapt anything which (1) he did not respect as a work of art, and (2) which he did not feel to be in line with his own aesthetic.
>
> The responsibility of the playwright is double— to the work adapted and to the stage as an art form. He must sometimes alter a work radically, so that no change will seem to have taken place

when it is moved from the page to the stage. He
must make a work belong between curtains as
much as it ever did between covers . . .[2]

What Albee says is true enough. But in putting his en-
deavor among the legitimate adaptations of Shakespeare,
Sophocles, *et al.,* he plays a curious sleight of hand on both
his audience and himself. Those artists imposed a vision on
old tales. The stories they adapted were catalysts for their
imaginations, not simply ends in themselves. In a creative
adaptation, the original text is the playwright's point of departure. The process can be educational and constructive,
allowing the playwright to solidify his language and ideas
around a pre-established framework. Albee's succession of
plays, however, has shown no development and even less
sense of craft. Albee's ability to mount these plays on Broadway attests to Dorothy Parker's dictum about America's
neurotic gauge of talent: "It is our national joy to mistake
for the first-rate, the fecund rate."

Albee's most successful adaptation, *The Ballad of the
Sad Café,* offers in its ballad genre a form which glosses his
inability to structure a play on anything but the most ele-
mental skeleton, drawing his force from yoking together
obvious dramatic encounters. As a "ballad," the play can be
effective while being simple, sentimental, and undramatic.
The tale recounts the sadness of Miss Amelia Evans, a tough
backwoods bootlegger, who turns her house into a café,
when her cousin, Lymon, a hunchbacked dwarf, appears
and befriends her. Miss Amelia shares her life with Cousin
Lymon, who poses no sexual threat and offers a comfortable companionship. She does not tell him of her first marriage to a reformed town hellion, Marvin Macy, how she
rebuffed him on their wedding night, and finally drove him
from her house and back to a world of crime. Her happiness

is shattered when Marvin, out of the penitentiary, returns
for his revenge. He does ritual battle with Amelia and leaves
with her cousin, wrecking her small community and leaving
her alone in private humiliation. Whatever touching moments there are, whatever glimmer of humor slips through
the pontifical sadness, the Narrator in the play stifles any
drama or metaphoric qualities. The tale is never allowed to
be more than itself. The ritual dance accompanying the
ballad is explained artlessly in its stage use.

> Oh, but Henry Macy was wrong, for Marvin did
> not move on. He stayed in the town and every
> night the café was open he would arrive for dinner
> . . . and bring his liquor for which he never paid
> a cent. And during these nights, which stretched
> into weeks, Miss Amelia did nothing. She did
> nothing at all, except to stand to one side and
> watch . . . Once every night, sometimes for no
> reason at all . . . Miss Amelia and Marvin Macy
> would approach each other, their fists clenched,
> and they would circle one another, and it was
> during these rituals that the townspeople expected
> blows to be struck . . . but it never happened . . .
> One night, though, nearly three months after
> Marvin Macy returned to town, there occurred an
> event which set the sure course to calamity . . .[3]

In this play, narrative never gives way to drama; but
here, as in no other Albee adaptation, the literary quality
is acceptable. There is a place in the theater for the lyric
potential of the ballad but its limitations are embodied in its
form—a miniature, an epiphany of sadness or a moment
of light, a vision never larger than the contents of its story.

Ballad tries to confront themes which Albee never quite
faces in his other plays. Where *Who's Afraid of Virginia*

Woolf? was a game of sexual domination, Albee has sought a clearer image of human cannibalism, a neurotic obsession which he has, as yet, not been able to channel into art. In *Ballad*, Miss Amelia brutalizes Marvin Macy, finally to be pulverized by him.

Purdy's *Malcolm* chronicles the adventures of an innocent preyed upon by society's vultures, who try to swallow him whole, ultimately glutting him with their flesh: Malcolm is screwed to death. In the same way, *Everything in the Garden* appeals to Albee because it offers a stage image of the affluent outsider (Jack) made a sacrificial victim by a guilt-ridden society. He is murdered on stage. Behind this fascination with cannibalism is a homosexual impulse which Albee tries to keep muted in his plays and which accounts for much of their hollowness. Cousin Lymon's interest in Marvin Macy is apparent in his reactions toward criminals:

MISS AMELIA: A bunch of common criminals, chained together by the ankle, workin' on the roads in the broilin' sun, a guard standin' over 'em with a gun.

COUSIN LYMON: Yes! Yes! Yes! Amelia!

MISS AMELIA: Cousin Lymon . . . they common criminals, they . . . they got no freedom.

COUSIN LYMON (*pleading*): I know Amelia . . . but they *together* . . .

MISS AMELIA: An' . . . an' we got a good life together.

COUSIN LYMON: Oh, yes, of course, Amelia. (*The ecstasy returns.*) An' they are together, those men . . . An' how they *sing*. Amelia! You hear them sing, Amelia? . . .

Malcolm's passivity, which betrays him to a variety of vipers, rarely confronts the homosexual innuendo so hilarious and threatening in Purdy's fable. Albee concentrates instead on a sentimental vision of Malcolm's aimless, "fatherless" condition. Albee seems convinced that Malcolm is an orphan, where Purdy never allows his reader the certainty of any identity. Sentimentality necessarily distorts reality, never confronting life with a clear focus. (*Everything in the Garden* loses its grip on the real world because it is constipated with a feminine loathing which will not admit its origins. The women in this suburban tale of prostitution are depicted not merely as threats but as the embodiment of psychological and spiritual castration.)

Albee's peckish attitude toward critics skirts the issue of his theatrical craft: "With James Purdy's book, I have wandered further in specifics than I did with McCullers', but I have come back as far . . ."[4] Defending himself against all contingencies, Albee overlooks the text. The failure of *Malcolm* on stage was not that Albee had attempted the outrageous, but that he had plumbed for too little, unsettling the episodic situations of the novel and dialogue already richly dramatic in Purdy's dead-pan style. What happened with *Malcolm* is precisely the watered-down metamorphosis Albee sees in other plays, but not his own. As he told the *Paris Review:* "I've seen an awful lot of plays that I'd read before they were put into production and been shocked by what happened to them. In the attempt to make them straightforward and commercially successful, a lot of things had to go out the window."[5] *Malcolm,* a fable whose humor and insight thrives on a murky ambiguity, cannot be transformed by Albee into its stage correlative, quite simply because Albee is not at home with complexity or nuance. The evil which Purdy seeks to define in Malcolm's peregrinations is a cool one—unstated, omnivorous, a trap lurking behind every smile and benevolent touch of the people whose "addresses" he visits. Purdy's triumph is one of comic style which transcends the simple event. He is inventive, creating a fable from language at once objective and concrete. This gives the tale its density and control. Albee's adaptation appreciates the quality of Purdy's effort and his vision, but lacks the verbal control which comes from an all-encompassing vision of Malcolm's relation to the world. Albee responds to what he believes intellectually to be the case, but what he cannot feel.

Malcolm is introduced to the world by Mr. Cox, a man he meets one day while waiting on a park bench, the only spot which holds Malcolm to the geography of the world. Purdy's dialogue is filled with sexual innuendo and an ironic tone which create richness on the page.

> "There's only one thing for you to do now," the astrologer exclaimed. "Give yourself up to things!"
>
> "Give myself up to . . . things?" and he got clear up this time from the bench and one could see that Malcolm was neither tall nor short for his age, but looked as if he had always been this height and would continue to be.
>
> Mr. Cox was also rather surprised to see how strong Malcolm looked physically in comparison with the somewhat weaker development of his mental powers.
>
> "Please be seated at once," Mr. Cox commanded.
>
> Malcolm sat down.
>
> "The whole crux of the matter," Mr. Cox continued, "is your father gave you all he had including his undying affection, I gather, and what have you done with such *largesse?*
>
> "*Largesse?*" Malcolm wondered.
>
> "I thought you knew French," Mr. Cox assailed him. "*Largesse* is the horn of plenty; it's *everything.*"[6]

In putting the same situation on the stage, Albee strips away everything but the most serviceable plot points.

MALCOLM: But, what is there to do?

MR. COX: You must . . . give yourself up to things.

MALCOLM (*rises, a little apprehensive*): Give myself up to
. . . things?

MR. COX (*stern*): Be seated; at once. (*Malcolm sits.*) The crux of the matter is, your father gave you all that he had, including his undying affection, I gather, but what have you *done?*[7]

Malcolm becomes the emotional crutch for each person he encounters on his visits. Madame Girard Girard, one of the "addresses," is bound to him with a passionate devotion. Malcolm finds both her and her husband appealing. When Girard Girard informs his wife that he is going to divorce her, Madame Girard realizes that she will lose his famous, wealthy name. Purdy's evocation of the scene is economical and hilarious—a perspective which is a triumph of style counterpointing vision.

> Suddenly she kissed his shoes.
> "Leave me with what I was," she begged. "Leave me *Madame Girard.*"
> She saw the shoes withdraw from her embrace, and a moment later she heard the closing of the massive outside door.

The sense of outrageousness conveyed by the style is transformed by Albee into a much more literal make-believe situation, where the tension between the concrete and the surreal is lost. Madame Girard confronts her husband's voice, like Dorothy at the Emerald City:

MADAME GIRARD: When I gave you your victory, Girard
    Girard? The night I surrendered myself to your bland-
    ishments and agreed to become your wife.
GIRARD GIRARD'S VOICE: That very night.
MADAME GIRARD: I recall it. I gave up . . . everything, my
    life, in return for but one thing, which I now cherish:
    my name—Madame Girard.
GIRARD GIRARD'S VOICE: It is that which I propose to take
    from you now.
MADAME GIRARD: I do not think . . . I hear you well . . .
    Girard! Girard! The Name!! The NAME IS MINE!!
GIRARD GIRARD'S VOICE: No longer, my dear. You are his-
    tory. (*Lights out on Mme. Girard.*)
MADAME GIRARD'S VOICE: GIRARD GIRARD!! GIRARD
    GIRARD!!

Albee is caught between styles, attempting to incorporate
Purdy's careful, formal diction into a situation no longer
subtle enough for that language, and mixed with his own
fustian additions. Malcolm falls into the voluptuary clutches
of Melba, a pop singer, and finally dies of sexual exhaustion
and drink, debauched by the world. Where Purdy does not
allow Malcolm's death to be either certain or to ripple the
surface of evil, Albee tacks on a facile conclusion which
explains a situation and an experience more elusive than his
imagination can encompass. On this stage deathbed, Malcolm speaks words never uttered in the novel:

MALCOLM (*lying back, a little delirious*): I've . . . lost so
    much, I've . . . lost so very much. (*Madame Girard
    gets up, moves a little away, doesn't look at Malcolm.*)
    And . . . everyone has . . . swept by . . . Kermit and,
    and Girard Girard . . . (*Madame Girard stiffens a
    little.*) . . . even Mr. Cox, and . . . I've lost Madame
    Girard . . . (*She thinks to speak; does not.*) . . . and . . .
    my father . . . my FATHER! . . . What . . . (*softly*)
    what have I not lost?

In Purdy's novel, Malcolm's last breath, his final moments of life, are ironically missed by Madame Girard who sits by him.

> Returning to Malcolm's bed, she put her hand to his cheek.
> "Prince!" she called out, feeling the iciness of his flesh.
> She had missed, she saw immediately, his last single minute: Malcolm's short long life was at an end.

Through the density of fact, Purdy leaves the experience uncertain.

> . . . The florists of the town discussed Madame Girard's funeral expenditures for years to come. She had, for instance, ordered—even if she perhaps did not quite get—a quarter ton of roses, and an equal amount of violets, so that Malcolm's last hours above earth were passed in a green house of sweetness and foliage . . . The only flaw in the ceremony was the repeated insistence of the local coroner and the undertaker—later they were both silenced, it is said, by money—that there had been no corpse at all, and that nobody was buried in the ceremony . . .

Albee, however, concludes with a vision which seems impossible for anyone who has read the book with a critical appreciation of its content and style. Madame Girard is talking to her husband about Malcolm's portrait. As she speaks, gradually fading into a voice, all those objects from his past, like the park bench on which he sat awaiting his "addresses," appear before the audience. The question of his identity is raised with an artless insistence:

MADAME GIRARD: You . . . you can come and see this portrait . . . if you care. (*Subdued, sad.*) It is . . . not much.
But . . . it will have to do. That's all that's left. Just
that. Nothing more.

*The golden bench, center, raised, begins to glow. As
it brightens, Madame Girard goes to darkness. The
golden bench is bathed in golden light.*

MALCOLM'S VOICE (*a trusting boy, a little scared*): Father?
MADAME GIRARD'S VOICE: Just that.
MALCOLM'S VOICE: Father?
MADAME GIRARD'S VOICE: Nothing more.
MALCOLM'S VOICE: Father?
Silence. The golden bench slowly fades into darkness.

Albee's lack of critical ability, his failure to focus on the
core of the novel are the reasons for the failure of the stage
adaptation. His sentimental instincts reflect his helplessness
in confronting so complex a theme with hard-headed perception. He is guilty of the same kind of literalness he
criticizes in others, settling for an exterior drama without
the interior density of poetry. It is precisely because Albee
is not a poet that he is forced to rely on a technical bag of
tricks, as neat as they are unsatisfying.

Perhaps the most outrageous example of this failure,
hinted at in the first two adaptations, is *Everything in the
Garden*. Albee has said, "The good writer creates his
audience and the bad writer creates himself out of the whole
cloth of his view of himself as perpetuator of the intellectual
status quo."[8] The words are prophetic; and Albee's *Everything in the Garden* is the work of an artist creating in a
vacuum, cut off from society and lacking a healthy sense of
himself. Albee's adaptation is a work of poverty or arrogance—or both. Albee's statements about the play illustrate

how his pride pushes him into artistic corners from which the only escape is easy popularity.

> ... Then something happened, and by the time I was finished with my work there was hardly a word left to the original. This was neither madness nor immodesty on my part but merely that Cooper's play became a catalyst and set me working my variations on his theme.[9]

Albee has taken Cooper's caustic play about the consequences of the suburban pipe dream and turned it into a synthetic pageant of decadence. While every playwright must have his failures, such blatant prostitution of Cooper's talent reduces Albee in a gesture from one of America's significant writers to a strolling player, a mere journeyman selling what he can while there is still a market. In both versions the wife becomes a high-class prostitute to supplement the family income. Albee's version is itself a reminder that prostitution is not limited to bored suburban housewives.

Albee, despite his disclaimers, adds almost nothing to the content of Cooper's work. What he has changed is an interesting indication of his imagination and ambiguous intentions. He moves through most of Cooper's plot points with cat-like tread; the lines which he claims are *his* coinage are too frequently dredged from the original, the big laughs turn out to be Cooper's, and, most important, Albee's sense of the antiseptic bestiality in middle-class life is a tepid imitation of Cooper's less sentimental, more deeply felt work.

Everything in the Garden (the American version) becomes a finger exercise in which the playwright adds nothing to his craft, relying on an agility often mistaken for genius. Albee has made adaptations of two major characters. Both plays contain a bachelor neighbor, Jack, and both introduce the Madame into the machinations. In Albee's version, Mrs. Toothe, who keeps no lists of her stable, is just a wooden cog in the plot. She tempts Jenny, model housewife, with an embossed card and a wad of bills (£50 in the English version; $1,000 to satisfy Broadway fantasies). Albee's Madame exudes no strength, only a cool hardness. She has her philosophy, a kind of Pollyanna Polly Adler. Albee's change is not in name alone. In the English version, the Madame is a Polish Jew; in the American reading, she's bland English. Why the change? In eliminating her uncomfortable ethnic identity, he does not offend his Westchester audience. He pleases easily, but never clarifies the Madame's motivation or the question of human value at the heart of the play. In Cooper's version, the Madame justifies her licentiousness with a philosophical materialism:

> You think all this lasts forever, and it lasts for you? I tell you something. This house, it don't know you're here, nothing knows about you, nothing cares; what you do is up to you. Once there was a time when I thought the way you think now, but I am Polish. I was in a camp at your age.[10]

Albee takes only one of the lines Cooper puts in the mouth of his Madame, "nothing is disgusting unless you are disgusted." He whitewashes the character to fit a more fastidious American public.

The Madame has adapted, as Jenny and her reptilian friends will make their silent compromises. There is a poetry and a tightness of argument in Cooper's language which Albee breaks down but never bothers to reassemble.

Albee's other addition is equally destructive to both Cooper's intentions and his own. Jack, who discovers Jenny's

little pastime at a cocktail party among suburban friends
who are also in the flesh game and is killed by the group,
becomes an extension of the Albee Fool—fast-talking, glib,
insinuating. Like Claire (clairvoyant) in *A Delicate Balance,* he is a pointer, and his spirit appears in Albee's
original version to speak the play's moral with such ho-hum
prose that even Hamlet's ghost would pale. However, Albee
has had as much difficulty with his ending as Cooper did in
eliminating the heavy-handed conclusion. Jack cajoles the
audience but stops the play's momentum. Where Cooper
presents an experience which twists with surprises as hap-
hazard as life, Albee settles for a tour de force, allowing
Jack a clarity which life never offers, and turns a comic
drama into a melodrama as mechanical as situation comedy:

> Now look at Richard there . . . He's alive.
> Struggles, raises a family. Oh, by the way, I did
> what I said I was going to do. Remember? Re-
> member what I told you? (*Nods.*) I made my will
> . . . and left the whole kaboodle to Jenny and
> Richard . . .[11]

The voice is lipsmacking and wooden; its insertion over-
simplifies the experience on the stage. This is not a ballad,
drawing its strength from fable, but drama, nurtured on
Cooper's sense of treacherous life.

Where Cooper's play evokes the boredom which counterpoints suburban longing, Albee opts for a quasi-sociological
analysis of the country club set. Albee himself has articu-
lated this flaw in others:

> . . . Are creative writers making society rather
> than man himself their subject, leaning too heav-
> ily on the social sciences and psychology? Can we
> make use of the facts—the ingredients of truth—
> without becoming their public servants? . . .[12]

His own play is too much on the surface not to tell all. Says Richard, whose wife will soon find a way of making ends meet: "You live in a forty-thousand-dollar house, and you have to smoke bad cigarettes to get the coupon so you can afford a good vacuum so you can clean it . . ." The terrain is too familiar, and Albee never gets further than a line-up of social offenders. They are as transparent and lifeless as a poolside canasta foursome.

In Cooper's play, it is Jenny who demands that Jack's discovery be silenced with death. In Albee's version, the group handles the killing, smothering him with language which works faster than the actors on stage. ("Don't bother, he's dead!" "What do you mean he's dead?") Albee's play cannot absorb the contradiction implicit in such an act, because it does not thrive on complexity. Cooper is questioning the very nature of conformity. Albee is simply chronicling it. Where Cooper is hardheaded, Albee is strangely sentimental. Mrs. Toothe observes: "The grass will grow over; the earth will be rich and soon—eventually, everything in the garden—will be as it was." How different from Cooper's Madame with her perverse integrity:

> . . . You must forget if you want to live . . . We all
> must live in the way we want to live, and forget
> what does not help us so to do. This you know.
> You are men of family and education . . .

In the end, Richard, like his wife, conforms to the pattern; both are unwitting pawns to the logical conclusions of their gilt dreams. They set up a bordello in the suburbs when the police in the city make work difficult.

There are moments of genuine humor in *Everything in the Garden*. The audience laughs loudest when Richard receives the first parcel of money from an apparently anonymous donor. But the laughs and much of the language are too close to Cooper not to be more fully acknowledged. Here is Cooper:

BERNARD (*baffled*): Money!
JENNY: Money?
BERNARD: Notes. Look.
JENNY: How much?
BERNARD: It's incredible. (*He starts to count.*) One . . . etc. . . . One-hundred and ninety-eight pounds.
JENNY: Not two hundred?

Here is Albee:

RICHARD: Jenny, it's money. It's a great deal of money.
JENNY: Well, for . . . for heaven's sake.
RICHARD: Jenny, it's . . . hundred dollar bills. It's all hundred dollar bills.
JENNY: Well . . . how much? How much is there?
RICHARD (*counting*): One . . . etc. . . . eight.
JENNY: How . . . how incredible. Hundred dollar bills.
RICHARD: . . . Forty-five . . . etc. . . . forty-nine.
JENNY: Forty-nine?
RICHARD: Jenny, there's almost five thousand dollars here. Four thousand nine hundred dollars. Jenny! Four thousand nine hundred dollars!
JENNY: Well, that's incredible! Not five thousand?

Albee claims he has changed nearly every word, but grafting nouns and adjectives does not make an original work. His jokes are rarely as good as Cooper's because he overwrites them, the emotional overtones are muted to a shallower soul. He will no doubt be prepared to argue that he has written his own play, not Cooper's, and that comparison is fatuous. But this is merely the blur of rhetoric for he has not really written a play at all.

Albee's strutting dignity is too often mistaken for significance. His adaptations, however, illustrate that his instincts are not so much that of the artist as the entertainer. There is a dignity in that role, but Albee will never accept it. As W. H. Auden has pointed out, entertainment is not an unworthy art; "it demands a higher standard of technique and a greater lack of self-regard than the average man is prepared to attempt. There have been, and are, many writers of excellent sensibility whose work is spoiled by a bogus vision which deprives it of the entertainment value it otherwise would have had . . ." The hollowness of Albee's adaptations and later plays reflect this hypocrisy. Straining for importance, Albee has become that saddest of public performers, whose work and personality are "tall by standing on tip-toes."

3

The Street Scene:
Playing for Keeps

*W*hen theater goes into the streets of America, its function and its tactic must change. The streets are not polite; they are silent monuments to boredom and despair, reminders that melodrama or song-and-dance do not approach an existence torn from squalor. In the open, the theater leaves its own conventional environment—controlled, safe, predictable—and faces what the world has created. That moment brings the insight—for to be valid as theater it must be true to the life experience of the people. Where television can speak for the aspirations of white, middle-class America, street theater goes deeper into the cultural complex of a city, drawing on its most vulnerable emotions, finding a successful form *only* when it has understood the unique elements of the local geography. To acknowledge the people, instead of forgetting them, is to become political.

The bourgeois conception of art has nothing to do with the life of a street. On 104th Street in East Harlem, the bongo drums tell Enrique Vargas, the organizer of the Gut Theater, the tempo of the moment. "They sit on the window sills or the rooftops playing. By the sound, you can tell if things are easy, if there's a Narco inspector around, or a shortage of heroin."[1] What speaks in the street is not the reflective polish of a refined Western tradition, but something which confesses the brutality of hard-core poverty. When Joseph Papp tried to bring his Mobile Theater into Morningside Park in Harlem in 1964, ghetto youths, obeying their own territorial imperative, threw rocks. Four years later, they sat respectfully through a performance of a black *Hamlet* only to heave chairs into the empty wooden rows after the performance or lob beer bottles over the park fence in the darkness. The intruder is not merely the white man, but a life-style with its implied economic superiority. A black *Hamlet* does more for Shakespeare than the ghetto, adding a resonance to the soliloquies but little relevance to the poor. Papp himself questions the efficacy of his Mobile Theater. He is hamstrung between his private liberalism and an artistic mentality which will not give up its concepts for the people. As a result, his theater misses its audience. He confesses his impotence in the face of radical social change

in America which needs a new theatrical language to encompass it.

PAPP: There was a time when doing Shakespeare seemed
    all right. It doesn't seem so right now. In the last few
    years, it hasn't seemed right.
INTERVIEWER: Maybe that's because of the political situ-
    ation?
PAPP: Absolutely. Everything's changed to such a degree.
    I had a big argument with LeRoi Jones one time.
    "Shit," he said, "they don't need *Hamlet*. Give them
    plays about their lives."
INTERVIEWER: I think he might be right.
PAPP: He's partly right; but someone else would have to
    do that. It's not for us to do.
INTERVIEWER: Why isn't it for the New York Public
    Theater to do?
PAPP: Well, first of all, I wouldn't know what to do. We had
    Bobby Hooks go out one time—in an all Negro group
    with a thing called *We Real Cool*. We didn't create it;
    Hooks did it and we toured it. I wouldn't know what
    material to do.[2]

Papp, a liberal dedicated to the theater, was never able to
focus on the ghetto, like most of bourgeois America. He
does not understand the world he would improve—neither
the humor of the streets nor its demands. If he is concerned
about the problem, his willingness to meet it balks when
action moves outside art to a more dangerous commitment.
The real street theater is indigenous to the community it
serves rather than a form lopped onto it from out of date
concepts of the existing social situation. The myopic planning of most street events indicates the breach between the
white-collar ideas of the streets and the vulgar reality. Papp,
surveying his audiences after a Shakespearean evening, confides, half-expectantly, "Only a revolution can change this."

His theater, despite its technical expertise, fails in the streets because it is too tepid to stand up for change while wistfully toying with the idea.

The Mobile Unit was conceived to play middle- and upper-income neighborhoods as well as ghetto areas. The two worlds do not mix. In Papp's production, Hamlet beats up a policeman, entering in his uniform and talking a hard-line "To be or not to be . . ." But a street audience, struggling with words or sensing an idea behind them, demands more than fine phrases. It does not want the culture of a world alien to its own; it cannot abide the condescension which comes with most cultural forays into its universe.

Enrique Vargas's theater, on the other hand, is more carefully planned. It does not arrive with a controlled environment like the Mobile Unit, or elaborate machinery (lights, microphones, etc.) which cuts off the *fact* of the streets rather than acknowledging it. If his work is a service, making the community aware of itself and its potential, the theater also respects the public imagination. Vargas never plays a street without casing it for a few days, observing the habits and rhythms of the people at different hours of the day. Because of his own work with local youths, his theater comes out of an understanding of their games, a fantasy world where the children do not play cowboys and Indians, but cops and junkies. "They kill everybody and then kill themselves in a shoot-out," explains Vargas. "I also study the game of tag, the magical words and different places of touch. You've got to know the architecture of the community, what are the most conducive kinds of communication. In East Harlem, drums and the Latin sound speak to the people. There is also a special kind of humor. Chaplin is much closer to our humor than, say, the Marx Brothers who belong to an English buffoon tradition. In Chaplin, the people see the harlequin, the servant who outwits the master. You've got to know what touches the people. What they laugh at, what they read; what comic strips are preferred; what approaches the local preachers use to reach them."

Most street theater discounts the lack of self-respect engendered by poverty or the impulse of an audience not bred to "culture." In order to "control" its audience, the Mobile Unit usually performs in fenced-in environments; there is an age restriction of sixteen years, and younger children must come with an adult. Ushers from the community patrol the aisles and the atmosphere becomes as fearful and repressive as that which the theater would transform. In the summer of 1968, New York's Mayor John V. Lindsay inaugurated his own concept of a street event called "Broadway in the Streets," reflecting a Republican booster impulse which trusts the Establishment and "professionalism,"—concepts strangely alien to the ghetto population. Lindsay's statement about his street enterprise illustrates the moral cross-purposes that confuse placating the poor with sustaining their development. Sounding like George Babbitt at an Elks meeting, Lindsay announced in a press release:

> New York City is the capital of the entertainment industry. We have the finest in Broadway, night club, and recording artists. And yet with this abundant talent, there are thousands of youths in the ghetto areas of the city who have never seen live performances given by quality entertainers.
>
> For this reason I am urging all our friends in the performing arts to join with me in the unique and vital opportunity to bring Broadway to the streets.

The attitude of *noblesse oblige* creeps into every public statement. What, indeed, is the Mayor bringing to the city slums? An image of wealth and success which reminds the audience of its own impoverishment; a moment in their daily struggle, communicating an excitement which quickly vanishes. Joel Grey, Jerry Orbach, Larry Blyden, Jule Styne—talented and well-intentioned—can only perform from the position of success they represent so gaudily. They have made it in the commercial world; the people who watch in Bedford-Stuyvesant have not.

"Broadway in the Streets," complete with Rotarian format (master of ceremonies, etc.), only reinforces the gap between the underprivileged and the middle-class. There is no sense of "quality" in living off the garbage of affluence. Instead of building local unity or struggling for a community redefinition of purpose, "Broadway in the Streets" asks its audience to have fun, to escape from the streets, when that prison is the one undeniable fact of life. The street audience —tough, cynical, and hungry—has been betrayed too often. "Whenever 'Broadway in the Streets' tries to come down here, they'll get booed out," explains Vargas. "It's like getting Jerry Lewis to do a show for the Viet Cong. There's a different reality here. The mere presence of 'Broadway in the Streets' is like a Madison Avenue advertisement—a reality which is a lie."

Despite its ridiculousness, "Broadway in the Streets" is certainly an improvement over the 1967 summer production of *The Ox Cart,* a melodrama about Puerto Rican life which toured under the auspices of Mayor Lindsay's Task Force. The tale traced a Puerto Rican family through their journey to the urban world and their subsequent disenchantment with America. In the play, the family erodes before our eyes: one son is killed in a factory, another is locked up in reform school, and the daughter goes on the game. The final horrendous lines of the play were: "We must go back to where we came . . . it is the land that gives life."

Where El Teatro Campesino—the grape-picker's theater from Southern California which helped teach migrant laborers the language of resistance—educates its Latin brothers to exercise their rights and the Gut Theater works to unify Puerto Rican power, the city—predictably—chose to present a play which argued astoundingly for submission, rather than resilience and dignity. Where El Teatro or the Gut Theater can inspire laughter, rage, even joy to the streets, the more "sophisticated" Puerto Rican Traveling Theater could only reinforce the universal yawn between immigrant groups and the Establishment.

The emergence of street theater revives a much older impulse for a democratic event that haunted men like Diderot and Rousseau in other revolutionary times. A peoples' theater is just emerging in America after many fallow decades. Street theater at its best can call on the life-energy of the public, externalizing its inarticulate longings and confusions. An earlier poverty, unsure of itself and still clinging to a faith in the process of democratic government, founded the burlesque halls and vaudeville houses. Today there is no theater for the people. The showbiz fare does not reflect the hazards of their lives, while pricing them out of the theater-going community with seats on Broadway as high as $15 a ticket. The estheticians of the past were thinking of actual theaters and a literary *oeuvre*. Times have changed; what is effective literature changes in political crisis. "Poet friends of mine feel their poetry makes more sense if it is scribbled on walls," explains Vargas. "Calls to incite people, to get people going, can't be printed in hard-cover books. You know, $6.98—signed."

A theater for the people will never have the ideal conditions postulated by such theater dreamers as Romain Rolland (1866-1944) who began his speculation about such an enterprise, "Supposing that the capital is secured and the public ready." Street theater uses adversity as part of its emotional impact. There will be little security for the enterprise and the public will be as prepared as the material which arouses its interest. Diderot (1713-1784) suggested a type of theater for his time now possible in our best street theater:

> Shall we ever have anything of the sort on our stage? There we can never show more than one action, while in nature there are many simultaneous actions, which, if performed at the same time, would intensify the whole, and produce a truly terrible and wondrous effect . . . We are waiting for the genius who will combine pantomime with dialogue, mingling dumbshows with the spoken scenes, and render effective the combination; above all, the approach, terrible or comic, to such simultaneous scenes.[3]

Street theater is born out of a will to survive which needs its ethnic heritage as well as life's variety. At its best, the random elements of street life reinforce the dramatic event. Genius in street theater is not the *bon mot* nor the well-made plot, but the ability to judge the community and offer images which speak with force and passion to the problems which must be faced.

In the streets, the actor, too, must change his tactic. What succeeds on asphalt is energy and concern. Talent is an asset, but an artistic temperament is not. The actor who turns to the streets must acknowledge a more difficult relationship to his audience—where there is no reverence for the spoken word, where the audience may well talk back or throw something. In one performance of Papp's *Hamlet*, a small scuffle broke out in the second act. The actors remained on stage momentarily, with Laertes observing in character, "Violence disgusts me." In the end, the entire company left the stage in what amounted to an artistic flap. The momentum of the performance was lost; the trust in the actors and their enterprise totally dissolved by their arrogance. The actor must become an activist, putting the people before his performance, the intention of theater ahead of the "literary" content of the play. The audience keeps the performer honest. "If you're doing something bad and someone throws a tomato, get out," suggests Joe Walsh, founder and chief freak of the Anyplace Theater in Minneapolis. "If you're good, the community of the audience will put a stop to it."[4]

Many of the street events are rehearsed indoors for their outdoor activity. This is true of Papp's Mobile Unit and also Teatro en la Calle, produced with the support of the New York State Council on the Arts and the Rockefeller Foundation. In both cases, the impulse is hopelessly out of touch with the facts of the street. "It's like learning to swim by jumping in the air," suggests Vargas. More important to the hundreds of bored audiences who sit and hear performers speaking into microphones, the immediacy and energy of street theater is never communicated, only an electronic hum where the performer focuses his efforts on speaking directly into the equipment rather than connecting with the people. Teatro en la Calle is significant because of its foundation support and its unquestionable lack of quality. Instead of dealing with the moment, Teatro en la Calle adapts Chekhov and Molière stories for the street—an enterprise which would be annoying were it not laughable. Ancient fictions compounded with humor from some distant tradition and Spanish costumes from a Lupe Velez idea of Latin America cannot fool an audience which talks, laughs, and gazes at more interesting sights throughout most of the performance. Teatro en la Calle, like so many others, sets up an elaborate platform, speakers, equipment which cut the audience off from the event, and isolate the actors.

When street theater is effective, as with El Teatro Campesino or the Gut Theater, the performers are responding to the environment and using it to further their effect. The language of survival becomes the tempo of urban life. As Vargas maintains, "The whole rhythm and energy which is given by a performance should be equal or bigger than the rhythm of the street at that given moment. If you're performing in the street and you're not in complete control of everything around you—the kid that just yelled, the fire sirens two blocks away, a person that pushed you—you're not connecting with anyone, you're not in control and you'll be laughed at."

The impulse of most street theater is to control the audience response and to disregard it if it does not seem pertinent. Teatro en la Calle marshals in local children as masqueraders for a brief and formal moment; Papp's Mobile Unit likes to peer down at the crowd, slap a few happy hands, but never allows the rapport to muffle the words. This reaction is a significant hang-up of middle-class organizers who have not been taught to listen to their environment, because, insulated from ugliness, they have not struggled to stay alive. Vargas, who holds a degree in anthropology, knows the importance of understanding the patterns of his people. "The people around you are a chorus no matter what you think and cannot hear. You must perform *with* them rather than *at* them."

There seems to be no neutral ground in street theater: the art-oriented, middle-class ventures dwindle to mere caterwauling for lack of focus, balm for the performers' souls but superfluous to the life of the audience. The Task Forces, the "star" theaters, the myriad one-night stands become virtually useless, a lavish gesture to their own political myopia. Were the money squandered on such follies directed into community ventures—less attractive, more difficult, and even, perhaps, unsavory—the cause for liberty, for self-improvement, and the rights of the oppressed would be much more concretely aided. The presence of so many makeshift schemes merely confuses the hard task of organization, and convinces a bourgeois public which never dips its toe in unpleasantness that something is being done. This can also be true of radical groups like the San Francisco Mime Troupe, which modernizes the *commedia dell' arte* format. Their enterprise dwindles to a chic if exciting idea in the face of poverty, a derivative *commedia dell' arte* which becomes a museum theater with almost no relevance beyond the college campus.

To be totally effective, El Teatro Campesino (now El Central Campesino Cultural), like the Gut Theater, must become more than a street theater—a center for a new way of life. At the Gut Theater, local renovation problems and the lack of information have created the "Newspaper of the Truth," a whitewashed wall of a tenement where daily bulletins explain "what they think" and "what we think." The artist-workers for these organizations have denied the individualism of the Western artist. Enrique Vargas, explaining his approach, puts it this way: "The artist who comes from the Western traditions of prophets and kings is a vain, a very selfish person by definition. The art-worker cannot be vain. He has to redefine his whole course of action. Who is he working for? Why? What language is he using? What does he have to get rid of? That is not just a question of his own artistic language but a question of what is happening all around him."

On 104th Street, a block which has been nicknamed by the neighborhood "Junkie's Paradise," there is a world worth fighting for, but it seems far away. What's happening is dope addiction, city indifference, police harassment, swindles, ignorance, festering shame, and outrage. From the rooftop of the Gut Theater's tenement building, Penn-Central trains can be seen streaking safely to suburbia. On this roof, Vargas has posted warnings of the Revolution to scare commuters. He has also thought of choosing one train a day and, over a period of days, educating the window-gazers with information. Surrounded by rubble, encased by fences painted with words like "unity," "brotherhood," "power," is a squalor perpetuated by absentee ownership and a city's lethargy. Within the ghetto, the Gut Theater may be regarded with skepticism by the older members of the community, but among the young it is a vital, active force, certain of its own identity, in charge of a momentum. "We don't like to call it a community center because of bad implications—but rather a communal house. We don't do this because we're social workers or somebody's paying us. We do it because we've got to get together," Vargas said.

In the past, the theater has been a powerful force in bind-ing communities in a shared, articulate experience. Broad-way inculcates a passive acceptance of the bourgeois world in its entertainments. Gut Theater and its many smaller, disenfranchised prototypes throughout America are talking about revolutionary action, using the theater to begin a debate and then following it with serious organizing. In the spring of 1968, the Gut Theater played in the streets, trying to unify local opinion and action against renovation de-mands where the tenants, asked to evacuate (some after thirty-five years of occupancy), had no bargaining power and could not confront the landlords. Slowly, by showing that unity can have some effect, the Gut Theater can prove itself, just as El Teatro Campesino did—by bringing pres-sure against larger industries to alter their exploitation, by winning a union contract for the grape-pickers and traveling the country.

Like any valid street theater, the form must come from the needs and traditions of the environment. Vargas has special training for his workers. "One thing I insist is for people who work with me to go to an Evangelical or Pentecostal Church service. They usually begin with singing, movement, sound. The preachers know when the right time has come; the people begin to say 'Amen' together. This never happens at the beginning—they warm up. They're going to make something happen with their universe. It's done in complete connection with the congregation—and this is what theater is all about." The impulse of this street theater is to move its people forward politically by updating a theater form of the past. It can become a serious ritual, in much the same way as French drama in a decadent tradition caused Camus to write:

> In Athens there was nothing at all frivolous about theater; performances took place only two or three times a year. And in Paris? They want to go back to something dead. It is much better to create your own style of drama.[5]

Vargas's plays capitalize on the emotional truth of the ghetto experience. "I write them like an architect builds houses—if it's constructed right, the people always know where they're walking, they always feel right. The play allows people to conceptualize things they want to play with. The energy has to be there—otherwise it's useless." Vargas uses the popular fascination of Puerto Ricans with wrestling as a metaphor for oppression. Captain America, complete with gold brocade and rock music, is pitted against Poppo. Vargas plays the referee who looks the other way

while Poppo is being fouled. In his newest play, *The Bench,*
Vargas begins the event forty-five minutes before the actual
performance with bongo drums stationed around the block.
The beat gradually moves in on the arena, forming a
counterpoint between the stage action and the people. The
audience, sandwiched between stimuli, watch the play—a
"city official," his "wife," and a Puerto Rican "advance
man" try to give a speech on a bench made of police boards.
It starts with slapstick caricature, the "city official" beginning in a nervous benevolence and finally, in fear, refusing
to read his speech. The "wife" tries to speak, only to be
drowned out by drums. The speech begins, "How can you
people become better Americans?" While they talk, Puerto
Ricans begin to sit at the edge of the flimsy platform. At
first there is one, but finally, when the "advance man" joins
his brothers at one end of the platform, they are able to tip
it. Together, they have the power to shake things up. At this
point, the theater looks to its audience. "What do you
think? Is this our bench?" The answers come from the drums
and the people. The slapstick changes abruptly. "We bring
the audience to this point and then make them realize we're
talking for real. This is my first attempt to say '*Vaya!* You're
right, brother.' It's a race revival, a brotherhood. It means
unity and action." Those who respond to the play are given
pamphlets explaining how to organize themselves and sug-
gesting books to read. The educational function comes full
circle, moving from the imagination back into life.

The beauty of these events, on strike lines and in the
rubble of Spanish Harlem, is their gorgeous flowering in
arid terrain—the simplicity with which they discover the
dignity of the human will. No two street theaters can be
the same; each environment has its special metabolism.
But where the need is so immense and the communication
barriers so great, the fact of beginning is itself an important

step. Vargas's own axioms are general cornerstones on which to build:

1. KNOW WHO YOU ARE: If you know who you are, you'll know what to do.
2. WHAT IS THE BEST ROAD TO SURVIVAL? What are your best tools for communicating with groups (movement, sound, words)?
3. WHAT ARE THE BEST WAYS OF CONNECTING WITH THE COMMUNITY? Find the simple way which won't turn people off. *Begin where they're at.*

While so much of America's theater suffocates in its golden delusion, another dramatic tradition holds out the possibilities of a revitalized life, denying decorum and discovering the vernacular. Street theater revives a performing impulse almost lost—a mime for survival.

4

The Language
of Silence

I've got nothing to say but it's O.K.
Good morning, good morning,
good morning.
　　　　　—John Lennon and Paul McCartney

Go ahead, Houston. Apollo 8. Burn complete.
Our orbit 169.1 by 60.6—169.1 by 60.5.
　　　　　—Capt. James A. Lovell, Jr., to Earth.[1]

I

Floating in a blue and fathomless silence around the moon, an astronaut spoke to Earth 231,000 miles behind him. Ironically, he read from the Book of Genesis, a testament of faith from man's pristine history and a mockery of religion in the technological age. *"And the earth was without form, and void. . . ."* In the beginning

50

was the Word, made awesome by the silence from which language sluggishly emerged. Now, the void surrounding Earth begins to diminish. But not the silence, made more complicated by technology which has abandoned a cumbersome sensuous vocabulary for the *voiceless* precision of mathematics. In the same way, the machine—wheezing and sputtering in a mammoth imitation of human functions—gives way gradually to speeds and accomplishments beyond human correlative.

Silence is a concept alien to America, whose destiny was carved out of a noisy faith in human accomplishment. In silence there is no direction. Only now—with contemporary man farther from the center of his metaphysical world, increasingly displaced from nature, distrustful of moralities, suspicious of the State, unable to define for himself the new scientific momentum ruling society—has silence muscled in on the imagination.

"For one transitory enchanted moment man must have held his breath in the presence of this continent." In these words, F. Scott Fitzgerald described in *The Great Gatsby* the two impulses which coexist in silence: a sense of loss and of wonder. Silence implies both the fall and the recapturing of a primordial unity with the universe. "The fall is into language . . . and overcoming the consequences of the fall is speaking with tongue. Language carried to the extreme, to the end; a lapse into pre-lapsarian language; eating again of the tree of knowledge, a second fall into the second innocence; *verbum infans,* the infant or ineffable word."[2] The wonder with which Americans faced their new, would-be Eden still persists, but the silent stalemate Fitzgerald conceived held its glory only briefly. As they labored in this Eden, Americans borrowed and invented words childishly, new Adams imitating the first Adam's sensual speech.

The Lewis and Clark Expedition (1804-1806) added

over five hundred words to the American vocabulary (many of them Indian), creating instant terms for the flora and fauna they observed: "bayou," "hickory," "pecan," "sassafras," "squash," "tote," "prairie," "raccoon," "whippoorwill."

The nation was growing; so too was its vocabulary, carrying in its newness a sense of the unknown the frontiersman so willingly challenged. Early American speech was also marked by extravagance, creating nonsense words with no rational intention or connection: "guyascutus," "scalawag," "sockdolager," "rambunctious," "hornswoggle," "hunky-dory." This verbal invention reflected a vitality born out of a nation's battle with the silent forces of frontier living.

In this century, the language of science, analytic and less spontaneous, has merged with everyday speech ("libido," "id," "systems analysis," "input," "output"). The geography of the newest frontier is indicative; we speak of a "translunar" coast, a "transearth" coast, "libration points." Many artistic gestures—from the purity of James Joyce's *Finnegans Wake* to the nonsense sounds in *Hair* ("Good Morning, Starshine")—are struggling with the contemporary weight of meaninglessness in which proliferating communications have unified speech and devitalized the word. "To restore to words their full significance, as in dreams, to get the nonsense or thingness or silence back into words; to transcend the antinomy of sense and nonsense, silence and speech. It is a destruction of ordinary language, a victory over the reality principle."[3]

America has inflated words like its dreams—and the arts have suffered. Tall talk and the booster spirit which characterized early America were the seeds of the massive communications networks and advertising systems which dominate the language and the imagination of modern America. The nation, archetype for the new technological boom, has fallen victim to another kind of silence—a negative force in which the word has been gradually devalued, no longer evocative nor trenchant enough to pinpoint the new, more complex objects on the contemporary horizon. As Susan Sontag has pointed out, when "the prestige of language falls, that of silence rises."[4]

Every culture has its own attitudes toward silence. In Eastern religions, silence represents the abolition of mind, a state of peace where word and body are eliminated as intellectual divisions, where all becomes transparent, organic, and clear. In a state of silence the mind, acting on the outside world, falls into a harmonious balance with nature. One *Zenrin* poem explains the elimination of illusion:

> Sitting quietly, doing nothing
> Spring comes, and the grass grows by itself.

Man aspires to the realm of shadows: silent, diaphanous, totally void.

> Entering the forest he moves not the grass
> Entering the water he makes not a ripple.

While there can never be an absolute silence in nature, the silence of the mental process becomes a metaphor for spiritual revelation. *"Shantih shantih shantih,"* the concluding words of T. S. Eliot's *The Waste Land* from the *Upanishads,* reflect the "peace which passeth understanding," a silence glorious with revelation and beyond words.

But silence can also come from the din of noise, a numbing lack of connection with the world. In the modern Western literary tradition it has become, increasingly, a term for chaos and destruction, a symbol for the void where no possibilities exist. Silence has evolved out of a

mordant irony about modern man—"I want to be a
machine," said Andy Warhol—and an unwillingness to take
part in the bestialities of the political state. Silence may also
be the paradoxical testament of the brilliant mind refusing
to speak in order not to dilute its insight. "He who has the
final answers can no longer speak to the other, as he breaks
off genuine communication for the sake of what he believes
in."[5] (Karl Jaspers.) Language fails the poet as he approaches the radiance of the Godhead in the final cantos
of Dante's *Paradiso*; silence becomes the destiny of insane
revelation (Hölderlin, Artaud), and even the life style of
philosophical conclusions (Trappist monks, Beckett).

The best contemporary art has become a strategy for
silence. This is not a flirtation with nihilism, but an esthetic
attempt to revive the senses, numbed by noise and flaccid
speech which glosses experience rather than confronting it.
"Silence administered by the artist is part of a program of
perceptual and cultural therapy, often on the model of shock
therapy rather than persuasion."[6] Miss Sontag's observation
is apt. Audiences watching a member of the Living Theater
stand at attention for a quarter of an hour in *Mysteries and
Other Pieces* are not interested in the physical control or
state of mind which allow for such a feat; the silence offends
them. They want to be shown something, told something;
to experience the state of being is confusing to many. They
shout insults and try to force the performer to speak. At a
moment in history, loud with meanings and information, the
choice of silence is a brave refusal to accept the world. It is
not surprising, then, that sculpture has become "minimal,"
that directors speak of a "poor theater," "nonverbal language," and playwrights like Beckett and Pinter have reduced the conventional stage to a sparse and quiet dramatic
moment.

In modern fiction the finest prose stylists—Beckett,

Joyce, Kafka—have also aspired to a purity of form and language which verges on silence. The choice to reduce art to its essential elements is an attempt to revive the language and make it speak through the silence of its original sound. The tactic is often interpreted as arrogance by outsiders, but for the creator it is a practical means of survival. Kafka dramatizes this in *A Hunger Artist*. In this story, professional fasting, an art of abstinence, is on the decline, but the hunger artist tries to explain his acceptance of silence on humble and shattering human grounds.

> "But you shouldn't admire [the fasting]," said the hunger artist. "Well, then we don't admire it," said the overseer, "but why shouldn't we admire it?" "Because I have to fast, I can't help it," said the hunger artist. "What a fellow you are," said the overseer, "and why can't you help it?" "Because," said the hunger artist, lifting his head a little and speaking, with his lips pursed, as if for a kiss, right into the overseer's ear, so that no syllable might be lost, "because I couldn't find the food I liked. If I had found it, believe me, I should have made no fuss and stuffed myself like you or anyone else . . ."[7]

The freedom to be silent may be the only practical alternative for the artist.

Kafka's prose speaks in whispers; the hunger artist is vanishing before our eyes in total immobility. This is a contemporary metaphor: the silence of a Giacometti figure, a Beckett buffoon. In that silence is a mystery which can be constructed but never explained. The state of silence is a paradox: a death and birth, the end of speech and a beginning. It can be a negative force through which to appreciate positive energies.

> Heard melodies are sweet, but those unheard
> Are sweeter; therefore, ye soft pipes, play on;
> Not to the sensual ear, but more endear'd
> Pipe to the spirit ditties of no tone.
> —John Keats, "Ode to a Grecian Urn"

Keats' instinct is not far from Pinter's disavowal of theatrical experiences made literal through fustian language.

> Life is much more mysterious than plays make it
> out to be. And it is this mystery which fascinates
> me; what happens between the words, what happens when no words are spoken at all.[8]

Pinter acknowledges silence as an articulate energy which gives resonance to the spoken word. Between the spoken and the unheard lies the mystery of human confrontation. The silence is not radio's "dead time," but an active force, a breathtaking artistic choice which allows audience (and actor) to forego systematic meaning for total immersion in the living and unpredictable present. In these Pinter moments, the audience's consciousness fills the void with its complex associations. There is not one meaning but hundreds; there is a form, but the result of silence gives a sense of randomness to the event. Yet, in silence, each new theatrical moment brings the memory of the past into the present. The quiet affirms the void and filters into the irony of the barbed stage argot. Silence is the fulcrum of the stage creation.

II

Until the twentieth century, language and the visual arts had a confident and close relationship; from the first medieval illuminations, where the mysteries of a new typography were combined with carefully wrought and explicit graphic images, to silent films with printed dialogue. Pictures often illustrated literary axioms (Hogarth's "The Rake's Progress"). Often, Pre-Raphaelite poetry (and also some of William Blake's verse) was meant to be exhibited along with the canvas. This impulse reached its height with Victorian illustrators. Nineteenth-century graphic images were noisy with words, indicative of the importance of language at the center of the intellectual and emotive life. In *Language and Silence,* George Steiner has expanded on this tendency of painting and sculpture to correspond to language.

> A landscape, a still life, a portrait, an allegory, a depiction of some event out of history or legend are renditions in color, volume, and texture of realities which can be expressed in words. We can give a linguistic account of the subject of the work of art. The canvas and the statue have a title that relates to them as a verbal concept. We say: this is a portrait of a man with a golden helmet; or this is the Grand Canal at sunrise. In each case, even before we have seen the work, the words elicit in the mind a specific graphic equivalent.[9]

Most modern art has eliminated the verbal correlative from its canvases. Often numbered rather than titled, they deal with abstract visual properties (surface, edge) which cannot be discussed. The viewer is denied not only his language but the one-point perspective of realism which puts him and the artist on the same comforting wave length. The minimal object interrupts space, but does not fill it with noisy (and limited) explanations. Like silence, it is a specific fact, only appreciated on its own terms. Don Judd, explaining his objects, stresses their literalness:

> Most of the work involves new materials, either
> recent inventions or things not used before in
> art . . . Materials vary greatly and are simply
> materials—formica, aluminum, cold-rolled steel,
> plexiglass . . . They are specific. If they are used
> directly, they are more specific. Also, they are
> usually aggressive. There is an objectivity to an
> obdurate identity of material.[10]

The material of sculpture retreats, like the rest of the arts,
from verbal conception. The word, unable to sustain its
relationship with a technically complex world, falters. In
The Stoic Comedians, Hugh Kenner quotes from *Time*
magazine to illustrate yet another dilemma of a print-
oriented culture.

> On newsstands, the new Sunday paper had a
> clean, uncluttered look (six columns to the page
> instead of the customary eight) and it was cer-
> tainly easy to carry home (8 oz., *vs.* the 4 lb., 2 oz.
> of *The New York Times*) . . .

Kenner concludes that the passage has "moved from research through typewriter to printing press without the
intervention of human voice . . . a dense mosaic of factuality
behind each atom of which is alleged to stand a research-
er's guarantee that justification can be produced on demand.
Time, the *exhalation* of the linotype machine, does not talk,
it compresses."[11] The ultimate effect is a typographic tonelessness. "This means we have grown accustomed at last
not only to silent reading, but to reading matter that itself
implies nothing but silence."[12]

III

When Al Jolson spoke in *The Jazz Singer* (1927), his
words were prophetic for all technology. *"You ain't heard*

nothin' yet." Like the current information boom, the moving picture offered sound which would dwindle, often, to mere noise. The talking picture was commercial; in it the words of a nation became popularized and ultimately uniform. The sound brought to the film image a literalness which silent film, at its best, lacked. The impulse for realism denied silence while creating it. (In the contemporary cinema, the great innovators—Antonioni, Fellini, Bergman—have incorporated the silence of contemporary life into their films—*Blow-Up, Juliet of the Spirits*, and *The Silence.*)

The silent films were rarely silent. "It was the aim of the exhibitor to eradicate silence from silent pictures. A piano was at first sufficient to drown out the whirr of the camera. Soon even the cheapest theater could afford both a pianist and a violinist."[13] Silence was studiously avoided for the viewer, yet the actors found motivation on camera with mood music provided on the set by violinists. Technology brought to silent films a silence which stymied performers. One silent film actor recalls, "[When] talkies came in everything was soundproofed—everything was silent. The camera was sealed in a soundproofed booth and everybody kept absolutely quiet until the end of the take. In this complete silence we were at a complete loss."[14] In a burgeoning America whose noise was an aural indication of its progress, silence was discomforting. Raw energy had a rhythm; power had a sound which Walt Whitman's strong poetic voice first clarified. Silence implied a stasis which America's destiny denied.

> I hear America singing, the varied carols I hear
> Those of *mechanics*, each one singing his as it
>   should be blithe and strong . . .
> —*I Hear America Singing* (1860)

The talkies were an extension of Whitman's impulse to see and sing, to record the wonder of a new world. Whitman's voice is always conscious of silence ("Now, I will do nothing but listen") and of the fact that words can contain the world.

> Speech is the twin of my vision, it is
>   unequal to measure itself,
> It provokes me forever, it says sarcastically
> *Walt, you contain enough, why don't*
>   *you let it out then?*
>   —*Song of Myself* (1855)

Talkies took no notice of silence, matching words with objects but forgetting the void out of which they took their life. *Photoplay* magazine defended silence against the intrusion of sound. Silence, it maintained, was film's rarest and subtlest beauty.

> In its silence [film] more nearly approximates nature than any art save painting and sculpture. The greatest processes of the universe are those of silence . . . The talking picture will be made practical, but it will never supersede the motion picture without sound—the vision which, deprived of voice to ears of flesh, intones undisturbed the symphonies of the soul . . .[15]

Hollywood's superficial theorizing is unconscious of silence as a symbolic condition. Beckett's *Film* (1962) records the silence of objects and man's journey within himself. Beckett's film directions emphasize a ruthless economy and a gradual interiorization of experience.

> *Esse est percipi.*
>   All extraneous perception suppressed, animal, human, divine, self-perception maintains in being.

Search of non-being in flight from extraneous
perception breaking down in inescapability of
self-perception.[16]

IV

Technology has forced man back into himself. As the
circumference of his effectiveness shrinks, the process of
interiorization multiplies. The predicament has been a
major one for theater. Unlike the film, whose image (the
actual frame) is in the past, the stage event is composed
before our eyes. It is a thrust *into* life, an activity which
makes the silence of contemporary experience difficult to
examine in dramatic terms. (It is not surprising that much
contemporary theater tries to dramatize memory, the process
of interiorization which rarely reaches out to the audience.
Murray Schisgal's *Jimmy Shine,* Terrence McNally's *Sweet
Eros,* Anne Burr's *Huui, Huui* are unsuccessful as theater
pieces because the retreat into the characters becomes
cumbersome, robbing the stage of a living and *immediate*
reality.)

Artaud's speculations about theater began with a sense
of impending silence, a truth beyond words. Most contemporary theater has not taken up his lead. "In this theater
all creation comes from the stage and finds its expression
and its origins alike in a secret psychic impulse which is
Speech before words."[17] Conscious of an emptiness in life
as well as on stage, Artaud battled against literary theatrical
values, fearing the decline of language's evocative potential.
He wanted a theater of interior (silent) truth.

> In the theater, as we conceive it, the text is every-
> thing. It is understood and definitely admitted,
> and has passed into our habits of thinking, it is
> an established spiritual value that language of

words is *the* major language. But it must be admitted even from the Occidental point of view
that speech becomes ossified and that words, all
words, are frozen and cramped in their meanings,
in a restricted schematic terminology. For the
theater as it is practiced here, a written word has
as much value as the same word spoken. To certain theatrical amateurs this means that a play
read affords just as definite and as great satisfaction as a play performed. Everything concern-
ing the particular enunciation of a word and the
vibration it can set up in space escapes them, and
consequently, everything that it is capable of adding to the thought. A word thus understood has
little more than a discursive, i.e., elucidative
value . . . The word is used only to sidestep
thought; it encircles it, but terminates it; it is only
a conclusion . . .[18]

Silence acknowledges flux. It is obsessive and feeds the
interior experience Artaud wanted to externalize.

Stage events strain under the pressure of an emasculated
language. In the musical, lyrics no longer corner the fascinations of the moment or delight an audience in fillips of
verbal surprise. The language has lost its glitter; civilized
life is too complex for musicals to capture the veneer of the
moment as they did in their salad days of the twenties and
thirties. *Zorba* (1968), awkward and puerile as an entertainment, is indicative of the new breed—noise shrouding
emptiness with energy. Watching such an event is less in-
volving than an Ad Reinhardt white-on-white canvas. Reinhardt set out to achieve silence, a sense of timeless fluidity.
His painting is committed to total negation of convention
where *Zorba* exists to affirm the habitual. *Zorba* spins its
own cocoon of silence. It offers home truths which know
about boredom but cannot find a way to acknowledge it:

"Life is what you do/While you're waiting to die," says *Zorba's* author.

Many serious attempts at theater flounder because the linguistic and moral climate can no longer accept the premises of the event. Just as the great contemporary playwrights, men of dramatic words—Tennessee Williams, John Osborne, Arthur Miller—cannot locate their poetic targets in the sixties, attempts at classic grandeur like the Minnesota Theater Company's production of John Lewin's adaptation of Aeschylus's *House of Atreus* fail because the moral scope of Greek tragedy and the verbal power for it are not commensurate. In Tyrone Guthrie's Minneapolis production, the Greek method is once again attempted, but size is mistaken for significance. Gargantuan masks, boots which elevate each actor to mammoth proportions, recreate the visual aspects of Greek tragedy. Originally, this size gave the Greek actor visibility in the amphitheater as well as symbolic stature. The masks, far from being artificial, were part of the accepted and natural stage equipment. To a Greek audience, masks were more real than faces. The opposite is true in our culture. Giganticism in imitation of the past is an indubitable sign of impotence, the urgent (and perhaps final) attempt to force "significance" on an audience. This tale of Orestes's revenge on Clytemnestra asks moral questions diminished by the limitations of modern language.

In the time of the Greek tragedies, language was one of man's noblest tools, part of the dignity which separated him from the silence of animals. Words match man's tragic situation and encompass his knowledge of the world. In *Antigone,* the chorus reminds us: "Wonders are there many —none more wonderful than man . . . His is speech and windswept thought . . ." Swollen by masks and elephantine appendages, the *House of Atreus* becomes a wooden

spectacle. Without facial expressions and with gestures
obscured by massive costumes, only the voices create the
drama. The human element is lost. But words alone can no
longer sustain nor justify stage experience. When Orestes
claims that Apollo instructed him to kill his mother, the
Furies are angry.

CHORUS: If there is a crime—and there is—the arch criminal
    is you.
APOLLO: Explain that—and make it good.[19]

What words can approach the heroic timbre or erupt with
the fire of godlike rage? In its insufficiency, *House of Atreus*
reinforces the inability of modern man to approach the
tragic dimension. If the play and its production move into
areas of dance and musical harmony, its spectacle can never
convey beauty because the moral questions it poses and its
verbal means of dealing with them are no longer equal.

The inability of the modern American language to evoke
the past or to stimulate the senses affects the horizons for
new theater. What words encompass contemporary experience or tread the unknown, forcing us back to pristine
images of ourselves? The debacle of Rochelle Owens's
Beclch, an interminable daydream of a voracious white
African queen, is due to the enervating strain of finding a
valid, sensuous argot and an apt stage image. Miss Owens
fills her stage with pseudo-Elizabethan blood lust. Unwilling
to confront the silence of modern life, she yammers on, puff-
ing up her people with passion and outrage. Leprosy, nudity,
eating slaughtered flesh—any spectacle to fill the stage with
action. Her writing is not without its perverse sinew; her
nightmare begins with an awareness of the torment of
modern living, but she will not accept the silence which is
its symbolic conclusion. She quotes Arnold Toynbee as an
epigraph to her play: "As the process of disintegration

works itself out, the alternative choices tend to become more rigid in their limitations, more extreme in their divergence and more momentous in their consequences. That is to say, the spiritual experience of schism in the soul is a dynamic movement, not a static situation." But Miss Owens's language produces a sense of stasis; florid and orotund, it becomes a private jargon grafted on to transparent people. Queen Beclch has a pastoral reflection:

> A bird bringing a worm to the nest, to put in the mouths of the little birds . . . sensible, sensible mama bird . . . worm meat in the bodies of the little birds . . . worm meat passing down the little throats . . . Thank God for my sucking mouth! Fish, fruit, I've got it all—I'm a regular bigwig . . .[20]

Miss Owens wants a heroic voice, a gigantic resonance. When Beclch dies, threatening to expire in silence ("I want to drool like an animal without making a sound"), an attendant urges a monumental, impossible noise: "If you make any sound, Beclch . . . it will be a horse laugh; . . . loud enough to crack the dry earth." This colossal timbre contains a heady verbosity, which destroys the entire effect. The play, indicative of Toynbee's "extreme," does not recognize silence as an alternative. As a result, its vacuous language numbs the mind instead of informing it. *Beclch* is the product of a world which has created a metaphysical silence, and, in its inability to use that silence, it becomes its own victim.

V

Silence may be metaphoric and active. As an active force, it has many uses. Miss Sontag has outlined a few pertinent ones:

1. [Silence provides] time for the continuing and
    exploring of thought. Notably, speech closes
    off thought . . . Silence keeps things open . . .
2. [Silence furnishes and aids] speech to attain
    its maximum integrity and seriousness . . .
    When one talks less, one starts feeling more
    fully one's physical presence in a given space.
    Silence undermines bad speech . . . providing
    a kind of ballast, and even correcting language
    when it becomes inauthentic . . .[21]

These uses of silence refer directly to theater—the stage,
occupied with both visual and verbal problems, is able to
benefit most completely by them. Harold Pinter's *Landscape* is essentially a study in silence. Pinter has always
been conscious of silence in life and on stage. As Pinter
said:

> There are two silences. One when no word is
> spoken. The other when perhaps a torrent of lan-
> guage is employed. This speech is speaking a lan-
> guage locked beneath it. That is its continual
> reference. The speech we hear is an indication of
> that we don't hear. It is a necessary avoidance,
> a violent, sly, anguished or mocking smoke screen
> which keeps the other in its place. When true si-
> lence falls we are still left with echo but are nearer
> nakedness. One way of looking at speech is to say
> it is a constant stratagem to cover nakedness.[22]

Pinter's practical observations about silence imply an
intuition of the primal silence—the word which came with
man as he emerged from Eden, sinful, conscious of his
vulnerability, longing to cloak himself. The opaque, haunting specificity of Pinter's plays rests, like much of con-

temporary scultpure, on minimal intentions. "One of my main concerns is to get things down and down and down. Always paring away . . . People don't realize that the English language is extremely exciting; it means so much, so many different things at the same time."[23] Pinter's plays reduce experience to gestures and tones of voice so spare that they create a sense of their negative components. Each word spoken reflects the glacial silence beneath it. Pinter is able to offer an image of man's outer actions and his inner turmoil (his conscious and unconscious life) without pigeonholing motivation. "The doctrine of the unconscious, properly understood, is a doctrine of the falseness of all words, taken literally, at their face value, at the level of consciousness. The true psychic reality, which is the unconscious, cannot be put into words, cannot ever be translated by the silence into words. The unconscious is and will remain forever ineffable . . ."[24]

By allowing silence to exist on stage, Pinter's plays create a special relationship to their audience, similar to the effect of spectators entering a room of minimal sculpture. Speaking of "literalist" (minimal) art, art critic Michael Fried has discussed sculpture as theater:

> The beholder is confronted by a literalist work within a situation that he experiences as *his* . . . The work in question exists for him alone, even if he is not actually alone with the work at the time . . . Someone has merely to enter the room in which the literalist work has been placed to *become* the beholder, that audience of one, almost as though the work in question had been *waiting for him*. . . . And once he is in the room the work refuses obstinately to let him alone—which is to say, it refuses to stop confronting him, distancing him, isolating him . . .[25]

Pinter's later plays (*The Homecoming, Landscape, Silence*) are especially minimal; everything in them is before our eyes. Everything that happens does so in front of us. Language—the writer's metal—seems literal, concrete, specific; but the residue of silence allows the play to speak to each viewer in a unique way. There is no democracy of information. The crystalline quality of Pinter's best work, its uncompromised self-sufficiency, gives silence yet another dimension, which Miss Sontag has described as "a metaphor for a cleansed, non-interfering vision." With this silence, the art work exists (or seems to exist) uncompromised and undiminished by human observation. As Miss Sontag wrote:

> A landscape doesn't demand from the spectator his "understanding," his imputations of significance . . . it demands, rather, his absence, that he not add anything to it. Contemplation, strictly speaking, entails self-forgetfulness on the part of the spectator; an object worthy of contemplation is one which, in effect, annihilates the perceiving subject.[26]

In *Landscape,* two domestics, Duff (a steward) and Beth (a housekeeper) sit in the kitchen of a country house speaking in caverns of silence. This is not an eighteenth-century "landscape," a chronicle of a twittering and exterior nature. Duff may speak of the pond; Beth may follow her sensuous reverie of taking a lover on bleached beaches, but ultimately Pinter is dealing with an inner terrain, murky and inviolable. Instead of the confident order of a painted landscape, Pinter uncovers the chasm between perception and understanding, object and observer. Visually, Pinter arranges his characters to reflect this deadly but active stillness. Duff sits in a chair at the end of a long kitchen table; at the other end, but away from the table, is Beth's chair.

Physically, there is no through-line between them. The table surface, like Duff's words, extends toward her but drops off precipitously, leaving a blankness between them.

Speaking in tangents, Duff and Beth create from the silences built into conversation and reverie the emptiness of their lives, the pain, insensitivity, and even paranoia which have resulted. Duff's voice—vulgar, rough, a fist of blunt banality—contrasts with the lyrical and confused delicacy of Beth's. Duff speaks, as if into a void. Both characters seem natural, yet it is only their words which move toward the boundaries of "reality." Duff talks endlessly about walking to the pond, the very spot where, years before, he had walked with her after confessing adultery. His tone is matter-of-fact.

DUFF: The funny thing was, when I looked, when the shower was over, the man and woman under the trees on the other side of the pond had gone. There wasn't a soul in the park.

BETH: I wore a white robe. Underneath I was naked. (*Pause.*) There wasn't a soul on the beach. Very far away a man was sitting, on a breakwater. But even so he was only a pinpoint, in the sun. And even so I could only see him when I was standing, or on my way from the shore to the dune. When I lay down I could no longer see him, therefore he couldn't see me. (*Pause.*) . . . Snoozing how lovely I said to him. But I wasn't a fool, on that occasion. I lay quiet, by his side. (*Silence.*)

DUFF: Anyway . . .

BETH: My skin . . .

DUFF: I'm sleeping all right these days.

BETH: Was stinging.

DUFF: Right through the night, every night.

BETH: I'd been in the sea.

DUFF: Maybe it's something to do with the fishing. Getting
to learn more about fish.

BETH: Stinging in the sea by myself.

DUFF: They're very shy creatures. You've got to woo them.
You must never get excited with them. Or flurried.
Never.[27]

Out of this "conversation" emerges a violent indifference.
A woman whose femininity, sexuality, and dignity have been
gouged from her by Duff's dumb animality. His talk of fish
shows a concern he never exhibits for her. His chatter (Is it
to assuage his guilt? To fill his own loneliness?) becomes
itself a bludgeoning hollowness. Reminiscing about how
well Beth kept the house and how he once took the master
of the house up north, Duff recalls the nostalgia of returning
home.

> . . . You'd missed me. When I came into this room,
> you stopped still. I had to walk all the way over the
> floor towards you.
>
> (*Pause.*)
>
> I touched you.
>
> (*Pause.*)
>
> But I had something to say to you, didn't I? I waited,
> I didn't say it then, but I'd made up my mind to say it,
> I'd decided I would say it, and I did say it the next
> morning. Didn't I?
>
> (*Pause.*)
>
> I told you that I'd let you down. I'd been unfaithful to
> you.

By dramatizing an existential emptiness, Pinter shows the audience the silence in memory and deadness in language. Duff continually reiterates barroom conversations with others which, like wheels within wheels, move further from the actual dialogue. Duff's recollection becomes a pastiche of canceled linguistic energies. A zero.

DUFF: This beer is piss, he said. Undrinkable. There's nothing wrong with the beer, I said. Yes there is, he said, I just told you what was wrong with it. It's the best beer in the area, I said. No it isn't, this chap said, it's piss. The landlord picked up the mug and had a sip. Good beer, he said. Someone's made a mistake, this fellow said, someone's used this pintpot instead of the boghole.

Under this rich texture of chatter is a silence which Pinter uses to show a cold, intractable human experience. While steadfastly refusing to create a theater of symbolism, he has made it possible for words to become, once again, insinuating symbols. By stripping the word of its flaccid misuses, it becomes potent. As Norman O. Brown writes: "In a symbol there is concealment and yet revelation: hence, therefore, by silence and speech acting together, comes a double significance."[28]

VI

I use the words you taught me. If they don't mean anything anymore, teach me others. Or let me be silent.
—Samuel Beckett, *Endgame*[29]

Where Pinter's characters dramatize existential silence without them knowing it, the work of Samuel Beckett approaches an apocalyptic void. Language dies, like man, of habit; Beckett's characters struggle for the words to express the pain of living. No terms are sufficient. But, for them, words are the only means of clinging to the world. Language is an extension of man's cowardice, his unwillingness to accept the void and await the end. Beckett's prose style mirrors the dark laughter of his vision. Every sentence is an end and a beginning, compelled to continue without any reason to do so. The game of language is horribly comic:

> ... I can't go on, you must go on, I'll go on, you must say words, as long as there are any, until they find me, until they say me, strange pain, strange sin, you must go on, perhaps it's done already, perhaps they have said me already, perhaps they have carried me to the threshold of my story, before the door that opens on my story, that would surprise me, if it opens, it will be I, it will be the silence, where I am, I don't know, I'll never know, in the silence you don't know, you must go on, I can't go on, I'll go on.[30]

The human drama, like the stage images for it, becomes an "act without words." Where words become useless, man's gestures are miniscule in the void. Silence is the ultimate cosmic joke in a world longing for meanings, as seen in *Endgame:*

NAGG (*clasping his hands, closing his eyes in a gabble*): Our father which art . . .

HAMM: Silence! In silence. Where are your manners?[30]

Beckett's fictions move the novel relentlessly toward an interior reality, gambits for silence occurring in the mind of

their protagonists (Molloy, Malone, Watt, etc.) and trans-
ferred to the reader's mind. All of Beckett's characters talk
themselves out only (as in *The Unnamable*) to find a way
of breaking the tonelessness by uttering a sound. With this
sleight of hand, Beckett's fiction skirts the philosophical
impasse, yielding from the muck enough energy to speak
again. His books, plays, and *Film* become documents of
silence. No one—not even the faceless and elusive author
himself—can keep the discipline of Stoic solitude. Words
are arbitrary and impractical servants plumbing the morass
of consciousness—a failing appendage of the living—which
Beckett musters brilliantly to prove their intractability.

> There could be no things but nameless things, no
> names but thingless names . . . the world dies too,
> foully named. All I know is what the word knows,
> and the dead things, and makes a handsome little
> sum, with a beginning, a middle, and an end as in
> the well built phrase and the long sonata of the
> dead.[31]

Everything is, in Beckett's words, *"cosa mentale."* His
novels and plays follow a system in which each sentence is
a new silence. "There are many ways in which the thing I'm
trying to say be tried in vain to be said."[32] The repetition
calls attention to the continuum and a mathematical language beyond words. He deepens the paradox by calling
attention to the literal quality of his vocabulary.

> Do you find anything . . . bizarre about my way
> of speaking? I do not mean the voice. No, I mean
> the words. I use none but the simplest words, I
> hope, and yet I sometimes find my way of speak-
> ing very . . . bizarre.[33]

Hugh Kenner has argued that Beckett's fiction is a "closed field," a term derived from numbers theory. "A field, says the mathematician, contains a collection of elements and a system of laws for dealing with those elements. Once we have such a theory we can invent as many mathematical systems as we like, and so long as their elements are delimited and their laws internally consistent, their degree of correspondence with the familiar world, where space has three dimensions and every calculation can be verified by counting, is irrelevant. This line of reasoning sets mathematics free from our inescapable structure of intuitions about the familiar world."[34]

Beckett's game with fiction parallels other contemporary artists' intentions. Beckett, in an age inundated with print and data, is stingy with his information. Yet the little information which he does provide is repeated extensively to show the circularity of life. Repetition mirrors the technological world, potentially static, diminished in its "significance" to the repetitive rhythms where a change of emphasis yields whatever "content" is available.

Beckett's characters chatter into silence, while adhering to an "abstract" configuration appreciated by the author. Beckett once told London critic Harold Hobson, "I am interested in the shape of ideas even if I do not believe in them. There is a wonderful sentence in Augustine . . . 'Do not despair: one of the thieves was saved; do not presume: one of the thieves was damned.' That sentence has a wonderful shape. It is the shape that matters."[35] Beckett admires the contours of a vacuum where the subject cancels out the predicate, like the space between two opposite magnetic pulls.

In this abstract pattern, silence necessarily becomes a symbol for failure. Beckett has no heroes, and no voice which turns a consciously beautiful sentence to earn applause (the usual noisy means of approval). Beckett uses silence as a philosophical humiliation and the badge of one's humanity. Yet, emptiness can never be achieved. Silence engulfs the uneventful horizon of Vladimir and Estragon; Molloy's room is a bell-jar which cuts off the world and sends him into the vortex of his mind. There is always a voice which speaks after it has resolved to keep still; there is always a gesture which breaks the suicide pact, rebounding to sustain another day. The predicament is comical. Kenner sees Beckett's understanding of cosmic failure as going further than the fine arts:

> In the presence of art, however abstract, however self-denying, we have still, as Beckett phrases it, two familiar maladies: "The malady of wanting to know what to do and the malady of wanting to be able to do it " . . . Beckett advances the notion of utter and uncalculable incapacity, producing an art which is bereft of occasion in every shape and form, ideas as well as material. The theme of creation as well as the process becomes silence.[36]

VII

Our culture is a victim of the decorative. It looks back nostalgically to high-camp styles of fashion and design. Advertising twists language into frivolous shapes in order to titillate the consumer. Accustomed to the veneer of noise, to the shibboleths of promotion, public relations, and market research, society is suspicious of those who value silence. Pinter's refusal to publicly analyze his work and Beckett's mysterious inaccessibility are seen as arrogant and weird when they are merely means of survival. The printed and spoken word proliferate at an ever-spiraling pace. We are selling Telstar tracking stations to Africa and

putting men on the moon. But the inundation of language
by the media has not brought clarity, let alone literacy. It
is not McLuhan's prophecy of an electric technology by-
passing language which threatens contemporary man, but
Alexander Pope's vision of Night in *The Dunciad*, a linguistic silence where "light dies before the *uncreating* word":

> See Metaphysic call for aid of Sense!
> See Mystery to Mathematics fly!
> In vain! they gaze, turn giddy, rave and die.
> Thy hand great Dullness! lets the curtain fall,
> And universal Darkness covers all.

The acceleration of production through technology is a
crucial article of Utopian faith. Mankind existed by har-
nessing water power for 5,000 years, yet has outgrown
atomic energy in twenty. Material goods (especially in
America where they assume near-religious potency) are an
increasing clutter to the human geography. The machine,
an extension of man's sinew, has also become a testament to
his hubris, spewing forth products which testify to the blessings of the land and a nation's power. But there is an undeniable and encroaching threat in this noisy spectacle. As
Molloy observes: "To restore *silence* is the role of objects."

Inflation of every kind of currency (manpower, language,
gold) has been the natural result of a technological age.
The artistic process goes against the tempo of the times.
"The artistic tendency is not expansive but contractive. And
art is the apotheosis of solitude."[37]

The language of any powerful nation becomes debased
by public events. America has not yet suffered the sudden
and conclusive holocaust which reduced a language—like
German—to silence. Our wars can be turned off after the
eleven o'clock news; the effect on poetic argot is more

gradual but no less real. It is no coincidence that the minimalist tendency has come increasingly from Anglo-Saxon artists who bear the heritage of a language of oppression. "Worn threadbare, filed down, words have become the carcass of words, phantom words; everybody drearily chews and regurgitates the sound of them between their jaws."[38] This statement by Arthur Adamov, written after World War II, is applicable to our own chaotic moment in history. Once language is seen to cloak injustice, to go hand in glove with political betrayal, it increases the cynicism of a nation for its own tongue. The retreat toward silence, the appreciation of it as an active philosophical and human force, is a modern phenomenon. It is a lonely course, and a hard-headed one. But—to paraphrase Hugh Kenner—in courting a dead end, contemporary artists may be discovering a way *not* to die.

5

Jules Feiffer: Satire as Subversion

"*S*atire," George S. Kaufman once said, "is what closes Saturday night." His dollars and cents *bon mot* is not simply the slick wisdom of one of Broadway's most famous comic writers, but a distillation of commercial theater's disdain for satire's leering indictment. The attitude still exists. In a decade of political buffooneries and gargantuan excess, the number of plays even aspiring to satire can be counted on two hands. Faced with an uptown audience nervous about complexity, actors confused by ambiguity, directors opting for the literal, and critics ignorant of the genre, it is amazing that a satirist as talented and devastating as Jules Feiffer continues to write for the stage. His *Little Murders,* a brilliant analysis of the violence breeding in middle-class fear, was swatted down on Broadway by critics after seven performances (but has had a successful revival Off-Broadway); *God Bless,* a play aspiring to revolutionary parable, was roundly hooted at Yale and the Royal Shakespeare Company. Yet no stage writer has gone deeper into the paradoxes of middle-class America than Feiffer. Despite the fact that he must suffer arrogant dismissals in the name of stodgy decorum, he has added significantly to the debate of the nation's destiny as well as to its body of comic literature.

Feiffer's attitude toward stage satire is different from that of his predecessors:

> Satire basically has to be antagonistic to the system within which it's operating. I don't think of Noel Coward, for instance, as satire. They're pastiches, parodies. I don't mean this pejoratively; but satire is much more *subversive*.[1]

This contrasts with the spirit of acceptance which characterized burlesque entertainment as well as the literary satirists. Describing the *esprit* which led to such successful collaborations as *Merton of the Movies* and *Beggar on Horseback,* Marc Connelly recalls that he and Kaufman scoured New York as theater-reporters turned writers: "We greedily ate everything that looked like an appetizing dish. A piece of writing, a comedian, a serious actor or actress, fun for fun's sake. We were alert. I don't know whether we were shrewd in our judgments but we felt everything very keenly."[2] In the same way, the show business pundits who laughed at government were men with no axes to grind. Will Rogers claimed he never met a man he didn't like; Bob Hope ("Old Ski Nose") was always too safe to be angry. Only occasionally, as with S. J. Perelman's hilarious spoof on cultural prostitution, *The Beauty Part,* did a satirist take a healthy eighteenth-century swing at contemporary big-wigs. Perelman who, like Feiffer, has the satirist's asset of being a good hater, skewered a publisher called Emmett Stagg, a pipe-smoking punster for a publishing concern called Charnel House. Stagg is given to pronouncing en-comiums to potential film producers: "It'll be a tidal wave, and I'm letting you on my surfboard . . ." Perelman also gave his publicity-hungry publisher axioms for his faith in notoriety: "In the aristocracy of success there are no strangers."[3]

The satirist's venom and his vision generally spring from a conservative impulse, a distrust of the present, and a tacit hankering for the past. If this is true of Aristophanes, Swift, and Waugh, the Feiffer plays belong to the more progressive Shavian tradition, interested in criticizing the present in order to influence the future. Unlike Perelman, Feiffer is after much bigger game than Hollywood gar-goyles and literary phonies. His rogues' gallery extends into the political arena. Fascinated with the nation's moral myopia, he concocts situations which trace the confusions to their source. *Little Murders* becomes a parable for our Vietnams in the same way that *God Bless* focuses its audi-ence's attention on both the figures of authority and the ideas which become the rhetoric of political action. Yet, even the satirist's clinical instinct has its paradoxes. If satire is an underground activity, Feiffer acknowledges depths of subversion:

You can make a good living by being known as
anti-establishment. In the McCarthy fifties, being
anti-establishment was enough because the society was so repulsively conformist. Today, one
has to investigate his own approach to his particular brand of subversion and find out if he
can't dig still deeper.

Feiffer's plays have been assailed as cartoons, a fact he
accepts with irony. "For the first seven years I was doing
cartoons, people used to tell me that my drawings weren't
cartoons at all. I had to start writing plays for people to
discover I was a cartoonist." The pigeonholing of Feiffer's
plays is a critical fillip which hides their complexity. His
characters have an immense intellectual resonance, but not
necessarily a theatrical one. Performers find his plays difficult because they must perform in a strict and often ambiguous circumference of gestures and emotions. The
characters do not offer the actors a chance for emotional
self-revelation. Feiffer's people, like Jonson's Lovewits and
Congreve's Witwoulds, become an articulate amalgam of
general attitudes focused in a particular man. These are not
moral archetypes, but complex and human ones; they are
not literal caricatures or the subhuman banalities summoned
by the term "cartoon." Directors, too, often seem stumped
for means of creating a visual dimension for pyrotechnics
which live so vividly in print. Feiffer's plays demand a direc-
torial style which matches the ambiguity of his political
conclusions.

His images on stage can be broadly theatrical: the Washington Monument is toppled in revolutionary fervor during
God Bless; city noises shatter the calm of the Newquist
home in *Little Murders.* Yet, Feiffer's statement is never
primarily made with images in the way that Jean-Claude
van Itallie's *Motel* creates a sense of disgust and crude power

with papier-mâché giants, or which John Guare conjures in
Muzeeka when a woman sings headlines plucked from a
skirt made of *The New York Times.* Feiffer makes his point
with words, logic that spirals smoothly until, without knowing why, the audience confronts something menacing and
true. Feiffer himself looks on his plays as essays, an impulse
for which some critics might score him, but this is where
the real thrust of his dramatic power lies.

> The most interesting form today is probably the
> essay. It is what Godard puts on film and, God
> knows, they're exciting films. In many ways, it
> is what I try to do in the cartoon and I suppose
> it's what interests me in the theater. I want to
> frame an idea or ideas in characters who will
> interact, and I hope that interaction will present
> the idea to the audience. I don't mean one of
> my characters to be spokesman for the writer,
> walking frontstage and saying, "I know the
> trouble with us, the trouble with us is . . ." That's
> just too simple-minded. A character can't just
> stand on stage and tell us what's right and wrong.
> That sort of writing embarrasses me when I see
> it. What can happen is that characters can stand
> on stage and argue from various fixed points,
> none of which are absolutely right. And by lis-
> tening (and you are forced to listen if the argu-
> ments are interesting enough) the point of view
> emerges for the audience.

Feiffer, armed with the satirist's axiom to instruct by
pleasing, is able to use conventional theatrical formulas
against themselves, creating with inversion the shock of
reality. His satire is a confrontation, not an evasion. When
the curtain comes up on *Little Murders,* the audience knows
the terrain: attractive, clean, neat, middle-class New York

situation comedy. What occurs upsets their conditioned response. Instead of preaching the gospel of acceptance, Feiffer examines how the instincts of capitalism have warped the concept of democratic community in a land where the rich can buy protection or tip for better service. The idea of community—so important for laughter and, indeed, for America's dream—is lost in paradox: a nation believing at once that all men are equal and that every man deserves as much as he can get. By turning the conventional stage environment into a surreal geography, Feiffer consciously betrays the lie of bourgeois naturalism.

> I recently saw *Plaza Suite* and *The Price* on two successive nights, and I became aware that there is a whole chain of experiences that people assume to be real which have nothing to do with real life, only theatrical and movie lives. Confrontation scenes, for instance, in which everyone tells the truth about each other, never happen in real life. But we're so used to it in theater that, when it happens, we don't see it as a device. But nothing could be less natural.

Feiffer's satire aspires to pinpoint an emotional truth rather than use theatrical sleights of hand to avoid it. *Little Murders* was an experiment in yanking the carpet from under comfortable mythologies:

> In *Little Murders* I was trying to take those very familiar devices—the Andy Hardy family, the situation comedy—and set them loose in a country that's been living for a long period with a Cold War morality, the America of Vietnam. I find there is a great temptation to take traditional American theater rituals out of Kaufman, out of Neil Simon, and update them into the world of

reality. It's fascinating because what you're dealing with is the audience. You're giving them
something which has a relaxing familiarity, and
then showing them how it really is.

The intention of Feiffer's laughter, the twists he adds to
recognizable clichés, is easily seen in comparing the typical
"Jewish mother" in *Little Murders* with one by Neil Simon,
the slickest of contemporary Broadway comedy writers.
Satire's laughter is a deflation of conventional values; situation comedy is merely an extension of them. In *Barefoot in
the Park,* the newly-married daughter is giving her widowed
mother a marital pep talk.

CORIE: You know, underneath that army uniform, you're
    still a young vital woman . . . Do you know what I
    think you *really* need?

MOTHER: Yes, and I don't want to hear it. (*She gets up and
    moves away.*)

CORIE (*goes to her*): Because you're afraid to hear the
    truth.

MOTHER: It's not the truth I'm afraid to hear. It's the *word*
    you're going to use.

CORIE: You're darn right I'm going to use that word . . . It's
    love!

MOTHER: Oh . . . thank you.[4]

The joke in the Simon story is the same as the tenor of
his play. What is fearful to the mother is the grit of the
word. Is her daughter going to say "screw" or "fuck"? What
is funny and accessible to the middle-class audiences is the
sense of decorum which isolates and rationalizes truth on
stage. Feiffer can use this nervousness to zero in on hypoc-

risy. In *Little Murders,* the family sits down to dinner with their daughter's fiancé. Alfred is a photographer.

ALFRED: I take pictures of shit.

MOTHER: Young man, this is my table!

ALFRED: I don't mean to offend you, Mrs. Newquist. I've been shooting shit for a long time now.[5]

The facts of any situation have more ambiguity than a simple laugh line. Feiffer sees his tactic on stage as parallel to Lenny Bruce's.

> Bruce would create little situations. He'd be saying things to the girl and the girl would be saying things to him. They were marvels of discovery. The audience would hold its breath, laughing in a way that gave themselves away. They had been hit hard. It was rather marvelous to be there and be hit yourself. Lenny would say things that no one had ever said and the air was clarified. Suddenly, all your ghosts were out in the open and there was nothing to be afraid of, at least at the moment. It was a marvelous feeling.

Feiffer's satire liberates stage situations from convention. In *Little Murders,* the formula love duet is not grounded in a safe urban bower but pierced with shrill city sounds and anonymous telephone calls from The Breather. Feiffer's love interest, Patsy and Alfred, embrace in a typical Broadway boy-meets-girl first act finale. "My hero," Patsy says. "Aren't they an attractive couple," observes her mother. There is a gunshot; Patsy slumps in her lover's arms. Horrible but hilarious, the lie in the stage convention is exposed by an act of random violence. If the gesture is

unpredictable or outrageous, it approaches that nether
world which captivates the Feiffer imagination where in-
sanity lurks behind every rational structure and behind every
rhetorical statement of faith.

The human animal, for Feiffer, is continually betrayed by
his own cowardice, disguising his fear instead of confronting it. Mr. Newquist, who has the ambivalent first name of
Carol, speaks with a braggadocio certainty which masks his
vulnerability. His wife calls, "Carol," and he replies:

> (*Vicious.*) I *hate* that name! I told you never to
> call me that name. You deliberately do it to annoy
> me! (*Shouts.*) Call me "Dear!" (*Subsides.*) You
> refuse to look at the facts. This whole family.
> That's the trouble with it. I'm the only one that
> looks at the facts . . .

The father of the slain girl is a product of the American
spirit which holds onto a concept of democracy which, like
Newquist's virility, no longer fits the real situation. Mr.
Newquist bolts his doors, hawks photographs of his dead
daughter, and even ends up firing at passers-by with a rifle.
He never understands the moral confusion that, with each
gesture, creates the world he despises. The gun laws, which
the Newquist family exploit, allow men to defend themselves and their property against the threat (real or
imagined) of destruction. *Little Murders* becomes a parable
of contemporary fear, a crystalline image showing how
ostensibly harmless individuals contribute to slaughter.
Feiffer's allegory has its acerbic parallels in America's involvement in Vietnam, a solipsism brought up-to-date but
reminiscent of the Earl of Rochester's "Satire on Mankind":

> Whilst wretched Man, is still in arms for fear
> By fear, to fear, successively betray'd . . .

When *Little Murders* first opened, few middle-class audiences had lived with the violence Feiffer was chronicling. Now, with so many more slayings and omnipresent brutality, the violence has moved into the open.

> I think we're very slow in catching up with the obvious. And when we do catch up with it, we call somebody who saw it a year or two ago, prophetic. It's not prophetic at all. Is I. F. Stone prophetic because he saw we were in trouble three years before Robert McNamara? It was just that McNamara was stupid and misled by his own bullshit. So I think the ability to clear away the bullshit may be mistaken for prophetic powers.

Feiffer's satires explode the clichés of language. He never allows his audience the relaxation of comfortable dialogue and palatable caricature. His language has the spare, direct quality of the best satire. It is dry and delightfully tight-lipped, like Swift's "A Modest Proposal" or Donald Barthelme's modern salvos. Satire is an insidious tactic; it must parody and imply, but never state. The joke, which is on the audience, must also be discovered by them. According to Feiffer, "Satire is an attempt to get at the root of a situation and expose it by the extension of logic. By taking it to the point where it might become ridiculous, certain truths about situations can be revealed." Feiffer's stage language has a precision, the power to evoke a sense of fact which merges, finally, into fantasy. Critics scoff at this particularity in much the same way as Dr. Johnson underestimated Swift's *Gulliver's Travels*. Nothing in *Little Murders,* for instance, detracts from the artifice. Newquist fans the flames of violence by tipping the doorman for extra safety and passing out $5 bills to policemen. When the detective arrives on the scene (a third-act entrance which

challenges the Broadway formula that nothing new can be
introduced in the last ten minutes before curtain), he be-
moans the 345 unsolved murders with Walter Winchell
swagger:

> We are involved here in a far-reaching conspiracy
> to undermine our basic beliefs and most sacred
> institutions. Who is behind this conspiracy? Once
> again ask the question: Who has the most to gain?
> People in high places. Their names would astound
> you. People in low places. Concealing their activi-
> ties beneath a cloak of poverty. People in all
> walks of life. Left wing and right wing. Black and
> white. Students and scholars. A conspiracy of
> such ominous proportions that we may not know
> the whole truth in our lifetime and we will never
> be able to reveal all the facts. We are readying
> mass arrests.

We have heard the tone before, and have even seen this
conspiratorial view of history parodied. But Feiffer's strength
of mind and his inventiveness extend the rhetoric into a
network of social assumptions hilariously apt to the detective's conservative-heroic posing. The detective's speech
illustrates Feiffer's gift for parody. He can develop philosophical positions as logical and febrile as Swift's Aeolists
who, disdaining matter, walk with their eyes shut, bouncing
into objects whose existence they deny. Reverend Dupas
marries Alfred and Patsy. Dupas is so committed to existential freedom of choice that he has none:

> Why does one decide to marry? Social pressure?
> Boredom? Loneliness? Sexual appeasement—um,
> love? I don't put any of these reasons down. Each,
> in its own way, is adequate. Each is all right. I

married a musician last year who wanted to get
married in order to stop masturbating. (*Guests
stir.*) Please don't get startled. I am not putting
it down. That marriage did not work. But the man
tried. Now the man is separated, and still masturbating—but he is at peace with himself . . .

Feiffer is developing a dense literary comic style which
capitalizes on a national love of overstatement and a mysterious distrust of the complex. If he can impale right-wing
rhetoric in *Little Murders,* he can be can equally ruthless
to the left. In *God Bless,* the revolutionaries of the ALF
(American Liberation Front) have taken control of Washington. They deny the existing community in order to
establish one; their rebellion becomes an act of despair
rather than one of liberation and love. The creativity of
revolution preached by Camus develops into the slavery he
feared. The radicals mock the humanity they serve; their language becomes an appendage of arrogant simplification.
They too are betrayed into the pragmatism and cruelty of
the world they would reform.

Words cause cancer! The revolution rejects
words! It digs beneath the phoniness of words and
comes up with emotion. And then it digs beneath
the phoniness of emotions and comes up with
games! Ritual! It comes up with joy! Guerrilla
joy! We pollute the polluters with guerrilla joy—
we spray it like Mace! We adapt to a new vision
and begin to see what's really funny! Not jokes.
Jokes are words—they paralyze the spirit. Guns
are more humane than the jokes married couples
tell on each other. You know what's really funny?
A desk—(*Grins.*)—a time clock—(*Chuckles.*)
—a computer . . .

This is the muscle-flexing hysteria of the Yippie phenomenon, the psychology of the put-on, the group-grope,
the Living Theater, a radical event as humorless as it is
totalitarian. Feiffer's ear is not simply precise, he creates
a dramatic situation which comments on itself, haunting an
audience instead of haranguing it.

At Yale, where the play made its American debut, students accused Feiffer of taking no position. "What's being
said," counters Feiffer, "is that if I don't pick from labels
A, B, C, and D then I haven't picked anything. I don't
think those are the only choices. I don't really think the
choice is between Lyndon Johnson and Abbie Hoffman."

This moral tension between stage character and audience
sentiment is a tactic crucial to Feiffer's appreciation of
theater:

> The only real interest I have in theater, in writing
> plays, is to create drama between the actors and
> the stage on one hand and the audience on the
> other. So it's a two-way dialogue between what's
> happening on stage and the members of the audi-
> ence who are reacting to what's being said and
> arguing back, perhaps. I don't mean audience
> participation. If you have said "No" out loud
> inside a theater, there is very little chance that you
> will say "No" outside. But if you're arguing or
> befuddled or angry in the theater, it will go out-
> side with you and continue to disturb you. Plays
> which have meant something to me have dis-
> turbed me. That is something I'm trying to re-
> produce.

God Bless is about an elder statesman, William Brackman, who is 110 years old. Feiffer, in the one gesture of
Brackman dozing in his chair and waking to speak his past

into a taped interview, captures the ossified possibilities of pragmatic liberalism in America. The play was scored for its lack of theatricality, but no other playwright has tackled the American political tradition with such ruthless energy, defying stage etiquette for elaborate debate. At a time when the nation is led by a President who has shown no ostensible plans to move it forward, when Hubert Humphrey, having lost the election, lingers on the political scene clinging to the vestiges of power, Feiffer's concern with political tradition is exciting and useful. Other playwrights, especially John Guare in *Cop-Out,* have railed with outrageous images against a New World grown old. In *Cop-Out,* Marilyn Monroe is in bed with a succession of presidents who pop out of the sheets like Groucho Marx—a burlesque of evaporating energy.

> Oh, Woodrow, I feel so old.
> Oh, Calvin, say something.
> Harder harder harder Harding.
> To think one day Herbert Hoover would be mine.
> Oh, FDR; your braces are cold against my legs.
> You don't tell me, Harry, you learned that from Bess.
> Oh yes, Ike, you put me to sleep. Hold me,
>   Daddy Ike.
> Oh, Jack. We're young. You and I are young.
> (*She has turned into an old lady. She reaches
>   in hysteria for the phone.*)
> Bobby, answer the phone? Say I'm not old?
>   Say I'm young.
> Bobby, say we're both young? Say it? Say it?[6]

Feiffer's farce is more cerebral; his intention is not, like Guare's, to offer a vaudeville of fossilization, but to chart the process of a political philosophy grown rancid. In careful and literate sentences, Brackman expounds a history

of compromise. As he tells his story, he confides in the
President and also with revolutionaries who come to ask
for his support.

> Support? For what? The execution of army of-
> ficers—the cutting off of their ears? Support that?
> I don't know, I don't know. Norman, you were
> my student—what would you do in my place?

If Brackman has moral qualms about such violence, by
the end of the play he is negotiating with the revolutionaries
about how many cities are going to be bombed. The play
ends with Brackman talking into a tape recorder in his
nineteenth-century syntax:

> On my 110th birthday, the government of the
> United States was violently overthrown and there
> was at long last promise of a new dawn for
> America. Surprisingly, I found myself in a posi-
> tion of usefulness.

Brackman's pragmatism comes from superficially gen-
erous intentions. "He represents the liberal mentality which
chooses to be effective rather than woolly-minded, moralistic, and idealistic," explains Feiffer. "That effectiveness
has brought the U.S. to many betrayals, one of which is
Vietnam."

Politics, as the subject for an evening of theater, is usually
left to musicals like *Fiorello!* or nostalgic simplifications
like *Sunrise at Campobello.* Unlike them, *God Bless* is a
threat not only to those unfamiliar with the terrain of New
Politics, but also to those who know it too well.

Feiffer's theatrical sophistication has matured immeasur-
ably from his first stage effort, *Crawling Arnold.* As a

satirist, the theatricality of Feiffer's vision is continually being refined. His latest sketch, *Dick and Jane* (included in *Oh! Calcutta!*), is a more theatrically effective examination of sex, a theme he plans to develop in his next full-length play. Dick, anxious for new sex adventures and kinky thrills, comes to the conjugal bower equipped with a variety of stimulants—mask, whip, boots, basketball, watermelon, spray paint. Having built their discussion to a crescendo of painful cross-questioning, the special intercourse takes place—the triumph of ego over empathy.

> [*He*] *re-enters carrying phonograph and movie projector. Turns them on; deafening loud rock, accompanied by a light show. Light show intensifies, becomes blinding. The last action we see is* DICK *leaping through the air at* JANE, *an open umbrella in his hand. After a suitable lapse of time the rock record ends, the light show goes off, the room is black.*

DICK: O boy, O boy, O boy, O boy, O boy. Did you ever dream it could be that good. Don't you feel good, Jane? I feel good. Don't you feel loose, like your limbs are floating in air? Don't you, Jane? The best I ever had it. I'll have to tell you about the other times. Christ, we've got so much to talk about, Jane. You know, it's crazy, but I feel so close to you, as if for the first time I've seen your soul. And you've seen my soul, Jane. What does good or bad or ugly or sick mean when we've each other's souls . . . Would you believe it's me, Jane. Janie, honey, come lie in my arms for a minute. (*He lights a match.*) Jane. Where are you? . . . (DICK *rummages through the debris, calling out for his wife.*) Jane! Hey, Jane. Hey, weren't you here? Don't tell me you missed it! Jane! Jane! (*Opens door.*) Jane! (*Exits, his voice fading as he disappears down the hall.*) Jane! You should've been there! Jane![7]

The irony of hard-core hedonism! While Dick uses elaborate equipment to work up a climax, Feiffer is never so self-indulgent with his laughs.

Feiffer's stage future seems healthy. Firmly established as a humorist, Feiffer can hopefully withstand the slings and arrows of outrageous theatrical economics which defeat so many talents. The literary quality of his writing has never been in doubt; theater savvy is something only learned from experience. Most important, Feiffer is intimately involved with the world—inquisitive, bold, always probing the national consciousness. "Satire is the discovery of relationships in the society and it is always examining the society. There's so much material. The nation is literally up for grabs. It's a very exciting time and a very puzzling one."

In an America whose destiny teeters on the fulcrum of every current event, whose mythologies have been emasculated, and whose uniformity of experience increases daily, the satirist may become the only stage artist capable of dealing with the flux and political pratfalls of the future. Already blessed with a buffoon's resilience and the ability to take risks with his vision, Jules Feiffer has all the assets to become one of American theater's major craftsmen.

6

The End of
the Underground

Everybody's his own hipster.
—Lorraine Hansberry[1]

The protean style of self-process is characterized by an interminable series of experiments and explorations—some shallow, some profound—each of which may be readily abandoned in favor of still new psychological quests.
—Robert Jay Lifton[2]

I

*T*he American Underground is a unique phenomenon in the Land of Plenty: existing under a continual state of siege, yet it thrives by exporting its disenfranchisement like democracy. It is more embattled than the bohemia of the twenties, taking ferment quietly during the Eisenhower doldrums and rattling its shield mightily in the violent

95

upheavals of the sixties. True to historical tradition, the Underground has harbored the avant-garde in art and politics, and, under the banner of spiritual, intellectual, and political liberation, marched these ideals steadily against a recalcitrant Establishment. Unlike its dour philosophical predecessors in the European literary Resistance, our Underground has not been able to erase (or deny) its special national traits: the American Underground, for all its importance, is kinkier, more comfortable—and more fun, reflecting (perversely) the nation's special talkative booster buoyancy, its raw energy, and a national theatricality even in paranoia. But, in one of those rare historical quirks facilitated by the mass media, the Establishment and the Underground have acknowledged each other, bound together by similar pleasures (rock, grass) and dyspepsia over Vietnam, national politics, and the race question. The Underground, having forced a confrontation on major issues, has, in many ways, been accepted on minor ones. Without a truculent enemy, it must—in time—dissolve.

The archetypal Underground man has always been the outsider. In the fifties, he was the existential bum, Mailer's white Negro, half psychopath, half hipster. Then, it was a time of individual and distinct epiphanies: digging jazz, smoking pot, balling the neighborhood. It was a time of sliding from one pleasure to another, each with its own significance, each with its special frame of reference. Even the language which Mailer pointed out as characteristic of this search for energy—"how it is found, how it is lost"—had a kind of singularity: "Man, go, put down, make, beat, cool, swing, with it, crazy, dig, flip, creep, hip, square." The divisions were hard and fast, even for Mailer:

> One is Hip or one is Square (the alternative which
> each new generation is beginning to feel), one is

a rebel or one conforms, one is a frontiersman in
the Wild West of American night life, or else a
Square cell, trapped in the totalitarian tissues of
American society, doomed willy nilly to conform
if one is to succeed.[3]

Life in America has speeded up in the sixties; the Underground argot reflects the blurring of boundaries, the movement from single confrontations to many-in-one: "spaced,
groove, out of sight, flipped out, vibrations." The language
is more intense, more emotionally complete, more violent.
The Hippies and Yippies of today are the spiritual children
of the Beat Generation and hipsters whose subterranean
quest produced a literature, but not a sustained way of life.
Mailer's testament to them is important for understanding
the difference between the Beat Generation and the Underground of today. Then, the Beats were able to function and
live in their own society away from the mainstream; the
distance between the Underground life and bourgeois society
was unbreachable.

The beatnik, gentle, disembodied from the race,
is often a radical pacifist, he has sworn the vow of
no violence—in fact, his violence is sealed within,
and he has no way of using it. His act of violence
is to suicide even as the hipster's is toward murder, but in his mind-lost way, the beatnik is the
torchbearer of those all-but-lost values of freedom, self-expression and equality which first
turned him against the barren cultureless flats of
the middle class . . . For years now, they have
lived side by side, hipster and beatnik, white,
Negro, and crippled saint, their numbers increasing every month as the new ones come to
town . . .[4]

Mailer, like so many of the best Underground spokesmen, felt an emotional kinship to the community but was
never claimed by it. Already foreshadowing the sixties style,
he was everywhere and nowhere, impossible to predict, and,
consequently, always outrageous. He became, as the rest of
the Underground would, a protean figure, vociferously his
own hero. The destiny of the Underground fulfilled its
prophecy of discontent as American society floundered on
old axioms. The world began to adopt the Underground's
artistic expression of political disgust (but hedged on the
ideas behind it); Underground culture gradually became
one of the nation's most definable sights and sounds. In
an age of political cynicism, the Underground was jubilant;
after so many middle-class compromises, it was adamant.
Jerry Rubin remembers:

> It's 1969 already, and 1965 seems almost a child-
> hood memory. Then we were the conquerors of
> the world. No one could stop us. We were going
> to end the war. We were going to wipe out racism.
> We were going to mobilize the poor. We were
> going to take over the Universities . . . Check out
> the original hippie-digger poetry and manifestoes:
> euphoria, overflowing optimism, and expectation
> of immediate success. Wow, I still get high on it.[5]

The artistic revolution was easier to create than a political one. The people who formed the cornerstones of the
Underground brought to it a vision of the problems of the
future and new forms to convey them. It was impossible for
an Establishment so incapable of explaining its malaise,
so hungry to consume the new, to deny what the Underground harbored: The Living Theater, Bob Dylan, Joan
Baez, the Velvet Underground, Andy Warhol, Allen Gins-
berg, LeRoi Jones, Paul Goodman, William Burroughs,

John Cage, Paul Krassner, Timothy Leary, Jules Feiffer, Abbie Hoffman, Jerry Rubin, *et al.* Each had his own passion, each his alternative for a better world, which took on pertinence with each new Establishment political buffoonery. Folk rock became the soul of a nation's rebellion and its potential resilience. Man's consciousness was expanded not only by the electronic media but by the psychedelic experience. This synthetic vision was graphically available to the non-drug-taking public through records, posters, or movies like Kubrick's *2001.* The variety of expression matched the technological multiplicity.

The once arcane, isolated Underground became public spectacle—recreated, talked about, analyzed, and finally made available to the mass. And, in that curious American way, idealism cohabited with Big Business. But avant-garde materialism in the affluent society has nothing to do with the catcalls of "selling out." The Underground man merely lives "better" than his father, spending money on bell-bottoms instead of blazers, supporting the Movement instead of the fraternity. In an industrial state it is hard to avoid cash on hand when one becomes an industry.

The Underground has been the psychic home for the nation's uprooted. Dislocation was an intellectual decision in the fifties; today it is a fact. Mass communications inundate us with a plethora of images, allowing all classes to stare at one another. In one night, a television viewer could watch both the spectacle of RFK's primary victory *and* his assassination. The speed of the new technology has indubitably wrenched man into a new position: the man sitting still can be everywhere. The Underground, like the Establishment, had to acknowledge the protean nature of modern life— man's omniconsciousness. The Underground man could do more; he could experience many-things-at-once. The Underground became a well-publicized part of contemporary

geography. Psychiatrist Robert Jay Lifton has outlined how
this notoriety creates a unique and ambivalent situation:

> Each individual is touched by everything, but at
> the same time he is overwhelmed by superficial
> messages and undigested cultural elements, by
> headlines, and endless partial alternatives in every
> sphere of life. These alternatives moreover are
> universally and simultaneously shared, at least in
> the form of significant imagery.[6]

As a result, Underground activity has become neither
silent nor private, nor happily disenfranchised—a victim
not only of its good intentions to survive but of an omnivorous technology. The Underground has always had its
literary promoters (the *Village Voice, Evergreen Review,*
part of the fifties disenfranchisement; *EVO,* the *L.A. Free
Press* and *New York Free Press,* representing the psychedelic and political thrust of the sixties). But only recently
have mass media discovered it, unable to deny the Underground's cultural relevance by staying away. The TV audience could see the Yippies face the Pigs in Chicago as well
as life in a California commune; a documentary on LSD as
well as David Susskind interviewing the Fugs. Individualism,
once so hard-won from conventional society, is now retailed.
In an industrial society whose Establishment is emotionally
impoverished but all-powerful, freedom is both a titillating
threat and a marketable commodity. The result has been
an absurd cultural about-face by both the Establishment
and the Underground.

The Underground man, once the drop-out, can now handle himself on television, and be applauded for putting down
the white-imperialist-military-industrial complex at interviews. Technology and the mechanics of the industrial state

push him continually back into the Establishment society he has left—but *always on his own terms.* This becomes a deceptive gauge of society's sympathy.

In previous cultures, the breach between the Establishment and the avant-garde (Lenin: "the vanguard of revolutionary forces in our time," 1902) has been wide and clear. In Europe between 1840 and 1940, bourgeois society's artistic heroes had nothing to do with the renegades who disputed the orthodox (and usually academic) cultural scene. As British critic Douglas Cooper points out in the *Times Literary Supplement,* "The avant-garde made no effort to come to terms with it either emotionally or intellectually."[7] But the names now associated with pre-1940 European culture are primarily innovators, men who clung ruthlessly to their vision and passion for experiments *outside* conventional channels, and whose longevity of creation was assured by this very distance: Ibsen, Brecht, Rilke, Nietzsche, Eliot, Wagner, Bartók, Schoenberg, Marx, Einstein, Freud, Picasso, Braque, Matisse.

Where once the revolutionary experiment was disdained by the Establishment, in a "liberalized" America it has become the only thing worth supporting. The National Council for the Arts gives over $100,000 a year for experimental theater; the Rockefeller Foundation awards grants to "new playwrights," most of whom necessarily emerge from the Underground. The avant-garde, far from being the anathema which gives danger (and integrity) to its enterprise, has become an important cultural bric-a-brac. Its newest frustration is to be at once popular and curiously powerless. The element of surprise is lost to public habit; the healthy subversiveness, by becoming popular, loses its threat. The Underground life-style, once intended to be a shocking fist in the face of the Establishment, is now predictable because of publicity. In sharing the dynamic (promotion, distribution, profit, market research) of the Establishment, it must also assume part of the responsibility. By mixing with the enemy it becomes hard (impossible) to know where to point a finger. Norman Mailer forgot this very recent shift in attitude when he lectured at a benefit for the *New York Free Press.*

> Until every one of you is willing to get to that point where you recognize your life, your work, your movement, your whole vision will not succeed unless it becomes an art work, you've got nothing, you're the enemy. And you're working for them, for the Right.[8]

For a decade, the Underground life-style was measured against the Establishment. But the Underground battle for artistic liberation has been won, in part, by the Establishment. The pill has unleashed sex from its bourgeois repressions; marijuana is in the suburbs and on the battlefields. The schools are changing their organizations, introducing Afro-American curricula. There are still enemies, and causes (Vietnam, the ghettos) which are stubborn reminders of the country's sickness. But even here, amelioration seems possible, if improbable. As the targets *seem to recede,* so too does the purity of antagonism.

II

Popular culture has become the *serious* culture. Philip Roth's *Portnoy's Complaint,* like Dylan's songs, is not only million dollar business, but art as well. Nowhere are the permutations of this shift more interesting than in theater. Languishing a decade ago in the turgid naturalism of Arthur Miller and the eclecticism of Edward Albee, it has found new forms and a different audience. The Underground sense of irony has become public event. If the paying numbers have diminished, the national consciousness has never been more aware of theatrical metaphor. The sit-in, the protest march, the Yippie confrontations, are *dramatic,* calculated as theater to bring the artistic metaphor (and irony) out of the auditorium and into the street. The masks of Nixon worn at Nixon's inauguration were not only ghastly specters of disgust, but, over network television, a dramatic counterpoint to the well-scrubbed and whitewashed proceedings. The Yippies know about television; they *want to use it.* Jerry Rubin observed in the *New York Review of Books*(!):

> The Yippies love HUAC. For us it is a costume ball: a chance to project to the children of the world our secret fantasies, à la McLuhan. What a gas it was to see the headline: HUAC BARS SANTA CLAUS. HUAC is bullshit; it has no power.[9]

The Underground, once set off from the mass experience, has learned how to manipulate it. Abbie Hoffman knows how vividly his theatrical intentions register on the tube:

> The rhetoric of the Convention was allotted the fifty minutes of the hour, we were given the ten or less usually reserved for the commercials. *We were an advertisement for the revolution . . .* Watching the convention play out its boring drama, one could not help but be conscious of the revolution being played in the streets . . . That underlying tension builds up and the viewer becomes totally involved with what we are doing EVEN IF HE CANNOT SEE OR EXPERIENCE IT DIRECTLY. He makes up what's going on in the streets. He creates the Yippies,

cops, and other participants in his own image.
He constructs his own play. He fabricates his own
myth . . .[10]

If the Yippies brought out the latent ugliness on the
American terrain so that not even television could deny it,
they also became national news because their theatrical
adventures projected well over television. The journalists
pressed in for their story, demanding more events to meet
public interest. The Underground activity is bolstered by
the Establishment need. Hoffman reminisces:

> I constantly hustle the media. I make them pay as
> much as possible. Four cases of beer, limousine
> service, free dinner, press credentials. Once Chan-
> nel 2 in Boston (where I socked in the only
> "horseshit" ever heard on Boston television) gave
> me a blank airplane ticket to fly back to New
> York. I filled in "Chicago" . . . and cashed in on
> the difference. I suggested to *Life* Magazine that
> they could get some great photos if they threw
> 10,000 flowers out of a helicopter into Lincoln
> Park. They loved the idea . . .[11]

The effect on youth has been considerable. Rubin: "We
are stealing the youth of America right out of kindergartens
and elementary schools. We are the most exciting force in the
nation."[12] Exciting, in Rubin's terms, means theatrical. In
one sense theater has never been more available; in another,
it has never been more eclectic. This is the protean paradox
in an industrial state—reaching everywhere within the
society for new ways to comprehend and survive it.

The success of the public events (their ability to confront the real, not escape it) has been matched in more
conventional theatrical circles. Broadway's panache cannot

coat its artistic impoverishment. World events have caught up with its baroque halls; economics have limited its audience to the middle class, to whose banality it caters. But since Jean-Claude van Itallie's *America Hurrah* (1965), off-Broadway and off-off Broadway have become American theater. International attention has made it hard for even *The New York Times* to ignore them. In less than four years, this energy and relevance have also made Off-Broadway and Off-Off-Broadway supermarkets for talent, veering conspicuously away from the old Broadway route. In the Fall of 1968 two Off-Broadway institutions, Albee's Theater 1969 and Ted Mann's Circle in the Square, tried to bring Off-Broadway uptown, a fatuous transplant in which the badly bruised uptown body was bound to reject an alien object.

The barometer, however, is clear; the artistic phenomenon is fast becoming a commercial one. Almost all the Underground playwrights of merit are published; some, like the twenty-one year-old David Trainer, made it into print without a commercial production. La Mama Experimental Theater Group and the Open Theater, after many years of hand-to-mouth existence, have received sizable foundation grants. The Establishment has been eroded; the golden egg has been hatched by Underground fledglings. If off-Broadway's emergence into fashion makes tough-minded experiment more difficult, it also indicates that bourgeois fashion and Underground experiment are mixing.

The list of Off-Broadway gold mines is as long as it is awesome; Tom O'Horgan signed to a six-film contract by Carlo Ponti; Sam Shepard writing a film for Antonioni; Leonard Melfi adapting his slight psychological epiphany *Birdbath* as a vehicle for Monica Vitti; a film version of Rochelle Owens's *Futz;* Michael Schultz, after directing one brilliant production (*Song of the Lusitanean Bogey*), being offered and turning down a million-dollar film contract. The money has suddenly arrived. If it means fewer week-long stews on the stoves for young theater artists, it may also mean that their craft will be compromised by an easy success. *But it doesn't have to;* they can also use the system against itself. To call for total separation from the Establishment is an old Underground cry which denies their complicit relationship with (and need of) that Establishment. The Becks and Abbie Hoffman explain their philosophies to Merv Griffin on television; the Open Theater will not perform in a commercial production of *The Serpent,* but the script of their latest piece is published by Atheneum. Michael Smith, former critic for the *Village Voice,* calls for a revolution in his introduction to *The Best of Off-Off-Broadway:*

> A crisis is essential, but it calls for a difficult decision by the artists involved. They must abandon their desire for conventional success, especially when it comes within reach. It calls for sacrifice, without ego comforts of martyrdom, because the decision must be made for self-serving reasons. It is an incredibly hazardous moment: they must first create a new aesthetic and then a new institution to express it. Broadway won't die: it has to be assassinated.[13]

Yet Smith, who disdains the popularity of Off-Broadway, is writing about it in a book which *promotes* it! He is calling for a break with commercial habits at $1.95 a throw!

Richard Schechner's Performance Group, on the other hand, is not only raising an alternative Underground theater, but is capitalizing on the system to establish an economic structure which will allow the experiment to continue *without* the blessings of the Establishment. Schechner is marketing *Dionysus in 69* like Wheaties—a book will be published,

a film has already been made. The difference is that the
profit is not taken out of the theater, but *returned to it,*
not only insuring salaries, but sustaining the potential to
continue experimental work without financial pressure.
Schechner's idea may seem cynical to some, but, within the
culture, it is also shrewd. Foundation money is already
pulling back from the arts. The $90,000 given to La Mama
to construct a new building was not enough; the extra
$25,000 needed was not forthcoming from these bene-
factors, and as a result La Mama, having raised her aspirations to meet her new budget, had a six-month period
of *no activity.* This hurts theater. Those who deny the
system only hamper their ability to function effectively
against it; they cling to a noble Marxian concept of themselves already out of date in the modern state. (The Living
Theater, for instance, calls for anarchy in the name of a
non-materialist culture while three books are being published about them and they are earning $3,000 for an
evening's performance.) The paradox is not acknowledged,
resulting usually in a debate of slogans rather than soul-
searching. The Underground strains to maintain a subterranean image already seduced and abandoned.

III

America's fear of its old age has lent a reverence and
permissiveness to its youth, a mandate nervously given in
communal despair, and voraciously seized. *Greetings,* a
controversial feature film, is typical of an underground in
which the life it depicts is no longer separated from the
mainstream, bounded neither by geography nor income.
The film is a testament to the new "freedom," a modest
liberation (sexual, linguistic, political) in the face of terrifying events. The film begins and ends with LBJ glowering

like a haggard panda bear over the television: "I'M NOT SAYING YOU'VE NEVER HAD IT SO GOOD, BUT THAT IS A FACT, ISN'T IT?"

The arrogance of power is matched only by its obvious myopia. *Greetings* celebrates what is left of apple pie: random sex, draft finagling, groovy clothes, political paranoia, dancing, drugs, more sex. The three youths—Paul, Lloyd, and Jon—who are the focus of this film surround themselves with the clutter of Underground accoutrements: the *New York Review of Books* (which mixes the Black Panthers and Proust, Stokely Carmichael and Susan Sontag), Malcolm X posters, David Levine buttons, and RAT. This is the merchandise of rebellion. The background song intones the paradox of being an Underground and protean man in an affluent society: "So many things/So many places to go."

The Underground man is as much a consumer as a political being; his voraciousness in this film is reflected in his penchant for books, films, and voyeurism. Every emotion, every idea is available to his generation. He can study and cross-reference the Kennedy assassinations, like one young man in the film who takes his dazed, nude girlfriend, marking with a grease pencil the supposed point where the bullet entered. He can also watch America carry out its political decisions, creating a problem which even Lyndon Johnson can vaguely discern:

> Television brings into almost every home the most vivid pictures of foreign policy in action—in Europe, in Vietnam, in Panama, in the Middle East . . . There are many instant authorities now, with clear opinions on every crisis.[14]

Greetings starts with this fact, and extends it to its logical (and hilarious) conclusion, living out the fantasy of international voyeurism. The film ends with a mock television report from Vietnam where a Viet Cong soldier (a beautiful girl) is captured only to be asked to undress. The point is clearly made. Seventy million television sets and six hundred television channels have made us a nation of Peeping Toms: a sexual activity which gives an intimacy of experience and emotion never before available. The world bombards our brains. The audience knows too much to be satisfied and too little to match the mounting historical velocity: "They just don't know where to go/So little time to know." The song in the film follows a beautiful Underground urchin through the geography of her new mobility: the park, the Whitney Museum, a Village party where a Vietnam veteran talks about being stoned in the Delta.

The people in *Greetings* exist gaily around a patchwork of violence—violent sex, violent drugs, violent institutions, violent protest. Through a fractured cinematic form, the transience and fragility of their moment is conveyed, at once experimental—seeking new, briefer identities—and resilient. There is no time for pathos, let alone tragedy. In the fifties, Mailer's existentialist hipster was defined by the commitment of his subterranean quest. With no end in view, he still had to be specific about his inner turmoil.

> To be an existentialist, one must be able to feel oneself—one must know one's desires, one's rages, one's anguish, one must be aware of the character of one's frustration and know what would satisfy it.[15]

Greetings typifies an Underground life where no easy focus of rage is possible, although many are offered. Anguish and excitement come too fast, too enmeshed with each other to be so clinically or clearly separated. *Greetings*

is a world of old people, in which, like Beatles films, age
exists merely to be parodied. Paul, Lloyd, and Jon exult in
the fact of their youth without clear *rites du passage* to
adulthood, marriage, and death. The general appeal of
such films illustrates that the square world may also have
lost its rituals, even if it wishes to deny the validity of those
who establish new ones. Their love-hate affinity for the
young is also part of the protean paradox. As Robert Jay
Lifton points out,

> [protean man]—his being metaphorically and
> psychologically so young in spirit—has to do with
> his never ceasing quest for imagery of rebirth.
> He seeks such imagery from all sources: from
> ideas, techniques, religious and political systems,
> mass movements, and drugs; or from special indi-
> viduals whom he sees as possessing that problem-
> atic gift of his namesake, the gift of prophecy.[16]

Rock, high fashion, drugs, avant-garde literature—all are
extensions of this search for rebirth. Protean man no longer
expects an absolute, nor wants it. What is new, what is
different, is the rhythm of protean man's life. The Underground has been the vanguard of the nation's questioning of
its identity. As Lifton emphasizes:

> Political and religious movements, as they con-
> front protean man, are likely to experience *less
> difficulty* convincing him to alter previous con-
> victions than they do providing him with a set of
> beliefs which can command his allegiance for
> more than a brief experimental interlude . . .[17]

This intellectual transience makes the ethical position of
the Underground precarious; it also lays its discoveries open

to the criticism of novelty. Lifton's analysis illustrates that fashion itself may be the new universal.

IV

The death of Satan was a tragedy for the imagination . . . He was denied. Phantoms, what have you left? What underground?
—Wallace Stevens
"Esthétique du Mal"

The Underground has always been America's secular Styx in a land whose dream of paradise has been long lost. If it has been satanic—slightly mad, dangerous, inviting— it has also enriched the arid symbols of our society and invigorated those myths which have sustained a new genera- tion—privacy, quest, redemption through suffering. The output of the Underground has been phenomenal, providing not only new talent but new forms for it. Yet, the energy which brought the Underground into the open and changed its style is already being confused by the very Establishment which helped promote its visibility. The problem has been foreshadowed by Herbert Marcuse who sees this involve- ment as an inevitable desublimation, where alienation is robbed both of its ruthless loneliness and corrosive social force by being made palatable and safe through mass marketing.

> The absorbent power of society depletes the artistic dimension by assimilating its antagonistic contents. In the realm of culture, the new totali- tarianism manifests itself precisely in a harmon- izing pluralism, where the most contradictory works and truths peacefully coexist in indiffer- ence.[18]

Now that the Underground has been catapulted to whole-sale stardom it must also suffer the stigma of a "has-been" if it loses its direction—a new technological phenomenon, planned cultural obsolescence. In politics, repression (and worse, avoidance) can muffle accomplishment. Jerry Rubin, calling for "coordinated and very theatrical" demonstrations in the spring, admits:

> . . . Scores of our brothers have become inactive and cynical . . . It is just because we are striking so deep that, in every phase of the movement, arrests and trials and court appearances and jail have sapped [our] energy and demoralized [our] spirit.[19]

An earlier "liberal" indulgence created the inevitable backlash, a criticism of new directions when once that in itself was enough. Theater, which caught the first tide of the Underground popularity, has also been the first to be slapped. Robert Brustein, who three years ago called for a "Third Theater" in which *artistic license* was the alternative to commercial appeal, saw his prophecy turn to dollars and cents, while helping it along himself as Dean of the Yale Drama School by providing Off-Broadway with two Yale productions and Broadway with one. Having given a mandate to experiment, he has now limited it:

> But the more radical inventions of the new generation are nothing if they proceed from the same violent and mindless sources that originally brought our civilization to this terrifying juncture. We fail the future when we surrender what we know and value for the sake of fashion and influence . . .[20]

But, as Lifton points out, "renewal on a large scale is impossible to achieve without forays into danger, destruction, and negativity." The dilemma of the Underground is that of the child and the permissive parent. Slawomir Mrozek paints a hilarious modern picture of it in *Tango,* where a son tries to reorient his avant-garde family:

ARTHUR: Don't you see that you've deprived me of every last chance to revolt? You've been nonconformists so long that there aren't any conventions left to rebel against. You've left nothing for me . . . nothing! Your only norm is the absence of norms. The only thing left for me to rebel against is you . . . you and your immorality.

STOMIL: Go right ahead. Did I ever tell you not to?[21]

In this search for a "living idea," for order, the best of right and left are eliminated. The left loses itself in an esthetic revolt which forgets political intentions; the right destroys itself through its own impossible obsessions. The victor in Mrozek's allegory is Banality, the dumb animality of the servant, Eddie, who fills the vacuum with his mediocrity and brute power. While radicals are bludgeoned in the streets or struggle to control a theater event or create a new electronic sound, others plan their survival at the expense of Underground extremes. Americans, Constance Rourke has said, have always been constrained to perform against the backdrop of their nation. But the spectacle they may leave us with is precisely Mrozek's, where the best of Establishment and Underground camps are defeated in their gorgeous certainty. Mediocrity is already laying the foundations for its survival. The ad copy for *Avant-Garde* illustrates the cynical bastardization of the Underground:

Reading *Avant-Garde* . . . is total immersion in sensual pleasure. A graphic arts freak out. Rolling nude in the snow after a sauna—Love in a mink blanket. The tinkling of wind chimes . . . An orgasm of the mind . . . *Avant-Garde* is proud to be the National Liberation Front of American arts and letters.

The Underground, having been drawn into the game of slap-and-tickle with society, has teased itself into the inevitable seduction. There can no longer be charges of rape, nor even of bad faith. Everybody is contaminated; everybody has contributed.

The Underground dies slowly. Old sights and sounds will linger; but the ruling romantic passion will have moved on. How will it end? Perhaps on the pages of *Vogue* or the Late Night News or at a New School seminar. It may be that the Underground's mixed parentage will make it weak, and finally ineffective. However, its demise as a concept may yield a new, healthier synthesis. Having acknowledged a world where the terms of battle change with each current event, in which everything that rises on the public horizon must converge—the impulse to scream at the world, to choose easy sides and palm off cool lies can stop. If there is to be an alternative society, the materialism of the oppressors must be used against them. Institutions must parallel their efficiency but not their exploitation. The Underground must learn this; and there is time to turn its demand within the affluent society into a strong, institutional opposition. As a new generation understands its protean potential, it will discover the symbiotic relationship which makes an Underground an impressive accomplishment and an anachronism. It may also discover a humble revolutionary savvy—a guideline for the hipsters of the seventies.

7

The American Musical:
The Slavery of Escape

*T*he American musical is dying the slow, melodramatic death of a Barrymore. True to the middle-class
inclinations that created the genre and sustained it, the
musical splutters toward an ignominious demise, unable
to risk anything for change, too caught up in the language
of its own strangulation to see that the impulse of the form

115

must shift with the age. There is still talent and energy in the field; there is even, amazingly, money enough to meet the preposterous costs of this golden escape. Critics and audiences wait for each new season's offerings, hoping for the breathless, unsuspected thrill of uncovering a new Cole Porter, another George Gershwin. While they wait, producers return with paranoid certainty to the same themes and theater formulas that enthralled an audience a generation ago. Like a professional virgin after her wedding night, the musical has not yet learned how to cope with America's loss of innocence.

The philosopher John Dewey has observed:

> If our American culture is largely a pecuniary culture, it is not because the original or innate structure of human nature tends of itself to obtaining pecuniary profit. It is rather that a certain complex culture promotes and consolidates native tendencies so as to produce a certain pattern of desires and purposes.[1]

The musical's popularity fed on the faith of its audience in the principles of extravagance it embodied. The magnitude of the musical spectacle, the unerring panache of each production, reaffirmed the tenets of capitalism often confused with democracy. The musical has become the most powerful and indigenous American theater form precisely because it has been the obvious extension of America's middle-class dream. Just as earlier Americans spun tall tales, the musical became, in the prosperity of the twentieth century, the heir of this gargantuan dream of wealth, leisure, and safety. It inherited the cloak of words but went far beyond them in song and dance. The musical was the logical next step to the language of anticipation which historian Daniel J. Boorstin has brilliantly outlined in *The Americans: The National Experience*:

> There is a figure of rhetoric adopted by the Americans and much used in description," wrote the English traveler Morris Birkbeck in 1817; "it simply consists of the use of the present indicative instead of the future subjunctive; it is called anticipation. By its aid, what *may be* is contemplated as though it were in actual existence.[2]

The musical became the art of anticipation, whose baroque halls, with their gilt cornices and plush curtains, contained a world as lavish and affluent as their surroundings. In 1817, the rhetoric of anticipation could be used for a nation in transition, as unsure of its boundaries as it was of its untapped resources. The twentieth century, however, brought with it a new sense of power and clearer possibility; the American public which had survived for so long on a myth now wished it to life with a vengeance. With a dream so conspicuous, it is no wonder that the musicals, such as *West Side Story*, sing so confidently and eagerly about its arrival:

> Could it be?
> Yes it could
> Something's coming
> Something good—
> If I can wait.
> I don't know what it is
> But it is gonna be great . . .[3]

What the audiences heard in *West Side Story* (1957), they were being urged to believe decades earlier. While the comedians and performers generally came from America's

lower classes, the song writers (with rare exceptions) came
from solid middle-class backgrounds and wrote with a
faith and buoyancy which evolved with their urban up-
bringing. The music cajoled the audience, making it look
upon itself as the American Adam. There was still the
rainbow, and America still loomed as some profuse Eden in
which each person had only to wait his turn for satisfaction
("Will it be/Yes it will/Maybe just by *standing still*—it
will be there").[4]

The musical has not only wanted to sing away cares, but
also thought. The music haunts the communal imaginations of a society, subliminal advertisements for the American dream. John Dewey was one of the first thinkers to
understand the importance of the musical comedy imagination—which has told us for decades that the best things in
life are free, that everything is coming up roses, and that if
you don't have a dream how you gonna have a dream come
true.

> We are beginning to realize that emotions and
> imagination are more potent in shaping public
> sentiment and opinion than information and rea-
> son . . . Indeed, long before the present crisis
> [W. W. II] came into being, there was a saying
> that if one could control the songs of a nation, one
> need not care who made its laws.[5]

With only the public as its censor, the musical took on a
pertinent uniformity of intention. Max Beerbohm, discussing the musical stage of 1914, could have been talking
about the general output of 1968:

> One reason why the play (at the Gaiety Theater)
> is irresistible is that nowhere else do we feel that
> we are so far away, and so harmlessly and ele-

gantly far away from the realities of life. We are
translated into a sphere where the dwellers have
nothing whatever to think about, and would be
incapable of thought if there were need of it. All
the people (except the ladies of the chorus, whose
languor is part of the fun) are in the highest
spirits, with no chance of a reaction . . . Everyone
wants everyone else to have a good time, and tries
to make everything easy and simple all around.[6]

The musical, although looked upon as an escape from
reality, becomes the most tangible fulfillment of the American dream, the visible proof that opulence, capitalism, conflict, and peace can exist together. The musicals satisfied
the middle-class consumer mentality—its insatiable longing
for a destiny mistaken for cash on hand. Musicals provided
the certainty that the world would take care of its own—
or at least those it chose to sing about. The Gershwins would
focus on the heart's benevolence (1926):

Maybe I shall meet him Sunday
Maybe Monday—maybe not
Still I'm sure to meet him one day
Maybe Tuesday
Will be my good news day.[7]

The thrill in the American musical was undeniable, an
anticipation of excitement and mystery which took many
forms. It often focused on the panoply of urban life and
that most unobserved quantity of the melting pot—the
Negro. The first Negro Broadway musical *Shuffle Along*
(1920), catered to white stereotypes with such nostalgic
songs as "Bandana Days." The fashionable excitement of
Negro culture was translated into white "downtown" music
in unwittingly pejorative terms. Ira Gershwin's "Harlem

Serenade" distorted the facts of ghetto life, finding in the melodic beauty of the music the anticipation of adventure which squalor denied:

> Say! When you enter this new world
> This particular blue world,
> You'll begin giving in.
> All your cares are mislaid.
>
> Oh, stop! Look! Listen to that
> Uptown jungle wail!
> Book your passage to that
> Harlem Congo trail . . .[8]

The song urges an appreciation without acknowledging the basis for that "blue world" or wanting to change it.

Anticipation, so much a part of the American experience, easily gives in to acceptance. The paradox of social mobility in a working democracy is satirized by E. Y. Harburg in *Finian's Rainbow:*

> No one will see
> The Irish or the Slav in you
> Cause when you're on Park Avenue
> Cornelius and Mike look alike.[9]

Once assimilated, the passion for justice, the dignity of identity merges with a comfortable middle-class uniformity.

Harburg's insight is interesting when compared to the unwitting note of *noblesse oblige* which creeps into *Porgy and Bess.* The Negro will always stand out; and the white man's understanding of his plight can take curious turns—

> Oh, I got plenty o' nuttin',
> An' nuttin's plenty for me.
> I got my gal, got my song,

Got Hebben de whole day long.
(No use complainin'!)
Got my gal, got my Lawd, got my song.[10]

This brilliant lyric is convincingly complacent, beginning
with the reality of the black experience and then turning it,
unwittingly, into the reality of the white dream for the
black. This ethical confusion is everywhere in musical
comedy. Rodgers and Hammerstein's memorable "You'll
Never Walk Alone," written a decade later, still sang about
a comfortable universe which found the language for belief
in the terms of hard currency.

DOC: The world belongs to you as much as the next feller.
   Don't give it up . . . Jest keep your faith and courage
   and you'll come out all right . . .

At the end of a storm
Is a *golden* sky
And the sweet *silver* song
Of the lark.
Walk on
Walk on . . .[11] (Italics mine. J. L.)

The tempo of the music, the actuality of the spectacle,
are so polished that the audience exits with its mind confident of the state of grace the musical promises. The tune
lingers on in the communal imagination and is invoked in
times of trouble and uncertainty. Like so many Broadway
songs, it becomes "inspirational." But in this language of
anticipation, the individual is tacitly absolved from the
responsibility of rational questioning of the society. The
musical becomes a most subtle complement to the system,
creating a moral universe compatible with the worst instincts of middle-class life. As John Dewey has pointed out:

On the moralistic side, [democracy] has tended
to substitute emotional exhortation to act in ac-
cord with the Golden Rule for the discipline and
control afforded by incorporation of democratic
ideals into *all* the relations of life. Because of no
adequate theory of human nature in its relations
to democracy, attachment to democratic ends
and methods has tended to become a matter of
tradition and habit—an excellent thing as far as
it goes, but when it becomes routine is easily
undermined *when changes of conditions change
other habits.*[12] (Italics mine. J. L.)

Society has been changing; but most of the middle class
are still suspicious of change, trying to see in the future the
debilitating patterns of the past. The musical in 1968 still
holds to the conservative tenets of earlier decades. America
is no longer an isolated, pastoral retreat. With world power
comes a new responsibility that musical comedy will not
acknowledge. In its pleasure domes and its splendor, the
musical has become the symbol of America's conspicuous
waste. It sings about what is closest to America and yet,
while embodying largesse, mocks it. Foreign aid, for instance, is depicted by Irving Berlin in *Call Me Madam* as
absolute folly, with Ethel Merman belting out her cynical
clarion call in "Can You Use Any Money Today?":

Can you use any dollars today . . .

There are photographs on every one
Lincoln, Grant, and Washington
Or you might like the ones with Henry Clay.
Can you use any money today

Two million, four million, six million, eight
    million, ten
Take what you want
When it's gone you can come back again.

Take ten million and please don't fuss
If you find it can't be spent
You can lend it right back to us
And we'll pay you seven percent.[13]

In a country which cannot accept the fact of poverty, the musical art form denies anything but the most lavish of worlds and makes it more difficult for the facts of life to surface to the public conscience. The musical may be untalented; it may be boring—but it is always spectacular. The drama of the musical is still, in part, its financial investment. Every news release prints the price at which the show is capitalized. Nearly all musicals appeal to this soft underbelly of American experience. Economics can be joked about or incorporated into the theme (nearly everyone gets rich—the concomitant of success).

In *Carousel,* for instance, the famous "Soliloquy" never forgets the financial facts of life from a thriving, middle-class viewpoint:

I got to make certain that she
Won't be dragged up in slums
With a lot of bums
Like me!
She's got to be sheltered and fed, and dressed
In the best that money can buy!
I never knew how to get money
But I'll try . . .[14]

The Protestant ethic, with its emphasis on pluck 'n luck, wrenches at every heartstring with its built-in assumptions about the nature of poverty. Slums are equated with personal unworthiness—a middle-class myth palpably false.

The musical still clings to both a proscenium architecture and a theater of acceptance in which the performances, like the ideas, are kept in comfortable isolation from the audience. Pampered by the security of its nineteenth-century surroundings, a modern audience is coaxed into believing the validity of "escape"—that mindlessness which was once applauded but which now has become a slavery. There is a gaping flaw in the argument for escape, which its most articulate and suavest defender, George Jean Nathan, failed to acknowledge. Mr. Nathan pooh-poohed calls for change in the content and form of the musical.

> That no one thinks in musical comedy and would be incapable of thought if there were need for it, as Beerbohm observed, is its prime asset. There can be no romance where even one party to it brings his brain cells into action, and the best musical comedy authors wisely appreciate the fact. Romance is a tacit agreement by both parties not for a moment to analyze and think away their feelings. Even a touch of wit is perilous . . .
>
> The critical insistence upon books that lean to some intelligence and realism has done much to debilitate musical comedy. Posturing hostility to sentiment, the young critics currently in extensive practice have sought through manly sneers to exorcise it from the medium and to replace it with elements generally described as hardboiled.[15]

In claiming that the musical functions best as an outrageous make-believe, Nathan and so many apologists fail to see that the best musicals took their inspirations from the real world. When George Gershwin discussed his inspiration for *Rhapsody in Blue* he used terms which extended to the music he wrote for the stage. The fiber of the American experience—its pulse and aspirations—was being consciously distilled into the sounds, the emotional texture of the decade:

> I frequently hear music in the very heart of noise. And there I suddenly heard—and even saw on paper—the construction of a rhapsody, from beginning to end . . . I heard it as a sort of musical kaleidoscope of America—of our vast melting pot, of our unduplicated national pep, of our metropolitan madness . . .[16]

The Gershwin musicals from *Lady, Be Good* (1924) to *Girl Crazy* (1930) were all set in the playgrounds of the rich. In the same way, the stunning successes of the De Sylva, Brown, and Henderson musical comedies (*Hold Everything, Flying High, Good News*) took as their subject matter the contemporary *fascinations of the moment*—boxing, flying, golf. If they were stilted in plot, romantic in lyrics, they spoke to something immediate and undeniable in the society. This, too, was the time of the great comedians. No matter where the plot of the story veered, the Marx Brothers, Bobby Clark, Bert Lahr could bring the smirk of reality into the most fanciful make-believe. The elements of the musical that will remain for posterity are those which plumbed for something deeper in the American experience.

The rhythm of America has changed. The jaunty rag of the twenties, the suave urbanity of the thirties, the lacrimose sweetness and confidence of the Rodgers and Hammerstein era, no longer speak to *our* moment, although they spoke to *their own*. Yet, producers, unable to understand the shift in taste and in the pattern of American life from which the musical drew its form, try to cram the tempo of an old world down the craw of the public. Until *Hair*, no musical had attempted to come into this decade and puzzle out a new form for a new time. *Hallelujah, Baby*, which dealt with the civil rights problem, had all the splash and affluence which denied the cause. The play, produced and written by white men, captured none of the violence, cynicism, and disgust which have come into the national consciousness, but instead fitted the story of a performer, a "star," into a bogus sociological perspective. While demanding a heightened seriousness for the musical subject matter, the environment and the tradition of acceptance and anticipation made it hollow at the core. The story, which shows the history of a Negro girl's life in six decades of race relations, plays up to the middle-class sentiment it never goes beyond. "We even eats better than the boss," says the Aunt Jemima mother of the heroine. "And it's *their* food." The audience laughs. The joke assures them of something they've always suspected— that the help enjoy the pleasures of affluence more after the party's over than the masters do when it's on. The play ends on a note of anticipation and acceptance; the heroine is ensconced in an exclusive all-white apartment house. Secure in her affluence, she can sing:

> I'll get out in that happy place
> Where the faces look like one big face
> That's the place
> I'm going to see my face . . .
> Now's the time.[17]

The song is not only a decade behind the times in the innuendo of its musical rhythm but in the content of its social sentiment. What begins as a progressive intention ends as an oppressive one. Musicals in the last decade generally have steered away from contemporary America. *Hello, Dolly!, Funny Girl, Gypsy, George M.!*, and the revival of *Annie Get Your Gun* are entertainments nostalgic for an earlier time. They fit easily into the spirit of the Broadway architecture where everything is what it seems; they also reaffirm the moral foundations of their patrons. The fascination of Broadway with theater subjects is ironic. In its heyday, when the great musical talent was making its own humble, but significant, contribution to defining a still-vague national experience, the writers and performers concentrated on the present with a confidence in the future and a general indifference to the past. Now that the Broadway musical is in serious decline, the nostalgia and distortions of that period threaten to make heroes of them all—Fannie Brice, W. C. Fields, Fatty Arbuckle, Gypsy Rose Lee.

Broadway's obsession with its history is a confirmation of its decadence. The lionization of George M. Cohan is a good case in point. A great showman, an Irish bulldog whose confidence in country and self were unabashed, Cohan embodied that brassy resilience which came to be known as the "American spirit." Cohan's "tragedy" was that, as a theater producer he refused to hire members of Actors Equity in 1919. He retired temporarily from the theater and gave up his idea of show business rather than acknowledge a changing society. The 1968 *George M.!* sentimentalizes Cohan's myopia. He was a stage personality; his success rested not merely on his individuality, but on maintaining the ethic of "talent," and the laissez-faire which made him and so many others "stars." His reactionary instinct is confided in one of his most famous songs:

I want to hear a Yankee Doodle tune
Played by a military band
The only tune that I can understand.[18]

The focus of so many musicals on the lives of "stars" attempts to carry the bourgeois misconceptions of democracy into the last half of the century. The "star," still the superficial image of democracy's magic wand, whose career significantly charts the rise of a low-born citizen not merely to riches but to social mobility, is the most important aspect of the entertainment mythology. The musicals reiterate a faith that money breaks down class barriers; in fact, "stardom" becomes the public's special sleight of hand, at once affirmative and destructive, an elite in which the individual is separated from the society and placed by his public above financial or moral concerns. This is another aspect of a historical anticipation which the American public longs to see acted out daily, which confirms the motivation of their lives, but which is denied everywhere in the sordid pockets of American poverty.

A theater of escape asks us to accept life as it is or life as it has been. In *How to Succeed in Business Without Really Trying,* corporate backbiting and capitalism are nudged gently. The laughter forgives the conformity and sugary pragmatism through which the play's hero, Finch, climbs to power. It is not without interest that the play, geared to capitalize on public approval, points to the most tepid of morals. Finch tells his boss: "Remember, mediocrity is not a mortal sin." And, to go one better, the musical finally sings about a benevolent world it has denied on stage. The cynical wink is palmed off as fun; but it is more than that:

> Now, you may join the Elks, my friend,
> And I may join the Shriners.
> And other men may carry cards
> As members of the Diners.

> There is a brotherhood of man
> A benevolent brotherhood of man
> Oh, aren't you proud to be in that great fraternity;
> The great, big brotherhood of man.[19]

To a modern audience more conscious of current affairs, acceptance of such chaff becomes increasingly difficult; and to some, even abhorrent. Television has changed our emotional environment and the consciousness we bring to the theater. The middle classes can no longer hide from the world; it stalks them at every news broadcast. How can we believe, today, in the benevolence of the universe that Rodgers and Hammerstein once sang about? *Oklahoma!* (1943) offered an image of rural innocence being denied in the carnage of a world war abroad. Hammerstein, a man who wept when he heard "Surrey with the Fringe on Top," explained the song's appeal: "I think of two people who are looking forward that much to a ride in the surrey. I guess it's a kind of assurance of faith in people's overall goodness. I've met a couple of villains in my life, but most people are trying so hard—sometimes they fail, but they try—to be good to one another."[20] There have been too many villains since then; too many good men muffled by the onus of a society trained to acceptance, as confident in universal justice as they are in their nineteenth-century idea of American democracy. Can we believe, in 1970, *South Pacific's* vision of a romantic war (written just prior to the Korean conflict) after the camera's eye has shown heroism in Vietnam to be dumb luck, idyllic languor to be simply boredom? Can we accept the "liberal" sentiments of "You've Got to be Taught," while the play, at the same time, holds up the Polynesians to ridicule and creates other race myths? The answer to anyone without a static view of history, who doesn't adhere to the tenets of the Monroe Doctrine, is obviously "No."

Alexis de Tocqueville saw in 1835 just how America's middle-class instincts stifled drama. He could not account for an art form which would take pleasure in the very lack of conflict and ideas he observed in the country, channeling the energy of the New World daydream:

> The extreme regularity of habits and the great strictness of manners which are observable in the United States have as yet opposed additional obstacles to the growth of dramatic art. There are no dramatic subjects in a country which has witnessed no great political catastrophes and in which love invariably leads by a straight and easy road to matrimony. People who spend every day in the week in making money, and the Sunday in going to church, have nothing to invite the Muse of Comedy.[21]

If de Tocqueville could not foresee the clowns or the good spirits which spawned the musical, he clearly predicted the lack of variety in the American middle-class experience which has had its ossifying effects. America is no longer such a simple story; the country knows catastrophe and unrest. Searching for change and new images for a lifestyle, even de Tocqueville saw the proximity of the stage format to society's shape:

> No portion of literature is connected by closer or more numerous ties with the present condition of society than the drama. The drama of one period can never be suited to the following age if in the interval an important revolution has changed the manners and laws of the nation.[22]

The revolution gets closer; the pressure to change the fabric of society and the forms in which it sees itself has never been more vociferous. For most of the world, a stranger never appeared across a crowded room and even if one took heart, like Shoeless Joe from Hannibal, Mo., the system rarely provided the success or coherence it promised. With each jilting came a betrayal of the musical convention, a depletion of its resources for metaphor and pertinence, until it stands as a ghost town in a debased terrain.

The American rhythm is no longer the jaunty bounce that summons up scenes of city elegance. It has discovered pain and violence, disenfranchised now, but still energetic, wild, and unpredictable. It cannot tolerate the lyric lie. It has found a range for joy as well as despair, pushing beyond bourgeois convention. It is no longer the confident blare of a Big Band sound, but something more articulate and personal. The American rhythm is still extravagant, but tinged with a knowledge of the world. Where anticipation had marked a national vagueness, the rhythm now sees possibilities more clearly. The joy it uncovers comes from finding a beat in life rather than merely glossing experience in tepid fantasy. For the musical to survive, it must find something to sing about in reality, not make-believe. It must acknowledge not only a new pulse but a new world—violent, labyrinthine, uncertain, cruel, and thrilling.

Hair is the first musical to challenge any of the tested musical stage conventions. Its success may open up new ground for the musical and illustrate to a society firmly trained to passivity that escape in a world of emergent uniformity does not mean a distance from life, but contact with it.

Hair wants to bring the musical down to earth, into a human perspective where it once again becomes joyous and magical, yet drawing the sources of its merriment from

everyday life. *Hair* brings to the stage not a nostalgia for
the flesh, but the flesh itself; it finds in the vocabulary of
life a language which is free from cliché, which has a coinage
that is funny, surprising, and rich. As a musical its self-
indulgence has a rebellious point. Amid the chandeliers and
baroque angels of a Broadway pleasure dome, someone is
airing out gutter talk, calling us back to reality, and mock-
ing the Victorian double-standard the buildings embody:
"Fuck, fuck, fucky, fuck, fuck." The words dangle out
there until we get so used to them that the repressions vanish
and the wince disappears.

Instead of the true love, moon/June lyric bandied over
the footlights, the new lyrics demand an honest vocabulary
that jibes with life. Cole Porter's witty innuendoes wink at
sex but never confront it. The sophistication of "But In The
Morning No" is hilarious and precious:

HE: Are you good at figures, dear?
    Kindly tell me if so.

SHE: Yes, I'm good at figures, dear
    But in the morning no.

HE: D'you do Double Entry, dear?
    Kindly tell me if so.

SHE: I do Double Entry, dear
    But in the morning no . . .
    When my pet Pekinese
    Starts to mind her Q's and P's
    That's the time
    When I'm in low . . .[23]

Hair minces no words. In the song "Sodomy" every
saccharine protestation of affection is taken to task, a low
blow to the Shubert Office and the audiences who have

swallowed the bromides of middle-class sanctimony as eagerly as they do reducing pills. There is no time for Porter's propriety. Instead, the actors sing of fellatio, cunnilingus, and pederasty. The words break through guilt, trying to uncover something honest in sexual pleasure. In a chorus, the song asks why these words seem so nasty. They conclude that masturbation can be fun, something Cole Porter probably knew but never talked about.

The societal taboos which enforce the debasement of language as much as the unresponsiveness of the soul are being shaken out and finally thrown away on stage. This is no language of anticipation, of tall tales. The parody and satire bring back a human dimension. The vocabulary finally aspires to some special style, a dialect of personal experience which is ironically bleeped out on television and deleted in *The New York Times*, but which is transformed on stage into something thrilling. What seems as frivolous as yesterday's graffiti is really quite sensitive to language and its continual dehumanization. The song "Initials" makes the point about homogenized America, referring to the CIA, IRT, FBI, and LBJ.

At another point in the show, a protester appears with a sign that reads: SEE ETHEL MERMAN IN HAIR. There will be no Ethel Merman in this show because there are no stars. With a new kind of Broadway music, there will be no nostalgic legends in a theater piece which takes aim at all the dead performances palmed off as excellence and all the lies accepted as home truths. The old postures of the performer are turned (literally) on their heads. Actors sing in the aisles and surround the audience. The safe boundary of the proscenium is liberated, once and for all, from that distance which keeps the audience glancing at their watches and wondering about the 11:35 from Penn Station.

The brilliance of *Hair* rests in its honesty, its ability to find a form which argues for its vision with energy and satire. One may not agree with it, but it is impossible to deny the zany explosion of song, gesture, parody which gives the play a density and a momentum that approach carnival mayhem. The theater—for the first time since the great clowns graced the stage—becomes a fun fair, a gay place where the eye cannot take in all that is happening on stage, where the atmosphere becomes intimate and the grit of experience brings the audience back to a world from which they have exiled themselves.

Hair loosens up the musicals' formula for movement with acrobatics that go beyond conventional choreography to statement. Action becomes part of the meaning; the abstract configurations that director Tom O'Horgan evokes on stage move out at the audience from unexpected angles, microphones are held by performers' feet, experience confronts the audience at different visual planes, swirling before the eye. The spotlight no longer isolates the musical experience or orders objects. The musical surrounds the audience in the generosity of its spirits; the story is lost in the vortex of satire and movement. Some members of the audiences even missed the nude scene because they were watching a performer on the other side of the stage. O'Horgan's success is in finding an innocence which comes with experiment. There is nothing obscene in his musical because the textures of flesh, like the levels of language, are ordered by a higher ideal, a concept of new theater.

Social questions whitewashed in musical extravaganzas become the focus of incisive parody. There is no condescension; there is no nervous euphoria—merely something approaching honesty. *Hair* has no "Harlem Serenade," but the song "Abie Baby" the old rock-and-roll idiom, replete with the side-straddle-hop of all the great combos, satirizes the anticipation of freedom. A girl, dressed as Lincoln, sings the Gettysburg Address with the group.

Even that nervous sexual attraction of black to white handled so boringly in *No Strings* takes on a gutsy truth in a take-off of the Supremes called "White Boys Give Me Goosebumps."

Hair will have its influence, but most likely for the wrong reasons. Producers are only now realizing that the way to make money is to offer something fresh to an audience overfed and underprivileged by television. It may become fashionable to change the audience's perspective, to sing about life as lived, to try new performers in different functions. The obviousness of *Hair*'s success will teach producers what everyone knew—that the theater even as an escape is only excellent when it confronts something human and honest. Although *Hellzapoppin'* sent its comedians into the aisles, it did not offer with its amusement a view of the world. The stage images in *Hair* have a poetic force that emphasize the value of the moment. *Hair* does not give the audience an image of clear motivation, a history that is recognizable, or a life that is completely contained. It just happens—with life's absurd logic and unreasonable contradictions. And the audience gradually responds. The theater, once again, becomes a special place, the last refuge for immediacy and human contact. What *Hair* shows is how effective the musical can be in *improving* the caliber of the audience's life instead of merely affirming the status quo. The musical, like every art in our dark times, must live dangerously or die like an aging roué, slobbering in a posh senility.

Arthur Kopit's Indians:
Dramatizing National Amnesia

" 'Gosh! The things they write!"
—Col. William F. Cody upon reading a Beadle novel about himself.

*A*merica has always been fascinated by stories
about itself. Young and powerful, confused and hopeful, it
tries to understand its adolescence by reviving its idea of the
past. The West—that primordial barrier and golden hope
—remains one of our central, most resonant images. Advertising stalks the rugged cattleman into Marlboro country;

Hollywood balloons the frontiersman into an epic hero for his courage and resilience; and the government sees in the space program a new frontier as untamed and as promising of abundance as the pristine American wilderness. The West as an idea holds the seeds of democracy; the West as fact reflects the betrayal of capitalism. Between the striving for democracy and what actually happened there lies the process of myth making, a denial of history unmatched in any other culture. America's treatment of the West has been consistently chronicled in melodrama—a fact more significant than the banal plays it has produced. Arthur Kopit's *Indians* denies the formulae and conclusions of melodrama. His play explores, in Kopit's words, "the American capacity for 'built-in' amnesia . . . and the danger of changing what happened into a fable."[1]

In the popular imagination the West constitutes one of the most willful, persistent self-deceptions of the American mentality, the barometer of a growing paranoia. To television viewers the West is a blood bath of duels in the name of law and order. But the cattle towns from which Wild Bill Hickok, Bat Masterson, and Wes Hardin emerged had few high-noon dramas. Infamous Dodge City had only fifteen homicides in its heyday between 1870-1885. The grand total of deaths from Abilene, Ellsworth, Wichita, and Dodge City came to a sleepy 45 in the same period.[2] The straight shooters never toted a pistol with the accuracy of Gary Cooper. Most pioneer slayings were done in the back and at close range. The popular celluloid "peace treaties" with the Indians omit some astounding details which Alexis de Tocqueville footnoted ominously in 1834:

> In 1808 the Osages gave up 48,000,000 acres for an annual payment of $1,000. In 1818 the Quapaws yielded 20,000,000 acres for $4,000. They

> reserved for themselves a territory of 1,000,000
> acres for hunting ground. A solemn oath was
> taken that it should be respected but before long
> it was invaded like the rest.[3]

The American continent was the richest asset of the
society. Land was given away to anyone who could inhabit
it. Abundance was a fact, not a fantasy. America created
property owners with the same enthusiasm that was later
to encourage the growth of capitalism. Geography was the
key to a working democracy and the realization of revolutionary goals. De Tocqueville observed the significance of
territory to the American experiment: "Ancestors gave
them the love of equality and freedom: but God Himself
gave them the means of remaining equal and free by placing
them on a boundless continent." If there was temporary
hardship (and, in 1837, even depression), there was always
more land further west. Kopit's play questions the American
reinterpretation of its actions: "This country was founded
on anticipation. A dream. Yet this country refused to acknowledge that this dream was something other than what
it wanted. That had to happen. But the way in which we
took the country was not what we want to know. Our dream
of glory wasn't the nightmare of destruction, of willfulness,
of greed, of perjury, of murder, which it became . . ."
Melodrama is a form which gives structure to vague
aspirations and justifies capitalist ideals. The demands of
the genre reinforce the imagined lost values of the frontier.
In melodrama, the sides of "good" and "evil," "virtue" and
"vice," are clearly and completely drawn. The sins of character are attributed to personal eccentricities and never to
the pressures of society. With its felicitous endings and
moral tableaux, melodrama reiterates the conclusions of
the Protestant ethos, which, with its faith in work, helped

to clear the frontier and fostered the idea that Providence will take care of the virtuous as long as their case is just. American theater as well as its history have strained to assert moral certainty in the face of outrageous injustice. The uniform banality of the fictions of the West, their conspicuous falsehood and indubitable impact on the national identity raise important questions for the theater as well as society. Why does a nation seek to hide from history by transforming the sins of its past into the hopes of the future?

I

When I fell into a trance a great and grand eagle came and carried me over a great hill where there was a village such as we used to have before the whites came into the country. The teepees were all made of buffalo hides and we made use of the bow and arrow, there being nothing of the white man's manufacture there.[4]

—Little Wound recalling his dream

When the frontier became the subject of dime novels and public spectacle, it was already moribund. Hunters and trappers had lost some of their contact with the land. The new machinery of a more sophisticated economy cluttered the romantic vistas of America. The thrill of vast economic horizons and courageous explorations (which stimulated such poet-adventurers as Joaquin Miller to be "inflamed with love for action, adventure, glory and great deeds away out yonder under the path of the setting sun") were now modified by industry. Railroads not only stimulated business; they populated the lands that they owned. Agrarian subsistence was giving way to industrial development. Equality, once thought so close to the need for property, would be diminished by industrial control of land and human resources.

Indians focuses on one of the West's archetypal heroes, Buffalo Bill, emphasizing his emergence at a time when the language of the Great Plains was changing from that of adventure to that of profit. Cody does not seek fame. He is discovered, promoted, and developed by a new economy which claims him in the name of democracy while destroying the possibility of its enactment:

BUNTLINE: . . . Look: de West is changin', right? Well, people wanna know about it. Wanna *feel* . . . part o'things. I t'ink *you're* what dey need. Someone t'listen to, identify wid. No, no, really! I been studyin' you very carefully.

BUFFALO BILL: You have?

BUNTLINE: I t'ink you could be de inspiration o' dis land.[5]

Cody represents the ambiguity of the West. Once involved in the authentic agrarian expansion—as scout, Pony Express rider, hunter—he later turned to marketing the West's past in show business. His paradox, and the source of his paranoia, is his attempt to be cast in an heroic mold while being associated with capitalism. A Plains jingle quoted by Dixon Wecter in *The Hero in America* strained to bridge the gap between the hunter of ritual power and the reason for his search. He no longer served the community of settlers, but a larger labor force:

> Buffalo Bill, Buffalo Bill
> Never missed and never will;
> Always aims and shoots to kill
> And the company pays his buffalo bill.

Indians, a mosaic of Buffalo Bill's memories, dramatizes the intellectual confusion which results in mythical obfuscation. Buffalo Bill, riddled with guilt over the Indians and his new business, is bombarded by fragments from his past and historical justifications of the future. Thus we become conscious of the process through which he rose to fame and its moral confusions. His Wild West Show was theater in which fantasy was made flesh and blood, where the spectacle of the West reaffirmed attitudes toward American life which no longer had a firm basis in fact. The emphasis was on verisimilitude: *real* Indians from the battle of Little Big Horn, the *real* Deadwood Stage, the *real* Buffalo Bill, riding in a dumb show of his dime-novel heroism. Tall in the saddle, blazing his six-shooter, he entered the arena with the loudspeaker blaring his words: "Fear not, fair maid; by heavens, you are safe at last with Wild Bill, who is ever ready to risk life and die if need be in defense of helpless womanhood." Buffalo Bill was rich and famous. His show capitalized on national desires. The spectacle filled the need for a primitive proving ground, and a violent and evil enemy that had to be violently (and unjustly) subdued. By 1883, both this adversary and the buffalo who loped through the arena had become almost a fiction. The West became an idea ruthlessly pursued and hopelessly reenacted.

Kopit's play counterpoints this public event which commercialized a once-authentic struggle with private despair. Buffalo Bill is confused and haunted by the Indian, and his anxiety is the fear of a man rationalizing his new urban role. Prototype of the scout, he reveled in his pristine role while destroying the wildlife that made it possible. A professed friend to the Indians, he killed their source of food, forcing the tribes to retreat, to separate, and to die. Buffalo Bill's schizophrenia comes from the split-personality of the land. Behind his promotion of the West is the inkling that the authenticity of its ideals has been lost in popularization. The hunter and the pathfinder become capitalists exploiting human resources for gain, but at the same time believing that they are doing good. Kopit handles the moral complexity with exquisite delicacy. In a hilarious scene where Buffalo Bill and Wild Bill Hickok recreate a Buntline[6] melodrama for the Old Time President, Kopit stresses Buffalo Bill's pragmatism:

> BUFFALO BILL (*talking to Hickok*): When a man . . . has a talent, a God-given talent, I think it's his godly duty t'make the most of it . . . Ya see, Bill, what you fail to understand is that I'm not being false to what I *was*. I'm simply *drawin'* on what I was . . . and liftin' it to a higher level.

Cody is talking progress. He is the quintessential American; excessive in the face of protean economic horizons; fascinated with new technology and trends. He uses the rifle to slaughter buffalo; he uses himself to package faith in the West. He is vague about the deeds which will win him a very specific fame, just as the nation was uncertain about the boundaries of the land over which it asserted such firm moral authority. In an industrial age, Buffalo Bill offered a glimpse of pioneer life: a folksy, agreeable country style to whet urban appetites (in the East he was often called "Bison William"). Kopit has Buffalo Bill explain his dream this way:

> My dream . . . is to help people. I mean great numbers of them. The nation. Everyone in the nation. And . . . whatever I do to help, for it they will name towns after me. Counties. States. I will be as famous as Dan'l Boone. And somewhere on top of a beautiful mountain, there'll be a statue of me sittin' on a great white horse. An' I'll be wavin' my hat to everyone below. Thankin' 'em for havin' done whatever it is I'm gonna do for 'em all.

He sees himself as savior and hero. He acts out of a sentimental faith in goodness, but lacks the means to achieve it. He is a friend of the Indian. When called upon to play a key role in treaty negotiations he finds himself torn between genuine sympathy for the Indians' plight and his own rationalist impulse, an offspring of the seduction of the capitalist society. He is no longer a man of instinct (was he ever?) or of ideals. Kopit brings Buffalo Bill back to the West to find his friend Wild Bill Hickok and help him bargain with the Indians, thus reaffirming his sense of an authentic West. Buffalo Bill returns to a Dodge City saloon. As Kopit first conceived the scene it was a parody of the Hollywood barroom. But in following the process of Buffalo Bill's decline, Kopit made an interesting discovery. As Buffalo Bill talks with Wild Bill, his good intentions and the commercial facts of life are in continual conflict. His language is no longer alive with the eccentricity and verve of the frontier; now, it is a curious amalgam of town and prairie:

> I dunno what's happenin' . . . to me. Things seem to've gotten beyond my . . . control. I . . . see them everywhere. In the pale grass, the rock . . . the branches of dead trees.
>
> (*Pause. Indian faces appear in the distance.*)
>
> . . . I wiped out their food, you see. I didn't mean to, of course. The railroad men needed food. They . . . hired me to . . . find 'em food. I just didn't realize the buffalo reproduced so slowly. Or . . . that I was makin' it into a kind of sport.

But the pioneer honesty Cody expects from Hickok has gone. Hickok too has caught the spirit of modern America. He has a plan—but not to help Indians. He confronts Buffalo Bill with four men who are replicas of Cody. In this gesture, Kopit finds the theatrical equivalent to capitalism's process of profit—repetition. Hickok speaks:

> You get fifty percent off the top . . . Of course, if at any time you aren't happy you can leave. Take your business elsewhere. That's written in. Keeps us on our toes . . . I can even now envision the great national good it will do. For example, some of you could concentrate on your theatrical ventures. Meanwhile, others of you could visit reservations . . . My God, but there must be millions —well maybe not millions but anyway thousands —yes thousands who could benefit by your presence. Your simultaneous presence.

Hickok is talking the language of mass production and capitalist enterprise—efficiency and service. Buffalo Bill understood the marketing concept. He had become a phenomenon of packaging, a man who lent his name to hats, gloves, rifles, dime novels, as well as being the star of his own Western Show. Kopit says: "I wanted to take Buffalo Bill out of a John Ford cow palace and put him into a Henry Ford production line . . . This grotesque duplication has a special meaning in terms of American democracy and capitalism. Two men making the most of things—that good old American expression."

Indians does not hitch Marxian economics to a Wild West star. It incarnates the relationship of myth to the national guilt over its territorial misdemeanors, as it does the romantic heroes made necessary by the capitalist syndrome. Between 1850 and 1890, as railroads shrank the continent and industry took root, plays and novels abounded with Western heroes and—the antithesis to the rationalist (capitalist) order—the Indian "savage." One early theater commentator, James Rees, observed as early as 1845 that "the

Indian plays have become a perfect nuisance."[7] Buffalo Bill himself capitalized on the fad, creating *The Scouts of the Plains* and *The Red Right Hand; or Buffalo Bill's First Scalp for Custer*. Buffalo Bill's heroics were forged in fiction, not in fact. His desire to please public taste compromised any true heroism. In the end, Buffalo Bill betrayed both the Indians and his own integrity—the paradox of a vain heroism in a society firmly grounded in supply and demand. The economist Joseph Schumpeter has described the problem of heroism in a capitalist age—an absurdity which affected not only Buffalo Bill, but an entire nation yearning to believe in its moral worth and courageous roots:

> Capitalist civilization is rationalistic and "antiheroic." The two go together, of course. Success in industry and commerce requires a lot of stamina, yet industrial and commercial activity is essentially unheroic in the knight's sense—no flourishing of swords about it, not much physical prowess, no chance to gallop the armored horse into the enemy, preferably heretic or heathen . . .[8]

II

"Cowboys and Indians" became wish fulfillment for a modern economy. Instinctive instead of institutionalized, fearless instead of fragmented, "Cowboys and Indians" embodied a world apart from the new civilization of bookkeeping. The nation's theatrical (and later celluloid) fantasy never admitted the dark side of capitalism: creating poverty with abundance. The Indian and the black man were pauperized. Yet the white settlers never doubted that the economic impetus of American civilization would overcome all obstacles. The painter, George Catlin, one of the first to chronicle the Indian, observed: "I have stood amidst these

unsophisticated people and contemplated with feelings of
deepest regret the certain approach of this overwhelming
system which will inevitably march on and prosper."⁹ Yet
the heroes of nineteenth-century theatrical melodrama (and
even Hemingway's romantic adventures) are *uneconomic*
men who obtain their mobility with no mention of money.
They may be outlaws or ranchers, wanderers or lawmen but
their job is never seen as ordinary. They are not bound by
the humdrum of conventional labor. The theatrical illusion
kept gainful employment (and motive) vague in front of the
footlights because it was not heroic. Buffalo Bill (like the
stars of today) was paid *not* to be absorbed in economic
tedium. Buffalo Bill represents a largesse beyond bravery.
As Buntline admits to the Old Time President, in his mock-
heroic introduction to their play:

> I saw the nation profit more than us;
> For with each one o'my stories
> Cody grew t'represent its Glories.

The American conscience did not want to admit greed along
with goodness, poverty with progress. As one critic of melodrama has pointed out:

> If a European setting were used, heroes were kings
> or nobles, but in America, though every good
> male was supposed to work, social and moral pre-
> conceptions about different professions made no
> job wholly suitable for the hero . . . Presumably,
> they were not idle, but because job opportunities
> did not jibe with melodrama's preconceptions,
> dramatists made little mention of how the Amer-
> ican hero earned his living . . .¹⁰

Kopit's Buffalo Bill does not speak of money, although profit is a recurring pressure in his mind. His language is increasingly practical in counterpoint to the active imagery of the Indians. Buffalo Bill's theater and his fame are based on a grim fact: exploitation of the Indians for profit. Kopit cunningly understates this impulse. The potential evil is beyond Buffalo Bill's understanding; but, nonetheless, it is built into the society which promotes him. Sitting Bull, appearing to him in a nightmare of his consciousness, makes clear the humiliation, acknowledging the oppression and the economic myopia of American ideals. He comprehends the process as an outsider. Buffalo Bill has been fooled into forgetting it.

BUFFALO BILL: It was fun though, wasn't it?

SITTING BULL: Oh, yes. And that is the terrible thing. We had all surrendered. We were on reservations. We could not fight, or hunt. We could do nothing. It was humiliating. For sometimes we could almost imagine it was real.

Cody's breakdown comes from an intuition of the false use of his myth. The hero gave focus and force to a new land. Kopit creates a world of jarring tension, in which a man is caught between the processes of capitalism and myth. What the audience experiences is an elusive American rhythm: the exploitation of the American experience to recast its ambiguity in an easy heroic mold.

III

. . . The Americans have accomplished this two-fold purpose (of annihilating the Indian and denying him his rights) with singular felicity, tran-

quilly, legally, philanthropically, without shedding
blood and without violating a single principle of
morality in the eyes of the world. *It is impossible
to destroy men with more respect for the laws of
humanity.*[11]

                       —Alexis de Tocqueville

Although the white man virtually eliminated the Indian
from North America, the theatrical and literary images have
always stressed the death toll of the *whites*. (Similarly, the
ghetto riots have frozen white Americans into fantasies of
fear although it is the black people who are the victims.)
The paranoiac reversal stems from America's furious attempt
to justify the means of colonization by the ends of democracy: to sustain the myth of unlimited economic horizons;
the need of capitalism to maintain an enemy to function
efficiently. Kopit's play is ostensibly about America's first
"enemy," but the Indians are prototypes for our hysterical
reaction to other "alien forces." Buffalo Bill dramatizes the
schizophrenia that leads to scapegoats. Uncertain of the
past, unhappy with the future, he blames not society but
identifiable outsiders. As Daniel J. Boorstin has pointed
out: "The more uncertain the destiny, the more necessary
to declare it manifest."[12]
Kopit's Buffalo Bill fits into this dilemma. At the peak of
his hysteria, he retreats to an entrenched position:

> I am sick and tired of these sentimental humani-
> tarians who take no account of the difficulties
> under which the government has labored in its
> efforts to deal fairly with the Indians, nor of the
> countless lives we have lost and atrocities endured
> at savage hands.

The rhetoric is familiar; it guards the neurosis which leads
to all our wars. The Indians were never a match for the

carbine. They were the national "enemy"; yet the white man had given them whatever tactical fighting strength they had: the horse and the rifle. They were impediments to affluence, not only because they inhabited "productive" land which was not being "utilized," but because their cosmology would not be "efficiently" assimilated into capitalism. The Indians were men of the chase, not of the market. For white America, the Indians stood in the way of democracy. They seemed to impede affluence, the hope of every American to have *his* fair share. The Indians sought to enjoy the land, not transform it for gain. Having destroyed the ecology of the wilderness, the white man demanded that the Indian become economic in his use of resources. The white man wanted to export his democracy, which meant (as it does now) grafting on a capitalist economy since abundance is a cornerstone of the democratic ideal. Kopit is brilliantly concise in his treatment of this. In one treaty discussion, where the Indians are speaking to a governmental committee with Buffalo Bill as interlocutor, the economic dilemma is stated:

> . . . I am going to talk about what the Great Father told us a long time ago. He told us to give up hunting and start farming. So we did as he said, and our people grew hungry. For the land was suited to grazing, not farming, and even if we'd been farmers, nothing would have grown.

Buffalo Bill explains Indian customs which made such pacification as hopeless in the West as it is now in Vietnam:

> Now the real problem is not poor soil. The real problem is . . . plowin'. Ya see, the Indian believes the earth is sacred and sees plowin' as a sacrilegious act. Well, if ya can't get them to plow, how can you teach 'em farmin'? Impossible.

Fertile land's another problem. There just ain't
much of it, an' what there is, the Indians prefer to
use for pony racin'. . .

The Indian is termed "savage" because he is antithetical
to the process of bureaucracy. The Indian, unlike the planta-
tion black, was never within the economic system. He was
more than a symbolic outsider; he was a spanner in the
works of industrial growth. This phantom enemy, provoked
to guerrilla tactics, was the impetus for technological invention. In the official program for Buffalo Bill's Wild West
Show (1904) there is this important generalization:

> The bullet is the pioneer of civilization, for it has
> gone hand in hand with the axe that cleared the
> forest, and the family Bible and school-book.
> Deadly as has been its mission in one sense, it
> has been merciful in another; for without the rifle
> ball America would not be today in the possession
> of a free and united country mighty in its strength.

Programmed fear is a cornerstone of capitalism. The
ABM missile system and space exploration are both defense programs and, more important, highly developed
industries.

Most American playwrights are not at home with ambiguity; Kopit does not reveal everything. He lets the stage
world create the irony and the audience draw connections.
His play demands complexity, not simplicity of vision. In
the melodramatic tradition, the Indian was the violent
opponent. The theater catered to popular fantasy. The act
of distortion was also an exercise in anticipation, an escape
instead of an examination. Kopit illustrates this with Buffalo Bill and his Wild West Show. The sense of safety in
the structure of melodrama (the bad guy would always get

"what was coming to him") fed a sense of destiny which justified violence. When Indians lived happily within the white community, the moral was quickly drawn. In *Pocahontas, or The Settlers of Virginia* (1830), the warrior chief, Powhatan, speaks the play's final lines in a tableau of integration. He gives Pocahontas as bride to the alabaster Captain John Smith:

> Looking thro' a long vista of futurity, to the time when these wild regions shall become the ancient and honour'd part of a great and glorious American Empire . . .

When the white man played at being an Indian he always made things easier on himself. Indian women became the subject of a love story only after having converted to Christianity and having their skin lightened! Thus in *New World Planted*:

> I know she's browner than European dames
> But whiter far than other natives are,
> And modest blushes oft adorn her cheeks.[13]

Melodrama reflected a Rousseau concept of nature which was imported to America. "The voice of nature spoke to all, but if truly heard, it always reiterated social preconceptions. The melodrama's categorical imperative was that anyone of unperverted feeling would *innately perceive* the rightness of accepted moral standards."[14] Indians, like the Viet Cong, become "savages." What is important about Kopit's *Indians* is not simply that it goes beyond such tepid clichés but, in telling an entertaining story, contrasts the ambiguous American theatrical concept of "good" with real-life political buffooneries.

IV

Buffalo Bill is not a man given to foresight. He
doesn't look into possible repercussions of his
actions. He becomes famous and he does enjoy
pleasing people. The irony is that he wants to help
people. He has a kind of undefined sense of goodness. (Kopit)

Law and order, success, safety, wealth are all part of
Buffalo Bill's sense of good. But in seeking to justify his
unnatural actions, goodness became a chameleon for self-
interest. In melodrama the "good" man always took *direct*
action.

But before he could again bend his hot, sensual
face toward her pure lips, a horse and rider came
rushing down the street with the speed of a winged
bird . . . "Oh, sir, you are so brave and so good, I
would have died before he should kiss me."
                    —A description of Buffalo Bill
                    in a Beadle dime novel.[15]

The nature of good is not only defined by its opposite—
the uncompromising enemy—but by the quality of its victory. Buffalo Bill's rodeo serves Kopit's theatrical intentions,
becoming a microcosm of American history. Richard Hofstadter has explained a process which the Wild West Show
symbolized:

. . . The American frame of mind has created a
long history that encouraged our belief that we
have an almost magical capacity to have our way
in the world, that the national will can be made
entirely effective, as against other peoples', at a

relatively small price . . . Free victories, decisive triumphs . . .[16]

Resplendent in buckskin, guiding his frisky stallion with a sure hand, Buffalo Bill embodies the magical appeal of the dream and its essential betrayal. He is overwhelmed by the nightmare of the great chiefs dying. As their voices haunt him, his arguments fend off their shadowy indictment:

BUFFALO BILL: For the truth is, the Indians never had any real title to the soil of the country . . . All the Indians were the temporary occupants of the land. They had to be vanquished by us! It was, in fact, our *moral obligation.*

CRAZY HORSE: Crazy Horse is, once again, dying.

BUFFALO BILL: For the earth was given to mankind to support the greatest number of which it is capable; and no tribe or people have a right to withhold from the wants of others.

Here Kopit illustrates how the "good" and economics interrelate. He also shows a man wrestling to preserve his identity and integrity. The magic of Buffalo Bill's fantasy life, the continual victories in the name of good, do not bring the long-dreamed-for rebirth. For Kopit's Buffalo Bill the truth is hidden by the myths of the nation. He has helped build them and define them, but he wants to see something else. He must make the Indian an enemy in order to make himself just. Kopit's concern is not so much with the fate of the Indians as with the process which continues to mushroom into political suicide:

The danger isn't what happened. That's already fact. The danger is the way in which it happened.

America becomes its own image. A Frankenstein
monster becoming its own creation, forgetting it
made the whole thing up. It's how we can equate
Vietnam with Korea when there are such clear
differences.

Buffalo Bill's ultimate breakdown concludes, as it must,
with a total denial of historical fact. "I'd better close," he
says. "I . . . just want to say that . . . anyone who thinks we
have done something wrong, is wrong!" The frontier spirit
which Buffalo Bill advertised is still selling America on self-
destruction. The pioneer challenge of the West is a justification for the Vietnam war, confusing masculinity with the
luck of the draw.

> Vietnam.
> Hot. Wet. Muddy. Perilous. To prove
> yourself here is to prove yourself
> to the world. No test is harder. No trial
> more demanding.
> But when a man serves here,
> he proves himself a man.
> To his country. To himself.
>
> —*Advertisement for the U.S. Army*

What emerges in *Indians* as evil is America's sense of
good. The provocation for Kopit's play was a statement by
General Westmoreland about Vietnamese citizens who had
been senselessly slaughtered. Westmoreland had said, "Our
hearts go out to the innocent victims." As Kopit recalls it:

> I was listening to Charles Ives' *Fourth Symphony*
> which combines this kind of seraphic American
> folk idiom with violent marching sounds. I read
> Westmoreland's article; I just sort of went berserk.

I thought: "No, our hearts do *not* go out to the innocent because there's something wrong." I didn't think Vietnam was the real problem but a symptom of something which went back much farther. It dealt with obfuscation. Then suddenly I thought that it was Indians and the white man, it was part of a struggle in which we had been fighting through our history against people whom we conceived as being spiritually, morally, economically, and intellectually our inferiors. We imposed our will on them and then justified our will morally, in terms of some godly sensation that we felt was for a general and moral good.

Buffalo Bill covers up his myopia with moral outrage. He assumes that any gesture which incorporates the exploited Indians will help their cause. "You know I actually thought my Wild West Show would make people understand things better." Naïve and earnest, he loves the lie which is the basis for his deepseated despair. Buffalo Bill, like any figure who fits into melodrama, believes that moral behavior is the pathway to happiness. He is confused when his goodness leads to destruction. The passion to be thought good ruled Lyndon Johnson, and also accounts for radical reversals of political positions. In a brilliant analysis of American politics, *An American Melodrama,* the political analysts explain, with special relevance to Kopit's theme, Ronald Reagan's shift from liberal to conservative. Like Cody, Reagan was a man whose fame came from acting out heroism:

> The real Reagan, like the celluloid Reagan, inhabits a world composed of "good guys" and "bad guys." Reagan, naturally, prefers to be a good guy. During the Depression and War

years, the Democrats had a firm hold on the good
guy image for a young man making his way. Then,
after the war, everything became complicated.
The ranks of the good guys were infiltrated with
bad guys; so the one-time good guys became
suckers, a very bad role in real or fantasy life.
Reagan felt that he was made to play it briefly,
and he did not like the action. He had no intellectual depth, no feeling for the complexity of
human affairs. He simply wanted to know where
the good guys were so he could be one again.[17]

The lines of political and moral action are not as clear
as we might wish them to be. Buffalo Bill begins by seeing
himself in a halo of goodness: "But I believe I am a hero.
A *goddam* HERO!" The guilt created a warped humanity,
a system clogged with the waste of its mythic confusions.
America is a society told to dream the impossible dream,
always looking over the rainbow for the silver lining. Kopit's
orchestrated nightmare returns us to the root of the problem implicit in such a sanguine tendency. His vision is
too flexible, too well-informed, too close to the historical
pattern of white America, to be overlooked. The myth of
our heritage replaces the facts of it in every political speech,
in every rationale for injustice or technological expansion.
Consider Richard Nixon on election eve 1960. With his
words, stage melodrama moves into the public arena:

. . . My friends, it is because we are on the side of
right; it is because we are on God's side: that
America will meet this challenge and that we will
build a better America at home and that that
better America will lead the forces of freedom in
building a new world.[18]

VI

Indians is not a protest play, but a process play. With its uniquely American energy, it is both elusive and delightfully specific, a spectacle as well as a haunting vision. On a very basic level, the material surprises an audience with the freshness of its sights and sounds: Indian chants, ritual ceremony, three-ring pageantry, Western bravado. Its subject matter is a reservoir of memories and associations which link each American (subconsciously) to his past. Kopit, with an engineer's delight for delicacy, dramatizes the creation of mythology. There is also an internal drama for, in order to interpret the whirlpool of events swamping Buffalo Bill, each member of the audience must become aware of the accumulated weight of his own private national fantasy.

With *Indians,* Kopit has found a form to match his enthusiasm and insight. The loose, fragmented structure allows him to imply the uncertainty at the core of America's sense of destiny without the play becoming vague or poorly defined. The play benefits from an element of farce which gives it added momentum. There are a handful of plays in the last two decades which equal Kopit's technical skill (*Death of a Salesman, A Streetcar Named Desire, Who's Afraid of Virginia Woolf?*); but none matches the scope of his inquiry. *Indians* tackles the gigantic themes of American history and channels them into art.

9

The Open Theater's
Serpent*

I

*M*ore impressed by the articulate abyss than by the non-verbal energies to transcend it, American theater has often confused significance with explanation. The plays which tell us everything do not always mean the most. When theater is illuminating, it creates its own irresistible logic and necessity, a process which beckons the viewer and per-

* Although *The Serpent* was "written" by Jean-Claude van Itallie, it represents the combined effort of the Open Theater ensemble with the playwright.

former back to a new beginning, a questioning of communal myths, a confrontation with morality. It is a delicate process, and rare. But when the serpent slinks into the Garden of Eden in the Open Theater's brilliant exploration of the Book of Genesis, it brings with it the visual richness, intellectual wonder, and surprise of a mystery play, whose function is to outline the boundaries of the human experience.

The serpent is not one but many. At first a writhing thicket of knees and elbows, producing apples in large and seductive arcs of the arm, it transforms itself into a pyramid of bodies. Legs and elbows sway; tongues flicker in counterpoint to words etched in silence:

SERPENT 1: It may be.

SERPENT 2: It may be that no garden

SERPENT 4: Is better than this one.

SERPENT 5: This garden.

SERPENT 4: It may be.

SERPENT 2: But you won't know

SERPENT 1: You can't know until you eat

SERPENT 2: How could you know.[1]

The serpent is playful and monumental. As the pyramid tilts from side to side, apples are dangled precariously by their stems. This is not merely temptation, but the tree. Unleashing associations beyond the vocabularies of reason, the configuration is exhilarating.

Actors perform with sounds that are not words; images speak vividly to the imagination, recalling the experiences of birth and death, longing and satisfaction. The opening processional directions indicate the variety of associations:

> After a few minutes the actors begin to move
> around the theater in a procession . . . The players
> don't use their voices, but they explore every
> other sound that can be made by the human body
> —slapping oneself, pounding one's chest, etc.
> The procession appears to be one of medieval
> mummers, and sounds like skeletons on the move.
> All at once all stop in a freeze. This happens three
> times during the procession. During a freeze each
> actor portrays one of the various motifs from the
> play such as: the sheep, the serpent, the presi-
> dent's wife's reaching gesture, Adam's movement,
> Cain's waiting movement, Eve's movement, the
> heron, and the old people.

The energy of the event becomes its theme, appealing
beyond the reasoning intellect, breaking physical and intellectual boundaries. *The Serpent* washes over the viewer,
not with the realistic, everyday medieval rendering of Adam
and Eve (*Mystère d'Adam*), but in more stylized, abstract,
and elusive patterns, suiting our time, when the realities of
a teeming Hell seem farther away.

The thrill of *The Serpent* lies in its consistency as "primitive" ritual. Conceived in an eight-month experimentation
with the actors, director Joseph Chaikin, and playwright
Jean-Claude van Itallie, *The Serpent* aspires to the most holy
(and fundamental) theatrical impulse—to return the actors
and the audience to an intuition of the primordial state and
a fuller comprehension of the immediate moment, retracing
(to understand) the myths which shape Western consciousness.

Chaikin's theater, so acrobatic and incantory, finds a
private form and direction which grapples with the concept
of the absurd, the despair directly descended from Eve's
first bite of the apple. The Biblical apple opened Eve's eyes.

"Then their eyes were opened, and they knew that they were naked: and they sewed fig leaves together, and made themselves aprons." This self-consciousness (the seed of existential guilt in the Other), the knowledge of boundaries and perceptual limitation has its modern correlative in existential phenomenology. Sartre's *Being and Nothingness* arrives at a "reef of solipsism" through elaborate *perceptions* of the world and an analysis of human experience. Camus's dictum about the absurd in *The Myth of Sisyphus* comes to its final conclusions by assuming that what is perceived—even separation—is all the knowledge available to man. His explanation of the absurd indicates the mythic tensions which surround it:

> A world that can be explained by reasoning, however faulty, is a familiar world. But in a universe that is suddenly deprived of illusions and of light, man feels himself a stranger. His is an irremediable exile, because he is deprived of memories of a lost homeland as he lacks the hope of a promised land to come. This divorce between man and his life, the actor and his setting, truly constitutes the feeling of Absurdity.[2]

The antidote to *Angst* is action. The Open Theater works to put performer and audience back in touch with themselves. The absurd denies history; the Open Theater affirms the bond of myth which connects century to century. A chorus chants a litany of isolation surrounding the Kennedy assassinations:

> I was not involved.
> I am a small person.
> I hold no opinions.
> I stay alive.

I mind my own affairs.
I am a little man.
I lead a private life.
I stay alive.

I'm no assassin.
I'm no president.
I don't know who did the killing.
I stay alive . . .

There is no connection to the world, no testament to prove that the human gesture can affect public conscience. The Open Theater wrestles with this existential dichotomy and goes beyond it. The intention of the performance is to create a new totality in the actor, to call up a world intimately *connected* with the imaginative past as well as the concrete present. Created through improvisation, *The Serpent* is a theater event which forges its own environment and to which each actor commits himself as well as his entire performing mechanism. Chaikin orchestrates a density of sights and sounds, a multiplicity which denies limitation. Eden is filled with animals and the sounds of primordial life. Through silence and chorus, breathing rhythms and chants, a world emerges from *Genesis* we'd forgotten existed. The shock of recognition, the ability to conjure the past in the present, denies Nothingness—the conclusion of the existential intellect. It creates an experience which challenges the destiny of existential inquiry, a gauntlet thrown down in words by Wallace Stevens in *Esthétique du Mal:*

The moon is no longer these nor an
    anything
And nothing is left but comic ugliness
Or a lustred Nothingness . . .

To lose sensibility, to see what one
    sees,
As if sight had its own miraculous
    thrift,
To hear what one hears, one meaning
    alone,
As if the paradise of meaning ceased
To be paradise, it is this to be
    destitute . . .[3]

II

Among the many contemporary theatrical experiments, *The Serpent* seems the most positive and successful attempt to redefine American life. Like a tribal shaman, Chaikin and his actors grope backwards to mysterious beginnings. In the introduction to *The Serpent*, Chaikin wrote:

The collaboration requires that each person address to himself the major questions posited in the material: what are my own early pictures of Adam and Eve and the serpent, of the Garden of Eden, of Cain and Abel? These questions deal with a personal remembered "first time." They are questions we stopped asking after childhood. We stopped asking them because they were unanswerable (even though we gave or guessed at answers), and later we substituted "adult" answerable questions for them. The group must also go into those deeply dramatic questions of the "first man" and "first woman," "first discovery of sex," and also into the character of God in the Old Testament. I would state that the premise of the piece is that Man made God in his own image, and held up this God to determine his own, Man's, limits.

In reweaving this story and cross-cutting to mythic memories of assassinations and a chorus of present-day laments, the question of the contemporary moral direction is raised in what Chaikin calls "an ambience of entertainment." But its gorgeous primitive quality is connected to the yearning for Paradise, so important to American theater (and the nation's idea of itself) but rarely articulately defined. The Open Theater's esthetic, its demand for a special kind of theatrical magic transcending the limitations of speech and movement, has curious anthropological overtones with other primitive traditions. The Open Theater probes the animal in man, as well as the animal in Eden— a quest with far-reaching implications. One anthropologist, Mircea Eliade, has pointed out provocative parallels with the past:

> Friendship with the animals and knowledge of their language represents a "paradisal" syndrome . . . Before the "fall," such friendship was an integral part of the primordial situation. The shaman restores part of the "paradisal" situation of primordial man and he does this by recovering animal spontaneity (imitating animal behavior) and speaking animal language (imitation of animal sounds) . . .[4]

American theater has known this impulse with its buffoons. Bobby Clark, Bert Lahr, Buster Keaton were acrobats, whose gutteral ravings and pratfalls were intuitive mirrors to an unjust world, ritual appeals for a state of grace. *The Serpent* is an American event which extends the unique expression of individual performers—the clowns— to a larger troupe. If the clown is sometimes seen as a saint of unreason, the same holy terminology must apply to the Open Theater.

The Serpent is subtitled "A Ceremony." There is an imaginative (mystic) certainty about the performance. Chaikin maintains, "In *The Serpent*, the point of crossing a boundary is a point of transformation, and the whole company crosses a boundary. Because when one person crosses a forbidden line, nothing is the same after that." Existential circularity is denied in ritual communion. The alienation is healed by the mythic spectacle. The intention and the effect pertain to primitive traditions as well as the Open Theater. Just as the tree and the serpent are brought together in one image, the rupture between Heaven and Earth is mended in primitive rites. In the excitement of ceremony (modern actors perform in trance states as in primitive cultures), divisions are forgotten in ecstasy. The dreamlike free form of *The Serpent*, the mingling of random moments, fused by passionate involvement, destroys the conditions of man's fallen state—Time and History.

> There is a great difference between the situation of primordial man and that restored by the shaman during ecstasy; the shaman can only temporarily abolish the rupture between Heaven and Earth. He ascends to Heaven "in spirit," no longer *in concerto* as did primordial man. He does not abrogate death . . .[5]

III

FIRST WOMAN OF THE CHORUS: In the beginning anything is possible.

SECOND WOMAN: I've lost the beginning.

THIRD WOMAN: I'm in the middle.

FOURTH WOMAN: Knowing neither the end nor the beginning.

If the Open Theater coins a new vocabulary of gesture, the language in *The Serpent* is at once concrete and economical, allowing it the generalizing power of mythic speech.

> "In *The Serpent* there is a great deal of incantation, because there is no confrontation between one human being and another in a direct way. The problem with Adam and Eve was how do you get them to speak. The moment you have actors and actresses open their mouths in a naturalistic fashion, you've lost their mythic potential. How do godlike figures speak? How do images which are larger than life speak? The sound has to carry a lot of grandeur or extend a stage image."[6]

Jean-Claude van Itallie's explanation of the technical problem of writing is also pertinent to the terminology which acknowledges the mythic intention behind the words:

> I'm trying to do with words what Chaikin is trying to do with the actors—get to the very essence of things. It's the only extent to which you can reach the archetype.

In *The Serpent,* the Zapruder film of the Kennedy assassination is acted out; then, as if being replayed, actors move quickly backwards, then forwards, then backwards again. The effect is to freeze a tableau of horror, emphasizing the immortality of the film image: JFK slumping forwards, Jacqueline Kennedy grasping backwards, etc.—the picture is stamped indelibly on the public consciousness. The event contrasts the public assassination with the primal slaying of Abel by his brother Cain, where the idea of total destruction without the knowledge of means was first acted out. Then, murder was an undiscovered skill. On stage, Cain heaves Abel like a rock, hacks at his body, and finally kills him. Progress has now given us instruments of destruction and a climate of banal death far removed from that first thrilling and overwhelming impulse. *The Serpent* explores the differences in the quality of killing and the nature of violence, linked together by their mythological potential.

> I think the Kennedy assassination is in our heads —at least my head—almost mythologically. I mean it's an image that the Zapruder film made indelible, as strong as anything from the Bible. We tried to explore other kinds of myths—fairy tales like Cinderella—but it didn't have any *weight,* the *largeness* of the Kennedy thing.

Van Itallie's intention was to create in each moment a size and resonance beyond particular space and time. "What one is trying to show is an impression of all-at-once." He speaks of "vertical time," the pull of mythology back to imaginative first sources, not linear time which is the playwright's usual historical frame of reference. As a playwright learning from the improvisational technique, van Itallie has been influenced by Chaikin's desire to externalize internal states of being. The ability to make life transparent, to confront its complexity with the clarity of living symbols is also a mythological impulse, discovering connections in oneself and reconciling man with the abyss.

> What we're really experimenting with at the Open Theater is how to split the human being up, in different levels, in ways which the human being has never been split up before. In other words, to use the analogy of painting, instead of a natural-

istic canvas, an impressionistic one. That kind of
experimenting opens your mind up. You can see
what happens when you split reality up in an
unexpected way.

In confronting mythology and trying to find the center
of its power, the Open Theater has discovered a resonance
in performance and an untapped source of energy. As
Chaikin said:

> When we explored Adam and Eve, we found our-
> selves much more involved with these stories,
> these myths, than we imagined. It became clear
> that although we had rejected these stories as
> being true in any way, they still claimed us. We
> were absolutely surprised how personal the dis-
> cussion and the improvisations were for us. That's
> what made me continue to work on it. There was
> a visceral energy and it seemed important to fol-
> low and let it have its own autonomy. Why were
> we still so interested in these stories?[7]

For the actor, improvisation breaks down the boundaries
of perception, calling up ideas and responses deep in his
subconscious. The passion to re-experience life is in itself
a denial of boredom, or stasis. *The Serpent* redefines emotional boundaries, questioning the sources of guilt and test-
ing man's new freedom. The position is put by the serpents
to Eve:

SERPENT 2: Is the fruit God's property?

SERPENT 1: He says Adam and Eve may not eat. But are
Adam and Eve guests in this garden?

SERPENT 2: Are they guests?

SERPENT 1: Don't they live here?

SERPENT 2: May they not eat what they want?

The Serpent becomes a dialectic exploration of mythology, playing off conventional theological attitudes and discovering new import in old myths. As one of the chorus suggests in counterpoint to the Biblical scenes: "I'm concerned because what you reject can still run your life."

The words refer to the power of myth and its ability to reinforce unnecessary guilt. They also create a tension between past history and present experience. "The awful guilt of the apple," says van Itallie, "is something every one of us carries around. The speeches of the women in the chorus are intended to indicate what it is like to be alive now. It's very hard. And part of the myth thing, part of the Genesis thing, is to explore on another level what's going on with all of us . . . what's hanging us up . . . what images are we stuck at . . . what forms do we see ourselves in."

THIRD WOMAN: My home was Cleveland.
      Then I came to New York
      And I didn't have to account to anybody.
      I slept with men.
      I slept with women.
      I smoked: pot, hashish, opium.
      I slept with a man and a woman at the same time.
      But I'm a gentle person
      And I collapsed.

The process of discovery in *The Serpent* brought its special understanding of these ruling myths. Chaikin recalls:

We found a great, great anger at God as we worked through the piece. Sulky, willful, stub-

born. People are always guests in the Garden in a
sense. We're guests in the world. The sense of
being a "guest" is something we became really
mad at. It's a feeling that still persists in the world
today.

The Open Theater wants to inhabit the world as it does
the stage, acknowledging the capacities for joy as well as
mortality. The performers embrace their creation completely because it is a product of their communal discoveries.
They are not separate from their environment, but in
gorgeous control of it. Their theater piece is an argument
against the assumptions of authority and absolutes—a
vehicle which urges the observer (and actor) back into
himself, a process of self-definition. When Cain kills his
brother toward the end of the piece, there is a moment of
strategic decision. Cain has tried to stand his dead brother
up, placed grass in his lifeless hands to feed the sheep. He
moves from one side of the stage to the other. The stage
directions emphasize the pathos of his predicament:

> . . . waiting, waiting for life to start up again in
> Abel. The heron from the garden is back, and it
> wanders near . . . Cain, still watching the place
> where he put Abel's body on the sheep, continues
> to wait . . .

This is Vladimir and Estragon's situation, the existential
one. "All Cain has to do is wait; wait with a conscience
and a knowledge of the murder" (Chaikin). If Cain suffers
the guilt of taking a life, minutes later, after performing the
ritual begetting, the Open Theater focuses on the end of the
cycle—the death. Theatrically, the polarities of the absurd
—guilt and death—have been acted out. Actors, posing in
decrepit age, stare at the audience. Suddenly, the actors

break the somber rhythm—jumping, chanting, churning
with determined energy. In the final beats of performance,
they move out into the audience singing "Moonlight Bay."
The moment is a leap of faith. As Chaikin explains, "The
intention is a moment of celebration. The stillness of Cain's
waiting, the fact of death—you can really get dragged down
by that and die from it. Or you can just go another way."
The Open Theater opts for action, not resignation, a life
force instead of a death wish. This is, in itself, a gesture
beyond the Absurd.

IV

What distinguishes the Open Theater from other radical
departures in stage form (The Living Theater, The Performance Group) is its sense of audience. There is a gentleness in the performance, a humility arrived at in confronting
death. The performers evoke a sympathy which does not
alienate the imagination but lures it deeper into the game
of discovery. This texture is Chaikin's vision, a belief that
one must acknowledge death in order to attest to a new life.

> The thing about theater—more than anything else
> —is that the people are actually there. You can't
> confront being alive without confronting that
> you're mortal. This is what theater's about. You
> can't do it in the movies because the situation is
> on celluloid.

When Eve eats the apple, everyone eats. Apples are
tossed into the audience, new Adams bite into the fruits and
then pass them on. The audience takes part in the mythological fall, reliving it, drawn tangibly into the arena of
exploration. At the end of the event, after the movement
of celebration, the cast strolls through the audience singing

"Moonlight Bay." The audience, unwittingly, hums the captivating pastoral melody. Some sing with the performers. The actors stop; but the song is completed by people in the audience. The point is made. The society has changed and so, too, must its myths.

The mythologies of an ancient Paradise, a safe and silvery bower, weigh seductively on the imagination. The moment is evocative; the play is over, ending with this intense, but strangely sweet, scrutiny. The myth of the silver lining, the romantic lushness of the American dream, is exposed on levels below the rational. Our rhythms must evolve with a new world, our guiding passions must be modified with the facts of life. The Open Theater's encounter exists in the net of images which surround it. This relationship, as Chaikin maintains, "is caused neither by the actor, nor the audience, but the silence between them." The silence creates the resonance, the atmosphere in which metaphor presses against the bounds of imaginative possibility. That silence is the catalyst of mythmaking.

V

There is talk that the Open Theater will leave America. Such an exodus would be foolhardy, for their volcanic energy, their sense of unease, and their passion to burrow into their souls comes out of the American grain and feeds on it. If the buffoon's tradition has left us no ruling clowns, the Open Theater has absorbed their anarchic exhibition of energy and has begun to find in the metaphor of the body new acrobatic possibilities on stage. The sounds and gestures are a language unto themselves, locked within the special situation of the improvisation. It cannot be copied; it makes no sense outside their unique ensemble. This is as Chaikin would have it:

I'd like to see each play have its own code in the use of words. Each play is only involved in its special poetry. It would become a kind of language, with the syntax carrying a special kind of meaning. The words have special meaning to the audience and the actor. That's what the playwright, finally, has to do. I despair of conversation and conventional language. It just doesn't carry meaning any more. It's facile.

The theater is political in the most basic sense—it deals with individuals and their relationship to life. But the Open Theater steers away from propaganda on esthetic grounds; statement too often eliminates theatrical discovery.

It's too literal. It limits resonance to do blatantly political things. It makes you limit your vision. There is a lot of propaganda theater in the country that does very good things. Sometimes I feel guilty that we're not doing that kind of thing: but I don't really enjoy it. It's not enough to change the opinions. Everyone knows how much opinions are worth. It's something *behavioral* that one wants, to free yourself from a kind of boundary. In that sense, the theater we do is political.

The Serpent is intended to call up dreams, not answer immediate moral questions. The action and sounds spin around an audience, reweaving the rites of birth and death as well as the Original Sin and celebration. "Don't lose any thought wondering what connects the scenes or what logic applies from one scene to the other," wrote Chaikin in the program introduction. "The connections are in your head." What may seem absurd is only the first rung of a much deeper and unified exploration of self. The theater event turns from spectacle to creative mythology. As Joseph Campbell points out in *The Masks of God:*

> In art, in myth, in rites, we enter the sphere of dream awake. And as the imagery of dream will be on one level—local, personal, and historic, but at bottom rooted in the instincts, so also myth . . . The message of an effective living myth is delivered to the spheres of bliss of the deep unconscious, where it touches, wakes, and summons energies; so that symbols operating on that level are energy-releasing and chanelling stimuli. That is their function—their "meaning"—on the level of Deep Sleep.[8]

The intention of *The Serpent* is the dynamic of myth, "to let go the past, with its truths, its goals, its dogmas of 'meaning' and its gifts; to die to the world and to come to birth from within."[9] The event is left open-ended and unsummarized. The effect is haunting, like a dream unresolved. The theater aspires to a higher dimension, beyond the absurd. "Plays should be instruments to get into people's dreams," says Jean-Claude van Itallie. "If you can get into somebody's dream, that's exciting, perhaps the most profound change you can effect." *The Serpent* succeeds.

10

Pinter the
Spaceman

*The human condition, Heidegger
says, is to be there. Probably it is
the theater, more than any other
mode of representing reality,
which reproduces this situation
most naturally. The dramatic
character is on stage, that is his
primary quality: he is there . . .*
—*Alain Robbe-Grillet*[1]

While the new novel has set out to paint the
surfaces of the object world, doing for literature what primary structure has done for sculpture, the drama of Harold
Pinter has come closest to capturing the changed relationship between Man and Nature at the basis of the artistic
experiments in the other arts. Pinter is a storyteller, not a

scientist; but his images chronicle a world beyond the Newtonian perspective.

In the Renaissance, Shakespeare could make Hamlet tell the players the function of their drama—confident in Man's direct relation to Nature and dominance over it:

> . . . the purpose of playing, whose end, both at the first and now, was and is, to hold, as 'twere, the mirror up to nature; to show virtue her own feature, scorn her own image, and the very age and body of the time, his form and pressure . . .
> (III, ii, 20-23)

Language, like the stage, informs the audience of Man's sovereignty over the natural world, where he is both distinctive within it and, yet, apart from it. Newtonian physics changed that view, its implications reaching far into the art of the twentieth century and the responses of its audience.

> [It] saw in man a puny irrelevant spectator (so far as being wholly imprisoned in a dark room can be called such) of the vast mathematical system whose regular motions according to mechanical principles constituted the world of nature . . . The world that people had thought themselves living in—a world rich in color and sound, redolent with fragrance, filled with gladness, love and beauty, speaking everywhere a purposive harmony and creative ideals—was crowded into minute corners in the brains of scattered organic beings. The really important world outside was a world hard, cold, colorless, silent and dead . . .[2]

Armed with a faith in reason and the mathematical certainty of the universe, the arts imposed on their varied images boundaries of implied coherence. History could be recalled and clarified, the future carefully charted. If the novelist could scavenge his memory or society for "truth," the picture frame gave the painting a spatial order where the objects fitted smoothly into the environment of the canvas, limiting the spectator's vision and controlling it. The proscenium stage imposed a certain formula on performance as well as on the play. The well-made play, with its careful architecture, its "plot points," its clear motivation, was the embodiment of a scrupulous logic which affirmed a middle class in the passive stability of the world.

Harold Pinter denies the human animal its deterministic response; his characters are no longer stimulated to act out of a clearly defined past, but rather out of the vagaries of the moment. They defy theatrical convention—passing out on stage without being carted off, refusing to explain themselves, telling stories which merge ambiguously into fantasy. In denying explicit knowledge, Pinter finds laughter and dramatic content by inverting literary and stage clichés. His characters, caught in the web of their own rational powers, continually latch onto a certainty only to destroy it, root up objects only to find them change before their eyes. Although critics score Pinter for being "slow" or "unexciting," in fact, Pinter has released the world and its objects into a nervous uncertainty on stage which offers variety and surprise. Far from being "absurd," his plays mirror a world which modern science has confirmed. "Observation means interference with what we are observing . . . Observation disturbs reality."[3] Although the statement refers to the scrutiny of atomic particles, science has put into serious question the concept of an objective distance. "The act of observation is at the same time unavoidably an act of participation."[4] As a result, the uncertainty of objects is not merely a fashionable esthetic but a scientific fact. As Werner

Heisenberg, the formulator of the Uncertainty Principle, has pointed out:

> We are involved in the argument between nature and man in which science plays only a part, so that the common division of the world into subject and object, inner world and outer world, body and soul, is no longer adequate and leads us into difficulties. Thus even in science the object of research is no longer nature itself, but man's investigation of nature. Here, again, man confronts himself alone.[5]

Nature exists in Pinter's plays with no anthropomorphic overtones. It holds none of the lush benevolence of a Shakespearean bower nor does it offer the tenacious, personal challenge of a Hemingway safari. Nature is primarily a memory in a claustrophobic, urban world. The "pathetic fallacy" is not only forgotten; it is parodied. Goldberg, in *The Birthday Party*, recalls that pastoral moment: ". . . I can see it like yesterday. The sun falling behind the dog stadium. Ah!" When Lenny recalls the out-of-doors in *The Homecoming*, the purifying salvation of Nature is mocked by his specific fantasy of violence:

> I mean, I am very sensitive to atmosphere . . . For instance, last Christmas I decided to do a bit of snow-clearing for the Borough Council . . . What I anticipated with a good deal of pleasure was the brisk cold bite in the air in the morning . . . Bloody freezing. Well, the lorry came, I jumped on the tailboard, headlights on, dipped, and off we went. Got there, shovels up, fags on, and off we went, deep into the December snow, hours before cockcrow . . . an old lady approached me and asked me if I would give her a hand with

> her iron mangle . . . I said to her, now look here,
> why don't you stuff this iron mangle up your arse?
> Anyway, I said, they're out of date, you want to
> get a spin drier. I had a good mind to give her a
> workover there and then, but as I was feeling
> jubilant with the snow-clearing I just gave her a
> short-arm jab to the belly and jumped on a bus
> outside . . .[6]

The rooms which enclose Pinter's dramas are pierced with
no sounds from an outside world. There is no "breaking
string" to warn of impending chaos, no twitter of birds as a
harbinger of a new day. In Pinter's *Landscape,* the title implies that Pinter has finally taken his characters out-of-
doors. He hasn't; instead, he shows us the mind re-creating
the outside world, painting it vivid and soiled. Duff and
Beth speak, but do not listen to one another. Beth recreates
the golden stillness of a beach; Duff relates how he went
to the duck pond to feed the birds:

> Mind you, there was a lot of shit all over the
> place, all along the paths, by the pond. Dogshit,
> duckshit . . . all kinds of shit . . . all over the paths.
> The rain didn't clean it up. It made it even more
> treacherous. The ducks were well away, right
> over on their island. But I wouldn't have fed
> them, anyway. I could have fed the sparrows.[7]

The coarseness is hilarious, carefully counterpointed with
Beth, who in her dreamy delicacy doesn't hear it. The precision of Pinter's language paints Nature with graphic
clarity; but they are in a room, talking. Both worlds become
real; both characters are charged with a relationship the
audience can never verify. Does the landscape exist as they
see it? Is it totally apocryphal? What is most important is
only that they see it. Pinter's advantage over the new novel-

ists is the stage itself; he can show the breach between man and the objects of his environment, dramatize a very special understanding of the process of perception. Robbe-Grillet, with many of the same modern instincts—conscious of geometry (specific groupings in Pinter) and the object world —describes life outside the mind, not merely with microscopic particularity, but enmeshed in a cerebral vision. The difficulty of conjuring a sense of three-dimensional space on the page is immense, if not impossible. In Robbe-Grillet's *Jealousy,* for example, jungle noises are outlined with a precision which always seems to have designs upon the reader.

> Still, all these cries are alike; not that their common characteristic is easy to decide, but rather their common lack of characteristics; they do not seem to be cries of fright, or pain, or intimidation, or even love. They sound like mechanical cries, uttered without perceptible motive, expressing nothing, indicating only the existence, the position, the respective movements of each animal, whose trajectory through the night they punctuate . . .[8]

The contemplation does not startle; Nature is not *shown,* only described. The intention is diminished by the form. This is perhaps why Robbe-Grillet turned so effectively to film; and why Marguerite Duras has experimented with the stage. Objects in space are dramatic; man's reaction to them is theater.

In Pinter's plays, the perceiver is the active agent; his values and his actions are not comprehensible by some external behavioral pattern, an objective rational force. Pinter dramatizes what physiobiology has demonstrated, "that there can be no genuine understanding of behavior without an understanding of the *behaver—on his own terms*."[9] In Pinter, the audience only knows what it sees happening on stage; no sociological assumptions are allowed. *The Homecoming* seems elusive where it is merely being realistic; it refuses to offer up experience to the audience from one point of view. Instead, action is fractured by the complex, private manner in which each character reacts to what happens on stage. The play is beyond moral questions which demand precisely this single perspective. In *The Homecoming*, Ruth leaves her husband and children to live in Max's household. Pinter does not intend her to be a whore (although most American audiences reacted this way). She responds to life on private, ultimately inexplicable terms. Her life in America is arid, her husband egotistical and unthinking; but her eyes offer only hints of the bleakness which no one else (not even Teddy) can understand:

> I was born quite near here. (*Pause.*) Then . . .
> six years ago, I went to America. (*Pause.*) It's
> all rock. And sand. It stretches . . . so far . . .
> everywhere you look. And there's lots of insects
> there. (*Pause.*) And there's lots of insects there.
> (*Silence.*)[10]

Max stalks his domain, swinging his cane with the lingering memory of sexual potency. Hating women and fearing them, he lives in a perpetual state of siege and yet longs for contact:

> I'm not an old man. (*He looks up at her.*) Do
> you hear me? (*He raises his face to her.*) Kiss me.

Max's suspicions, the fear and violence which dominate his reactions, are never certain to the audience, only to him. They see only a man clinging tenaciously to a sense of his own virility (". . . I always had the smell of a good horse. I could smell him. And not only the colts, but the fillies . . ."), whose reactions go beyond sentiment, interpreting every action with a specific aggression. Sam, Max's brother and a chauffeur, insinuates that Max's wife and his best friend are having an affair. Late in the play, as Sam passes out on stage, he confesses that the friend made love to Max's wife, Jessie, in the back seat of his car while he drove. True or false? We don't know. What is important is that it seems true to Max, whose fear of it makes it real. Early in the play, Sam jabs him pointedly with a pause in which he chooses his words carefully.

MAX: Above having a good bang on the back seat, are you?

SAM: Yes, I leave that to others.

MAX: You leave it to others? What others? You paralysed prat!

SAM: I don't mess up my car! Or my . . . boss's car! Like other people.

MAX: Other people? What other people? (*Pause.*) What other people?

SAM: Other people.

The word "boss" is sounded out slowly by Sam; it is too close to "brother" not to upset Max and unleash his questions.

If Pinter's drama seems to diminish the possibilities of experience—a criticism often leveled against it—in fact, he opens up a new, more illuminating mode of stage action. Where Beckett's philosophy must finally reduce itself to voiceless inaction (he has written a thirty-second play), Pinter opens up the stage to the examination of a new dimension of Man's free will—smaller, perhaps, than the grand designs of earlier centuries, but one where variety, choice and personal value still have an interest and a validity. This parallels new scientific defections from Gestalt theory of perception, in which there is a mutual determination of form (organism) and environment.

> What is significant . . . is the thesis that the individual is in the fullest sense an *actor* (not a mere field or receptacle), who creatively determines his environment by selecting and reconstructing the materials of experience in terms of his own sensitivities and makeup—his unique personal perspective. "What the individual is," in G. H. Mead's words, "determines what the character of his environment will be . . ." Man sets the universe out there as like himself in matter and substance.[11]

Pinter is fascinated by the highly discriminating way in which Man chooses to see the world. Man reconstructs the world and its objects through carefully selected stimuli. Ruth, calling attention to her legs, illustrates the point precisely:

> . . . Look at me. I . . . move my leg. That's all it is. But I wear . . . underwear . . . which moves with me . . . it . . . captures your attention. Perhaps you misinterpret. The action is simple. It's a leg . . . moving. My lips move. Why don't you restrict . . . your observations to that? Perhaps the fact that they move is more significant . . . than the words which come through them. You must bear that . . . possibility . . . in mind.

Ruth's sexy legs make the audience and the characters salivate with lust. She makes her point. But Teddy is held

up for ridicule because, as a philosopher, he will not acknowledge the autonomy between the objects which surround Man, and Man himself. Objects in the world are
both nonreferable and mercurial ideas which he refuses to
comprehend:

> . . . There's no point in my sending you my
> works. You'd be lost. It's nothing to do with the
> question of intelligence. It's a way of being able to
> look at the world. It's a question of how far you
> can operate on things and not in things. I mean it's
> a question of your capacity to ally the two, to
> relate the two, to balance the two. To see, to be
> able to *see!* I'm the one who can see. That's why
> I can write my critical works. Might do you good
> . . . have a look at them . . . see how certain people
> can view . . . things . . . how certain people can
> maintain . . . intellectual equilibrium. Intellectual
> equilibrium. You're just objects. You just . . .
> move about. I can observe it. I can see what you
> do . . .

Pinter's irony is twofold: not only is Teddy cuckolded,
but the stage is inundated with situations which deny his
way of seeing. A glass of water turns into a sexual threat
("Lie on the floor. Go on. I'll pour it down your throat.");
a cheese roll is equated on a moral scale with a man's wife;
a large ash tray held by Ruth receives the ashes from each
of the men's cigars with a sexual longing that vanishes as
quickly as their configuration in front of it.

The sense of chance, the arbitrariness of Nature is shocking and visually breathtaking in Pinter's plays. He is able
to create an expectation of some large physical gesture as
the logical extension of the emotional tension on stage (a
brawl over the wife, for instance). He then turns table on

the audience by having his characters focus on something *small* (the cheese roll). This is not a technique special to Pinter, but he does it differently. In *Hamlet,* for instance, the Prince, realizing the sword has been poisoned, says: "The point envenom'd too!—Then venom, do thy work!" (V, ii). The sword is vitalized by Hamlet's purpose; Hamlet sees the poison and the sword as extensions of *his* revenge. The audience expects him to run the King through. He doesn't; he grazes the skin. The revenge has an intellectual satisfaction for Hamlet, in keeping with his cerebral temperament. The death will be slow, and savored. The King, by his own words, is merely "hurt"; Hamlet forces him to drink the poisoned wine which has killed his mother. The audience expects a large gesture—to see the King skewered and writhing in violent action. Instead, the gestures are small, almost intimate. The effect is overwhelming. The contrast yields its special insight.

Unlike Renaissance thought, Pinter will not allow his characters to see anything as the extension of their "purpose." The objects are silent; they offer no hint or omens, no final sense of connection in the chain of things. In *Landscape,* Beth makes a comment which elaborates Pinter's deep-seated distrust of an objective relationship to the world, and the insinuating appeal of such assumptions.

> I remember always, in drawing, the basic principles of shadow and light. Objects intercepting the light cast shadows. Shadow is deprivation of light. The shape of the shadow is determined by that of the object. But not always. Not always directly. Sometimes it is only indirectly affected by it. Sometimes the cause of the shadow cannot be found. But I always bore in mind the basic principles of drawing. (*Pause.*)
> So that I never lost track. Or heart.

The "principles" of drama, like the principles of Newtonian physics, offer an image of purpose, a clarity and
simplicity which has insulated Man from his world. In
streamlining his plays, pruning the clutter of objects as well
as words, Pinter focuses on the dynamics of perception,
isolating special objects more easily for public scrutiny.
"The only play which gets remotely near to a structural
entity which satisfies me is *The Homecoming*. *The Birthday
Party* and *The Caretaker* have too much writing. I want to
iron it down, eliminate things . . ."[12] The silences and pauses
have become bolder and more evocative in the process.
This structured counterpoint to Pinter's words and gestures
etch his unique world. The silences are different from those
of Beckett, not simply a cosmic void or the final humming
breakdown of "communication." Pinter's characters communicate clearly; people hear each other, only to misin-
terpret the words for their own emotional reasons. More
important, the silences emphasize the element of perception.
The characters are making decisions, weighing the balance,
as the action is in the process of unfolding. These are *active*
silences underscoring the intense inner life of Pinter's drama.

The artifice of immediacy is as important to Pinter's
vision as it is to the new novelists. Pinter's characters are
continually reconstructing the past from memory, unable
to verify it or be certain of any origins except the present.
Pinter's tactile, sensuous language insinuates a sense of
reality into their vague imaginings. Max remembers his
father with vivid words which have the sound of clarity, but
whose logic denies it.

> Our father? I remember him. Don't worry. You
> kid yourself. He used to come over to me and
> look down at me. My old man did. He'd bend
> right over me, then he'd pick me up. I was only

> that big. Then he'd dandle me. Give me the
> bottle. Wipe me clean. Give me a smile. Pat me
> on the bum. Pass me around, pass me from hand
> to hand. Toss me up in the air. Catch me coming
> down. I remember my father.

The graphic language flushes the past into the present—
or tries to. Pinter is able to create that rare sleight of hand
which conjures a sense of the past without having to bow to
history's chronology. Bombarded by stimuli, faced with a
stalemate between Man and the world, the present moment
is the only dramatic situation which is justified by the philo-
sophic implications of Pinter's vision. Similarly, Robbe-
Grillet, in discussing his film *Last Year at Marienbad,*
maintained significantly that:

> The Universe in which the entire film occurs
> is, characteristically, in a perpetual present which
> makes all recourse to memory impossible. This is
> a world without a past, a world which is self-
> sufficient at every moment and which obliterates
> itself as it proceeds.[13]

The same seems true of Pinter, except that on the stage
this intended immediacy comes closer to an audience's
responses. If memory is impossible, Man's reliance on it
and its misuse are an interesting focus of drama which
Pinter will not, wisely, disregard. In Pinter's closed rooms,
the threat is not simply physical violence but the thought
of change which takes place every second on stage. Pinter's
drama attests to Nathalie Sarraute's esthetic which seeks
"some precise dramatic action shown in slow motion,"
where "time was no longer the time of real life but of a
hugely amplified present."[14]

Pinter inverts the techniques of inner monologue. The

characters' soliloquies are never clear mirrors to their real feelings. Instead, the monologues teeter between private consciousness and public threat. In *The Homecoming,* Max comes downstairs, disturbed by the sounds coming from the parlor. He talks to his son, Lenny, in the third person, a manner of address which makes an audience wonder if Max is talking to himself or threatening Lenny.

MAX: ... He wakes me up in the middle of the night, I think we got burglars here, I think he's got a knife stuck in him, I come down here, he tells me to pop off.

Lenny sits down.

He was talking to someone. Who could he have been talking to? They're all asleep. He was having a con-versation with someone. He won't tell me who it was. He pretends he was thinking aloud. What are you doing, hiding someone here?

Neither the past nor the present is explained through Max's ruminations. The audience, however, is lured into the limbo of the ambiguous tone: an eternal present. The effect is different from the Elizabethan soliloquy, for instance, which usually brought the actor downstage away from the action. It was the external expression of an internal thought. When Hamlet speaks to the Ghost in front of his mother, the audience *sees* that he is talking to somebody; and that he is far from mad. His mother cannot see the Ghost. It is Hamlet's greatness and dignity that he can see further and more perceptively than those around him. The audience accepts this dichotomy; they are given a special access to "truth," hearing everything, seeing all the possibilities. The mirror is held up to Nature for *their* benefit; the tragic "catharsis" also affirms a unity.

In Pinter, the audience experiences only what the charac-

ters do. They are privy to no extra information, no other
choices. Pinter constructs a situation where fantasy has the
weight of fact; and fact has the metaphoric potential of
fantasy. There is no longer the Newtonian Chinese puzzle
about appearance and reality. The "subjective" world and
the "real" are not simply confused; they are combined. The
character has no significance beyond what is presented on
stage; he simply *exists*. Lenny's muscle-flexing tales of violence for Ruth, Max's monologue on Jessie's clothes (he
calls her a "slutbitch" seconds later) show the capriciousness
of imagination while focusing the audience's attention on
these changes of perception from moment to moment. The
only facts we can know are that the characters change their
minds, that they say one thing and do another, that their
dreams are not synonymous with their actions. Pinter refuses to comment on them, to favor one over another, because to do that would be to point to a moral or opt for a
certainty which his plays deny.

It is interesting that *Landscape* extends the technique of
dramatic inner monologue further than he has taken it
before. In this short play, Pinter indicates no concrete
theatrical gesture, only characters facing each other ob-
liquely, speaking in realistic argot which turns in on itself
and destroys the boundaries of the concrete. The mystery
and the "reality" of the characters develop as they explain
themselves, each speaking in his special tempo. Pinter indicates his intention in the stage directions:

> DUFF refers normally to BETH, but does not ap-
> pear to hear her voice. BETH never looks at DUFF
> and does not appear to hear his voice. Both char-
> acters are relaxed, in no sense rigid.

Pinter wants to retain the naturalism in order to work
against it, blurring reality's framework. How much of Beth's

romantic revery is make-believe? How many of Duff's bravura tales of pub life are true? Everything remains uncertain—experience riddled with sexual longing, loneliness, hope, violence, but never offering itself up neatly for easy consumption. The drama is in the language:

> This beer is piss, he said. Undrinkable. There's nothing wrong with the beer, I said. Yes there is, he said, I just told you what was wrong with it. It's the best beer in the area, I said. No it isn't, this chap said, it's piss. The landlord picked up the mug and had a sip. Good beer, he said. Someone's made a mistake, this fellow said, someone's used this pintpot instead of a boghole.

Experience and individuals are tumbled together; Duff's voice absorbs the world. The audience must struggle to keep identities clear.

Just as the stylized speech in *The Homecoming* kept the audience poised on the immediate moment of dramatic reference, waiting for the carefully spoken words, forgetting about the past to make sense of the present, *Landscape* shows Pinter toying with the relationship of the audience to the stage illusion. Unlike the impressionistic naturalism of Chekhov, Pinter deprives the audience of its traditional perspective—its distance—which can bring all the small strokes of the piece together in a coherent pattern. Pinter forces the audience toward the center of his drama, denying their position outside the conflict. Crammed close to the stage image, the audience can be inundated with stimuli without having the final say on the final experience, without being able to make "sense" of it, merely responding to the exigencies of action. With the present and the past, the imaginary and the real so carefully wedded, Pinter forges a unity which is undeniable. These are the "facts"; these are the ambiguities. That is all there is; and all we, as the audience, should demand to know. Like primary sculpture, the experience exists only within its *own context,* on its *own terms.* In refusing to discuss *The Homecoming,* Pinter has said: "I've nothing to say about *The Homecoming.* It exists and that's that."[15] His words are specific and in keeping with his vision. He talks about his play as an object in space in the same way as a sculptor or painter might. Pinter, who sees himself as a conventional playwright, has not completely disregarded the accoutrements of the past, but used them against themselves, employing illusion in order to destroy it. This idea is prevalent among the innovators in the visual arts who have, however, denied the past and illusion. As Frank Stella has maintained:

> I always get into arguments with people who want to retain the old values in painting—the humanistic values that they always find on the canvas. If you pin them down, they always end up asserting that there is something there besides the paint on canvas. My painting is based on the fact that only what can be seen there *is* there. It really is an object. Any painting is an object and anyone who gets involved enough in this finally has to face up to the objectness of whatever it is that he's doing. If the painting were lean enough, accurate enough or right enough, you would be able to look at it. All I want anyone to get out of my paintings, and all I ever get out of them, is the fact that you can see the whole idea without any confusion . . . What you see is what you see.[16]

In the same way, Don Judd's primary structures are based on an instinct which Pinter would concede—the autonomy of the object world. As a dramatist and an actor, Pinter responds to the stage environment and is conscious of his audience. In this sense his art differs from Judd's highly cerebral but pathfinding extension of sculptural possibilities. But the reaction to Newtonian physics is an articulate part of both arts.

JUDD: The qualities of European art so far. They're innumerable and complex, but the main way of saying it is that they're linked up with a philosophy—rationalism, rationalistic philosophy.

INTERVIEWER: Descartes?

JUDD: Yes.

INTERVIEWER: And you mean to say that your work is apart from rationalism?

JUDD: Yes. All that art is based on systems built beforehand, *a priori* systems; they express a certain type of thinking and logic which is pretty much discredited now as a way of finding out what the world's like.

INTERVIEWER: Discredited by whom? By empiricists?

JUDD: Scientists, both philosophers and scientists.[17]

Judd's objects are self-enclosed and nonillusory. Although people may walk around them, the object never is intended to say anything, except to indicate what it is. Like Robbe-Grillet, this becomes the sculpture of surfaces and geometrical relationships—a precise, irreducible object. Judd indicates his concept this way:

> A shape, a volume, a color, a surface is something itself. It shouldn't be concealed as part of a fairly different whole. The shapes and materials shouldn't be altered by their context. One or four boxes in a row, any single thing or such a series, is local order, just an arrangement, barely order

at all. The series is mine, someone's, and clearly
not some larger order. It has nothing to do with
either order or disorder in general. Both are
matters of fact. The series of four or six doesn't
change the galvanized iron or steel or whatever
the boxes are made of.[18]

The public often balks at art's attempt to show Man the
autonomy of things. When *The Homecoming* opened on
Broadway, *The New York Times* printed a fatuous piece
on what seven of the city's chic people thought was its
"meaning." Many of them listed their findings in numerical
order—precisely the way of thinking which Pinter's play
strains to break. In the same way, critics of Judd's sculpture
will not let it *be*; in observing it, they exhibit the fatal
tendencies which the art stands against.

If they (the gallery-goers) care to disobey the
rules, moreover, and meditate on the symbolism
of Judd's boxes, the possibilities are endless. What
is a box, they say, if not a coffin, a house, a treas-
ure chest? As for that series of boxes climbing
up the wall, what is it but a machine-produced,
twentieth-century revision of a medieval illumin-
ator's stairway to paradise?[19]

In moving away from an anthropomorphic art, Judd and
Pinter share similar instincts of the culture. Often attacked
as "boring," "monotonous," "cool," "inhuman," they are
the most human of artists, forcing open consciousness into
new ways of seeing. Both artists shy away from universal
"truths" in their respective work. "I couldn't begin to think
about the order of the universe, or the nature of American
society. I didn't want work that was general or universal in
the usual sense. I didn't want to claim too much."[20] Judd's

words illustrate the predicament of conscience at the basis of Pinter's theater. There is not much one can claim for the world, but only a smaller, private *détente* between its objects and oneself. As in Pinter's play, where no proscenium arch is able to limit the variables of action, the three-dimensional sculpture has an infinite variety of angles and perspectives. It cannot be identified; it does not affirm any order but its own interrelation of parts, color, scale, material. Where the earlier plays of Pinter evoked the environment and its insubstantiality, *Landscape* obscures that aspect of existence. The stage direction reads: "The background of sink, stove, etc., and a window is dim." Beth and Duff are not conscious of the boundaries of their room, but exist outside them. Part of the chimera of environment is not merely that it may change before one's eyes but that it may bear no relation to Man at all. This development seems to parallel Judd's interest in objects defining a three-dimensional space. "Obviously, anything in three dimensions can be any shape, regular or irregular, and can have any relation to the wall, floor, ceiling, room, rooms or exterior or *none at all* . . ."[21]

The stage allows Pinter to give this vision, shared by such a variety of artists in different fields, a scope and dimension the other experiments cannot claim: he can translate the *process* of Nature's ambiguity with a directness and immediacy that the others have, as yet, not been able to accomplish. It is his art which approaches the dynamic of scientific insight which so many of the genres invoke. He has not merely broken with the past, but used the conventions of an old world-view to illustrate their limitations. While Man exists on this planet, language and gesture, objects and esthetics will abound. Pinter, by showing the failures and strengths of the human equipment, hints more precisely at what is "out there." His plays demand of life no new meanings, simply new questions.

11

The Language
of Laughter

Stage laughter, once the gaudy barometer of America's feverish leap into the twentieth century, now limps in search of a new voice. The society on which it comments is still shackled with injustice; the grotesque has not been ironed out by prosperity. Yet, if comedy has the targets, it lacks the language to encompass contemporary

195

experience. The humor of America's great clowns owed its untamed brashness and variety to the street; today, the metropolis has been partially tamed by technology, and it is from the impulses of science that speech takes its pattern. Where immigrant tongues brought liveliness and variety to the stage action, the sense of immediacy with the contemporary moment has been lost to today's laughter since the real language of science must be mathematics, not words.

Language bears the scars of history. It was inevitable that the dialect humor of the early twentieth-century stage would vanish. World War II would put an end to the Baron von Münchausens, the civil rights struggle would banish the Amos 'n Andys. A sophisticated society would be more self-conscious in its use of words, and even the ghetto-born comedians would speak in the uninflected tones of modern, democratic America. The buffoon, who had responded to the language of his new land with wonder and laughter at its eccentricities, would give to the American stage an energy and an openness comparable to the Elizabethan merry-andrews. The rough language, like the violent broad gestures, bowed to the decorum of the times. Society now frowns upon pratfalls—man brought low—and winces at the vernacular. The mass media which replaced theatrical satire as "popular" entertainment brought with them a special censorship and a uniformity which would castrate the eccentric instincts of comedy. The inundation of the public by television has not moved language to life, but away from it. Comedy has been seriously hurt.

The hollowness of contemporary vernacular—its smooth, efficient banality—has a corporate ring. There is a *New York Times* style, a *Time* style, and a CBS style. Americans listen and read, assuming the inflections without realizing their effect on the way they see the world. Language no

longer vividly recreates life nor stimulates the imagination as
fully as in earlier eras. Too much rhetoric has been passed
off as truth, too many inequities have been foisted on the
public with the language of logic. Words which added richness and ambiguity to our language are lost because of ethnic
nervousness or political misuse. The politics of exploitation
undermine the country's speech. Can Americans use such
simple words as "black," "justice," "dream," "liberal,"
"peace," without demeaning their argument? In the same
way, as George Steiner has pointed out in *Language and
Silence*,[1] Hitler reduced the coinage of the German tongue
by the atrocities carried out in its words. Terms like "roll
back," "clean up," "break through," "victory," and "nation"
lost their poetic, evocative power. The after effects felt by
the German writers from Mann to Brecht are being felt by
satirists in America today.

The early twentieth-century argot—with its malaprop-
isms and ebullient idiocy—laughed at the world, but with
a kindness which acknowledged a faith in it. The language
of the streets, like the terms uttered to the groundlings at
the Globe, had a primitive responsiveness to the world
which spoke with the voice of the moment—one of longing,
of failure, of carnival indifference. The effect could be both
poignant and surprising.

TEACHER: Gladys, vot is de opposite of misery?

GLADYS: Happiness.

TEACHER: Dot's right. Now Abbey, tell me vot is de opposite of woe?

ABBEY: Giddyap!

—(A 1910 "school act")[2]

Death filters into the language and its misuse. The grit of experience is captured in the playfulness of the fun-makers, who would refer to routines as the "wop act," "the straight and the Jew," "double Dutch act," "blackface"—violent terms accepted for a brutal moment in history. The puns, the free-association of terms were part of the amusement and the curious wonder at the spoken word. "The Double Wop Act" epitomizes the intention:

STRAIGHT: I gotta good job for you.

COMIC: What doin'?

STRAIGHT: Manicurin boulevards.

COMIC: How mucha you pay?

STRAIGHT: Twenty-two dollars a week.

COMIC: Twenty-two dollars a week?

STRAIGHT: Yeh—two twos.

COMIC: Datsa nice. Whatsa the hours?

STRAIGHT: You start at eight in the morning and stop at six ata night.

COMIC: Datsa too much work.

STRAIGHT: Okay. I makea it easier for you. You start at six anda finish at eight.

COMIC: Datsa nice man. I go now and tella my friend at the city hole.

STRAIGHT: Whatsa your friendsa name?

COMIC: He lives at the city hole, I nunga remember hisa name. Hisa gotta name something like a horse.

STRAIGHT: You don't mean the mayor?

COMIC: Sure, datsa him, the mare . . .[3]

The American public still appreciates the outlandish wordplay of the Marx Brothers or Bert Lahr's inarticulate bellowing—"Gnong, gnong, gnong." Like the ad-lib wit, the noise was simply the random conjunction of guttural sounds which Lahr never understood. ("One day I did it; the audience laughed. So, I kept it in.") The comedians' response to language, their instinct for going beyond the bounds of the spoken word to express an emotional idea, was a special moment for American culture, and, indeed, an often impressive cultural phenomenon in other societies. As Otto Jespersen has pointed out in *Language: Its Nature, Development and Origin:*

> When we say that speech originated in song, what we mean is merely that our comparatively monotonous spoken language and our highly developed vocal music are differentiations of primitive utterances. These utterances were, at first, like the singing of birds and crooning of babies, exclamative, not communicative—that is, they came forth from an inner craving of the individual without any thought of any fellow-creatures . . .[4]

The urgency of American laughter evoked by the comedians was precisely this exclamatory function, conscious of its audience, but sounding out the boundaries of experience with honest and individual statement. The effectiveness of the malapropism was its vivid image and surprise. These word pictures, a relatively primitive form of language, would evolve to a more analytic, cerebral discourse in which experience was broken down into more elaborate, formal speech units. As Jespersen points out:

> Just as here the advance is due to a further analysis of language, smaller and smaller units of

speech being progressively represented by single
signs, in an exactly similar way, though not quite
so unmistakably, the history of language shows
us a progressive tendency toward analyzing into
smaller and smaller units that which in the earlier
stages was taken as an inseparable whole.[5]

The linguistic ossification of America by its mass media
has other historical parallels. The metaphysical wit that
gave language a bold inventiveness and comedy a raucous
flexibility in Elizabethan England (Shakespeare had a writing vocabulary of 21,000 words), gave way to the banal,
passive tone of a more scientific concept of wit. Ultimately,
this instinct would lead to the buffooneries of Grub Street,
which Alexander Pope skewers in *The Dunciad* where "light
dies before her uncreating word." It was not merely a
fascination with print technology which made language
uncreative; it was the instinct to reduce it to a streamlined
equation. As early as 1667, the impulse of science to
remodel language was being discussed. Thomas Sprat in his
History of the Royal Society chronicled the discussion of
reform, stripping English of its "vulgar" eccentricities and
metaphoric potential for something efficient and dry. Criticizing "those specious *Tropes* and *Figures* of imaginative
writing which result in only mists and uncertainties," the
Society felt that it was necessary to be "arm'd against all
enchantments of *Enthusiasm.*" The plan was straightforward:

[The members of the Society] have therefore
been most rigorous in putting into execution the
only Remedy that can be found for this extravagance: and that has been, a constant Resolution,
to reject all the amplifications, digressions, and
swellings of style: to return back to the primitive

purity, and shortness, when men deliver'd so
many *things,* almost in an equal number of *words.*
They have exacted from all their members, a
close, naked, natural way of speaking; positive
expressions; clearness; a native easiness; bringing
all things as near the *Mathematical plainness* as
they can.[6]

The language of Restoration and eighteenth-century
stage comedy reached a linguistic and emotional dead end
because it never confronted the reality of its environment
and never offered the stage the necessary immediacy. Jona-
than Swift satirized the folly in a language which opted for
the general and eschewed the particular and colloquial. In
Gulliver's Travels, a book which Dr. Johnson maintained
was "written in open defiance of truth and regularity," Swift
pricks the bubble of contemporary disenchantment:

We next went to the school of languages, where
three professors sat in consultation upon improving that of their own country.
    The first project was to shorten discourse by
cutting polysyllables into one, and leaving out
verbs and participles because in reality all things
imaginable are but nouns.

If this sounds suspiciously like the famous *New York
Times* pyramid style,[7] Gulliver would meet others reminiscent of present-day avant-gardery:

The other project was a scheme for abolishing
all words whatsoever; and this was urged with a
great advantage in point of health as well as
brevity . . . An expedient was therefore offered,
that since words are only the names of *things,*

> it would be more convenient for all men to carry
> about them such things as were necessary to ex-
> press the particular business they are to discuss
> on . . .

Swift understood the bondage of a language stripped of
variety and a tactile fascination with the world. Today, Man
is coaxed into believing he has free and liberal speech, that
American arts still represent a freedom and honesty in the
mass media. Kenneth Tynan, back from a New York
scouting party, reported in the March 17, 1968, London
Observer: "Say what you like about America, it can't be
denied that you can say what you like . . ."

Tynan misses the point. Language and life are not
honored. He is chanting the party line of mobility which is
simply not true. Television not only bleeps out the vulgari-
ties and jagged edges of life, but commissions plays in which
the playwright *by contract* is not allowed to use certain
political and commercial terms which might impede advertising as well as offend the audience! Worse still is the
language that is allowed: a consensus argot of market research where banalities generally blanket experience, sell
products as well as coat emotions. While theater, even in its
prolific Elizabethan days, had its censors, the paradox in a
society "free" of censorship is a language and commercial
theater without variety, where the uniformity of output
matches the uniformity of taste.

Vaclav Havel's *The Memorandum,* which made its
American debut in 1968, was interpreted by the majority of
critics as a statement about bureaucracy in Communist
countries. Although Havel is a Czech, he has fashioned a
tale of brilliant and acerbic universality in which man's
fragmentation is matched by a similar change in his lan-

guage. What Americans fail to realize is that bureaucratic efficiency is even more pervasive in America than in Russia or its satellites. If the price of technocracy is an increasing limitation of human potential, language becomes an extension of this dehumanized, split personality. In *The Memorandum*, a new language is introduced into the office—Ptydepe. The office workers must adopt the terminology or be eliminated. While Havel explores the dynamics of conformity, his inventiveness uncovers a language which exhibits the lack of wholeness, the loss of man's responsiveness to his total environment.

In the Ptydepe classroom, the teacher expounds the principles of the new vocabulary:

> Ptydepe, as you know, is a synthetic language, built on a strictly scientific basis. Its grammar is constructed with maximum rationality, its vocabulary is unusually broad. It is a thoroughly exact language, capable of expressing with far more precision than any current natural tongue all the minutest nuances in the formulation of important office documents . . .[8]

The language itself, intended to eliminate redundancy and ambiguity, is cumbersome, unevocative, and dead. If there is no hint of the street or of the flesh in Ptydepe, the absurdity of matching scientific complexity with words is ballooned into hilarity. Ptydepe becomes a scientific malapropism, a twenty-first-century burlesque. The exclamation, that primordial response to nature, becomes lost in convoluted terminology:

> And now I shall name, just for the sake of preliminary orientation, some of the most common

Ptydepe interjections. Well, then, our "ah!" becomes "zukybaj," our "ouch!" becomes "bykur,"
our "oh!" becomes "hayf dy doretob," English
"pish!" becomes "bolypak juz," the interjection
of surprise "well!" becomes "zyk," however, our
"well, well!" is not "zykzyk!" as some students
erroneously say, but "zykzym."

In the end, the attempt to make Ptydepe the organiza-
tional language is squashed when the managing director
finally gets his memorandum in Ptydepe translated. It an-
nounces that Ptydepe is a bastard tongue. There is a purge,
an apology, and a new language, Chorukor, is hatched. The
final irony of Havel's tale rests with language. The girl who
translates the memorandum loses her job; the managing
director will not repay her kindness by reinstating her. In
a final speech, he analyzes his condition with clinical
accuracy:

> . . . Manipulated, automatized, made into a fetish,
> Man loses the experience of his own totality; hor-
> rified, he stares as a stranger at himself, unable
> to be what he is not, nor to be what he is . . .

He speaks clearly, but he cannot act. His words set him
apart from his own experience. The girl, overwhelmed by
the weight and import of his language, accepts his gross inhumanity with wonder: "Nobody ever *talked* to me so nicely
before." This dumb acquiescence underscores passivity and
overlooks the cruel indifference of Ptydepe's proponents
locked into a system which manufactures its own staleness.

Havel's tale has great implications for American life and
the silent violence of its clichéd language. Lenny Bruce's
scurrilities were not merely low-blows to hypocrisy, but a

clearly defined search to make American humor break
through the synthetic language and responses which isolated
an audience and kept it from confronting reality. In his own
combination of gutter slang, Yiddish, and literacy, Bruce
melted stereotypes with language larger than the word,
images which shattered the careful decorum of contemporary speech.

The first sentence of his autobiography, *How to Talk
Dirty and Influence People,* raises the erotic folklore of the
streets to consciousness and cuts into contemporary America
with a jolt that brings the mind's eye back to life (and the
streets).

> Filipinos come quickly; colored men are built
> abnormally large ("Their wangs look like a baby's
> arm with an apple in its fist"); ladies with short
> hair are Lesbians; if you want to keep your man,
> rub alum on your pussy.[9]

Wild, unpredictable, using the vernacular of every aspect
of the culture to strafe society, Bruce's intention was to
explode the present, to make his audience immediately and
incontrovertibly aware of their moment in American life.
The instinct is much the same as the early twentieth-century
American clowns; it is perhaps more literate and more
cynical about the dream to which they aspired. There is a
confidence in his mission and a willingness to stand alone,
where the impulse for humor in earlier eras had been social
acceptance and mobility. Bruce's autobiography resounds
with a simple existential idea. "There is only what *is*. The
what-*should*-be never did exist, but people kept trying to live
up to it. There is only what *is*."[10] His comedy glories in the
particulars of life—the dialects, the outrageousness, the
inequities. The language is at once thrilling and difficult,

obsessed and oppressive—but it is the syntax of modern life with all its polyglot confusions. There is no way to escape the voice of the world—unless you kill it.

Bruce begins with reality and moves into the surreal world of his imagination where only brittle honesty can test experience in safety. His satire of the absurd repressiveness of language, divesting itself of possibility and pertinence because of self-conscious decorum, is reflected in his monologue on the evil aura of the term "hotel":

> It's a real hang-up, being divorced when you're on the road. Suppose it's three o'clock in the morning, I've just done the last show, I meet a girl, and I like her, and suppose I have a record I'd like her to hear, or I just want to talk to her—there's no lust, no carnal image—but because where I live is a dirty word, I can't say to her, "Would you come to my hotel?"
>
> And every healthy comedian has given "motel" such a dirty connotation that I couldn't ask my *grandmother* to go to a motel, say I want to give her a Gutenberg Bible at three in the morning.
>
> The next day at two in the afternoon, when the Kiwanis Club meets there, then "hotel" is clean. But at three o'clock in the morning, Jim . . . Christ, where the hell can you live that's clean? You can't say hotel to a chick, so you try to think, what won't offend? What is a clean word to society? What is a clean word that won't offend any chick? . . .
>
> Trailer. That's it, *trailer*.
>
> "Will you come to my trailer?"
>
> "All right, there's nothing dirty about trailers. Trailers are hunting and fishing and Salem cigarettes. Yes, of course, I'll come to your trailer. Where is it?"

"Inside my hotel room."

Why can't you just say, "I want to be with you,
and hug and kiss you." No, it's, "Come up while
I change my shirt." Or coffee. "Let's have a cup
of coffee."

In fifty years, coffee will be another dirty word.[11]

Bruce's language weaves in and out of experience; the
pratfalls are no longer physical but psychic. "What won't
offend" becomes a commercial call-word which strips away
honesty and enforces a humorless sterility. Without risks of
language as well as spirit nothing can be learned, no new
terrain charted.

The attempts at recent stage satire have been struggling
with the onus of the spoken word. Barbara Garson's *Mac-
Bird* looked to Elizabethan rhythms for a fresh voice for
humor; S. J. Perelman's masterful *The Beauty Part* brought
the satirist's eye for hypocrisy and his ear for the dead
phrase to the stage. With characters like Monroe Sweet-
meat, Harry Hubris, and Vernon Equinox, Perelman's gallery of gargoyles spoke in stylized tones which were funny
but indisputably *dead*. A typical exchange between the rich
Weatherwax parents and their Ivy League Candide has the
airy lightness of a thirties fillip for the jazz age:

OCTAVIA: Why, our twenty-year-old son, which he's home
from Yale on his midyears and don't suspicion his folks
are rifting.

MILO: Of course, of course. Reached man's estate already,
has he? Where is our cub at the present writing?

OCTAVIA: In the tack room, furbishing up the accoutrements of his polo ponies.

MILO (*acidly*): Far better to be furbishing up to his Euclid,
lest he drag the name of Weatherwax through the
scholastic mire.

LANCE: Dads! Mums!

OCTAVIA: Shush! Here he comes now. You had best handle
   this. I'm laying down on my chaise lounge with a
   vinegar compress. (*Exits.*)[12]

The alabaster inflections are original, the butchery of
diction amusing; but the effectiveness of Perelman's satire
for the American stage is minimized because his vernacular
humor is a glance backward at a society already slightly
passé. There are greater evils than movie moguls, more out-
rages than philistinism.

Part of the immediate appeal of *Boys in the Band* (1968),
an Off-Broadway study of homosexuality, is the complete
emotional and linguistic reversal of conventional response.
In arguing for social understanding, a pattern of movements
and vocabulary stretches the audience's concept of the
"real." The shock brings laughter. Commonplace words
take on a new weight. One gay lover flounces around a
cocktail party with a lapdog coyness, asking, "Who do you
have to fuck to get a drink around here?" The effect on
an audience is visceral and surprising. The drama has a
superficial glitter of language momentarily turned back on
life. "There's one thing about masturbation. You don't
have to look your best." The sadness and hilarity, the
admission of man's bondage to his own flesh has its moments
of insight. However, the ultimate effect of this flashy style,
like the homosexual fascination with clothes and a carefully
preened existence, is to skirt experience, painting over
anxiety with superficial sleights of hand. "Give me Librium
or give me Meth."[13]

The words amuse, but also foreshadow the limitations of
homosexual theater and its laughter. Everything returns to
the single, sexual obsession. What begins as wit moves into
the weird boredom of paranoia where life is tortured into

nightmare or a flossy camp—both of which lose sight of the world.

Homosexual laughter on stage gathers its peculiar force from the fact that it is comparatively rare. Playwrights dealing with more familiar terrain must resort to different tactics in confronting the new dimensions of contemporary life. Jean-Claude van Itallie's *Motel*—the last play in *America Hurrah*—changes man's proportions, creating papier-mâché giants in a ritual of mindless destruction. The figures act in the larger-than-human gestures of the clown, matching a mammoth and technically streamlined society. As the figures sport themselves in a world which is supra-human, tape-recorded voices mouth the commercial banalities of contemporary speech:

> There now . . . There's a push-button here for
> TV. The toilet flushes of its own accord. All
> you've got to do is get off.[14]

Van Itallie's image of vulgarity is beyond words. The rape of the room, like so much of the grotesque in American life, cannot be conveyed adequately by contemporary language.

The growing vapidity of the American vernacular, the hollowness of language to encompass the truth of experience, has been one of the key brickbats of satirists from Swift to Jules Feiffer. Swift's *A Modest Proposal* uses the syntax and vocabulary of his day to expose the hypocrisy of the uncreating word. Feiffer's brilliant *Little Murders* which ran for seven performances on Broadway in 1967, is one of the few thorough attempts to inch language into a more careful understanding of its own limitations. Feiffer's play, mounted for the very audience it wanted to chastise, went unappreciated because of their numbness to the subtle changes in the vocabulary of the life and society he was challenging. Feiffer's language is wily, building to surreal proportions while keeping the ring of everyday naturalness. When a police inspector comes on the scene after the love interest has been picked off by a sniper, he speaks in the rhythm of the public clichés of law and order which we have come to accept.

> We are involved here in a far-reaching conspiracy to undermine respect for our basic beliefs. Who is behind this conspiracy? Once again ask the question; Who has the most to gain? People in high places. Their names would astound you. People in low places. Concealing their activities beneath a cloak of poverty. People in all walks of life. Left wing and right wing. Black and white. Students and scholars. A conspiracy of such ominous proportions that we may not know the whole truth in our lifetime and we will never be able to reveal all the facts. We are readying mass arrests . . .[15]

The violence and ignorance which appeals to reason is deceptive, and Feiffer's effectiveness is in showing up both the language and the process which spreads its special pall over moral and social problems.

The erosion of language is now finally being met by playwrights in hand-to-hand combat with the mass media. The fact that in *Hair* one of the performers runs around a Broadway stage yelling "Fucky, fuck, fuck, fuck fuck," may be self-indulgent but also a necessary means of letting the grit of life, its wonder and ugliness, back into the dingy pleasure domes, a way of acknowledging that man is neither deodorized nor fitted out with chandeliers between his legs.

The misuse of the word creates false heroes and false terms for analyzing them. In John Guare's *Muzeeka* (1968), a fantasy about a dreamer who goes to work for a Muzak corporation and hopes to change the world with his special music only to find himself fighting for CBS in Vietnam, a death chorus makes the point about language. In an acerbic take-off on the Martha Raye mentality, a girl leaps out of her Marine jump suit, decked out in a skirt made of torn copies of *The New York Times*. She pulls at her skirt, singing the print as she reads each transient name:

> Bonnie & Clyde and Jesus Christ
> Governor Wallace and Jesus Christ
> Ronald Reagan and Jesus Christ
> Hubert Humphrey and Jesus Christ
> LBJ was Jesus Christ.[16]

Heroes are born anew with each headline; and after each betrayal, the words that praised them lose some of their essence. This instinct for satire is not, as it has so often been, a conservative argument for a return to the past. The stage laughter, when it is effective, argues for a progressive future and a new language to meet it. The emphasis, finally, is on freedom—a poetry composed of the artifacts of experience where object and idea counterpoint one another in glistening amusement and insight. The hero of *Muzeeka,* Jack Argue, states his vision of how to revitalize the world. It is a satirist's esthetic, a plan for change. He will pipe in his music and depend on the cocoon of the media to dull the mind:

> I'll wait till all humans are inured to the ever-present inescapable background ocean blandness of my music . . . then on a sudden day that is not especially Spring, not especially Summer, a day when the most exciting thing around is the new issue of the *Reader's Digest* and you read with

> interest an ad that says Campbell is putting out
> a new flavor soup. That kind of day. I'll strike.
> I'll pipe in my own secret music that I keep
> hidden here under my cortical overlay and I'll
> free all the Etruscans in all our brains . . . and
> the country will remember its Etruscan forebears
> and begin dancing . . .

The impulse is to return to Jack Argue the gift of response, to free him from repression and free the words with which he conveys his understanding of the world. American theater is in the process of rediscovering playfulness on stage and with it, new possibilities for words. For the first time since the clowns made mayhem with their own individual *patois,* the theater is returning to an intimate relationship between experience as lived and experience as played. What is needed in stage laughter is what is needed in the society—honesty, responsiveness, flexibility. There is reason to be hopeful that laughter on stage will return to the flair and variety of the madcaps' language for an earlier, more intimate type of American entertainment. As American society changes drastically in the next few years, it will demand new terms to convey its dynamism and skewer its myopia. As the mass media increase in popularity, the theater may become the last outpost for the eccentric and individual voice.

12

The New Theater:
A Retreat from Realism

There is a tendency to say that humanistic painting must contain human figures, but why? Since human thought is itself an abstracting process, there is no basic conflict between abstraction and humanism.

—T. S. Eliot

*T*he masquerade of democracy that America witnessed at the 1968 Democratic Convention will have its effect on all the arts, but most immediately on the theater. The repressiveness of the society, the symbolic armaments with which it smoothly protects itself from new ideas and fights off change are stamped on a public imagination

213

numb to brutality. The individual's integrity and even his words—so long upheld as a creative ideal on stage—are mocked by the force of a state whose police can take both law and justice into their own hands. The radical impulse toward which new theater has been moving can only be intensified by the prospect of four more years of tepid mediocrity. Ironically, the new theater emerging in the late sixties will move into the intensely political and private battles which abstract expressionism fought in the visual arts during the forties. Both are radical departures from the texture of American life, both answer up—in their own form—to the ethic of materialism, conformity, and a society structured beyond the possibility of significant, individual political statement.

The American Broadway theater, with its "picture stage," has ossified under a concept of realism long discarded in other arts. In trying to find different kinds of images, to forge a new relationship between the stage object and the audience, the avant-garde theater work of La Mama Troupe, the Open Theater, The Performance Group, and even Jerzy Grotowski's Polish Lab Theater, embodies the impulses of abstract expressionism and must bear the same initial hostility from a critical press whose values and sense of the world are threatened by their work. They too, like Jackson Pollock, Hans Hofmann, Arshile Gorky, are branded hoaxes—chic, abstruse, undisciplined. New American theater is tapping a healthy resource in much the same way as medieval drama —as an outgrowth of its audience's plastic imagination— gave the drama of cathedral sculpture three-dimensional life.

In the twentieth century, theater-makers are just realizing that there is no longer the revealed (or revealing) word; they have become fascinated with the process of creating theater which answers modern needs. The creation itself becomes an act of religion. Their theater aspires to magic—

a special kind of prestidigitation where images and ideas emerge in the act of *doing* them. Like the works of Pollock, de Kooning, and Gorky, this theater reflects its own eccentric and personal reconstruction of the world. Tom O'Horgan, then director of the La Mama Troupe, maintains, "What I've been working toward is a new naturalism where, like Pollock, part of the meaning is the gesture itself."[1] The director becomes the catalyst—by setting up situations within which the actors must improvise—and choreographer; the theater pieces aspire to the emotional totality of music. While some critics score this as self-indulgence, they neglect a modern world, spiraling in confusions, which cannot be captured by one-dimensional realism and conventional stage techniques. As the English psychologist R. D. Laing has maintained in his book *The Politics of Experience*:

> If there are no meanings, no values, no source of sustenance or help, then man, as creator, must invent, conjure up meanings and values, sustenance and succor out of nothing. He is a magician.[2]

Other media can tell a story or reproduce a precise fragment of life better than theater. The new performance theaters (Open Theater, La Mama Troupe, Performance Group) want to go below that surface in much the same way that Pollock realized painting had to find its own specific impulse. "The modern artist," Pollock explains, "is living in a mechanical age and we have a mechanical means of representing objects in nature such as the camera and photograph. The modern artist, it seems to me, is working and expressing an inner world—in other words—expressing the energy, the motion, and other inner forces."[3] The theater is much less malleable than painting; it is a clumsy art, full of extenuating circumstances and personal variables. Yet, to externalize some inner energy, some idea which cannot be verbalized in "human" language, is part of the new theater's intention. The stage not only acknowledges the object world, but also the special emotional life of the actor.

Where Pollock attacked his canvas, painting an inner landscape, the techniques of improvisation bring this same interior quality to the surface of performance. The artist is no longer giving a final order to the world, but externalizing his own immediate view of it. This is relatively new to theater (except for the great clowns of the American stage whose acrobatics often mirrored deeper intuitions), but not to painting. "The idea that nature is chaotic and that the artist puts order into it is a very absurd point of view, I think," observed Willem de Kooning. "All that we can hope for is to put some order into ourselves."[4] This personalization of art offends the democratic theater critic who believes that theater belongs to the audience and not the creator. The new theater pieces are generally performed for small audiences (Grotowski has no more than one hundred people at a performance) or in workshops. To a theater based on dollars and cents, this smacks of "amateurishness"; while the work may not always be outstanding, its impulse comes from a far greater need, where performing is not merely the inhabiting of a fictional personality but a process of self-discovery.

Performance theater has come under devastating attack in its first few years. *Futz, Tom Paine, Dionysus in 69* have been defined more by their detractors than by those who are seriously trying to build a new future for the theater. Robert Brustein, who boldly called for a third theater in which "artistic license" was the alternative to "commercial appeal," used that language to support such shallow and

easy political documents as *MacBird* and *Viet Rock*. But
the political impulse of new theater has gone farther than a
criticism of society; it has created a theater which makes
its own world and special rules for living in it. Having called
for a revolution, Mr. Brustein throws up his hands in the
face of a liberation from esthetic principles at the core of
his middle-class social concern. Discussing Tom O'Horgan's
production of *Futz*, Brustein made his disclaimer for the
movement he spawned in print:

> Two years ago, I spoke, in an article, of a third
> theater which would combine (the words are
> Synge's) reality and joy: let me say at once that
> this sort of thing is not what I meant at all. Mr.
> O'Horgan's theater strikes me as singularly joyless
> and mechanical—a theater which gives us erotic-
> ism without passion, frenzy without energy, ego-
> ism without identity . . .[5]

Whatever O'Horgan's excesses and failures in the production, he is on the side of experiment and evolution of
theater art. Mr. Brustein denies the process at work, shout-
ing down innovation in the name of conventional attitudes
toward beauty and love. His white heat will not allow for
growth, or, worse still, acknowledge the possibility of new
stage resources. Fortunately for the theater, the avant-
garde has moved beyond the caterwauling of *MacBird* and
Viet Rock, just as Jackson Pollock and his coterie eschewed
social realism. The performance theater's statement—its
isolation, its denial of the conventional contexts and responses of theater, is in itself a greater political gesture than
name-calling. Melding the insights of new music and art
into the stage experience is a destiny which was prophesied
by Stanislavski who saw, as early as 1905, that realism on
stage was a thing of the past. There must be a new kind of

audience response and a new type of performing to conjure it:

> ... realism and [depicting] the way of life have
> outlived their age. The time has come to stage the
> unreal. Not life itself, as it occurs in reality, but
> rather life as it is vaguely perceived in fantasies
> and visions at moments of lofty emotions. This is
> the spiritual situation that must be transmitted
> scenically, in the way that painters of the new
> school use cloth, musicians of the new trend write
> music, and the new poets, poetry . . . The power
> of the new art lies in its combinations of colors,
> lines, musical notes and the rhyming of words.
> They create general moods that carry over to the
> public unconsciously. They create hints that make
> the most unobservant person create with his own
> imagination.[6]

This, over a half century later, is the esthetic which the
performance theaters are developing. Their theater confronts the audience with its qualities as theater: energy,
spectacle, movement, flesh, emotion. There is nothing between the stage action and the audience—no fancy seats,
no romantic ideas or special lights, no scenery in the grand
tradition. This emphasis on the physical aspects of performance is precisely the impulse of abstract expressionism,
where the experience of paint—color, form, line—was the
primary instinct. Pollock points out: "Abstract painting is
abstract. It confronts you. There was a reviewer a while
back who wrote that my pictures didn't have any beginning
or any end. He didn't mean it as a compliment, but it was.
It was a fine compliment."[7]

Pollock's elaborate network of drippings plunged the
spectator into the spectacle of an artist drawing forth primal

images on a barren canvas. The effect on the viewer is not meant to be logical or fully comprehended, but rather to communicate the energy, spontaneity, and risk of committing paint to canvas. "I think (the audience)," says Pollock, "should not look *for,* but look passively—and try to receive what the painting has to offer and not bring a subject matter or preconceived idea of what they are looking for."[8] Pollock's breakthrough found a way out of the surrealist fantasies. In the same way, performance theater, with its emphasis on *doing,* is a response and an answer to the intellectual circle drawn by the drama of the absurd—itself a surreal canvas of Freudian implications and nightmare associations.

A theater of performance makes a spectacle of physical risk, not only in its acrobatics, but in the type of acting it requires, which is both personal and spontaneous. There is a jaggedness and a great possibility of failure, but the struggle becomes the real drama and it is something to keep alive. "As a director," explains Tom O'Horgan, "one of the main functions I find is to evolve procedures which will keep the real thing going. I keep playing the same game with myself, setting up very difficult situations for actors and then not solving them." The effect attempts to evince a feeling, a response that is not programmed or contrived.

This confrontation takes many forms. It can be by touch, which has been tried by the Open Theater *(Viet Rock)* and the Performance Group *(Dionysus in 69),* where the performers coax spectators out of their environmental perches to join the bacchanal, and later offer the hope of a fleshpile to anyone who will submit to massage. The confrontation can be created by the spectacle of movement as in La Mama productions where the stage is filled with images of actions; the eye can never focus on one spot, nor can we expect experience to be translated to the mind (as in a proscenium stage) from one-point perspective. Bodies tumble and combine, slither across the stage, clasping around the neck, under the legs.

In *Dionysus in 69,* a three-tiered environmental stage allows the performers to move around the audience, sustaining the artifice of the play while sweeping the audience into its intention. The picture which emerges is varied and weighty with implication because of this theater environment. As in life, stimuli compete for the spectator's attention; the responsibility of choice and comprehension is thrust back to the audience's imagination. This impulse is meant, like abstract expressionism, not to confuse or bludgeon audiences, but to make them come alive.

Speaking of Paul Foster's *Tom Paine,* O'Horgan points out: "The world of Paul Foster's theater is a highly contemporary one, fragmented, burning hot and cold, offering data and facts, noncommittal, without solutions. The audience is made to feel the urgency of responsibility." The impulse is to stimulate response and thought, not spoon-feed an audience with a spurious "significance."

Abstract expressionism placed its greatest emphasis on the physical gesture of painting, the commitment of the artist to his *act.* "When you're painting out of your unconscious, figures are bound to emerge," Pollock explained. "We're all of us influenced by Freud, I guess . . . Painting is a state of being . . . Painting is self-discovery. Every good artist paints what he is."[9] Pollock, moving around his canvas stretched beneath him on the floor, demanded spontaneity and directness in his work. Hofmann, Pollock, and de Kooning gave special importance to speed of execution and autographic gesture. Their work became an act of immediacy and urgency. It became an event, the drama of an artist's self-discovery. "Painting, I think, today—the more immediate, the more direct—the greater the possibilities of making a direct—of making a statement,"[10] Pollock maintained. Like performance theater, abstract expressionism emphasized action and its ritualistic overtones. In painting, the terms of discussion took on the language of theater, which the theater is only now fulfilling.

Describing Willem de Kooning's work, art critic Harold Rosenberg uses the language and instinct of a theatrical reporter:

> Through the action of de Kooning's brush, things, persons, scenes, feelings are recorded in shifting forms that record themselves in the eye of the spectator as on a strip of film; one, looking at a de Kooning, never sees the same image twice . . . The gestures that brought the painting into being subsist in it not only through vestiges of energy— swipes of paint, splashes, smears—but through a constant forcing together of the visual ingredients of the painting . . .
>
> De Kooning's performance is also an "act" in the arena of art history, a display of skill and imagination put on before an imaginary gallery of the great masters.[11]

Abstract painting never creates its ideas for the viewer instantly; theater does, and performance theater not only strives for a similar improvisational revelation, but also a sense of acting against the framework of a larger theater history. Gesture, whatever its limitations in the new American theater, is meant to move the performer farther toward personal statement. Tom O'Horgan, discussing his approach to the actor, maintains:

> It is not easy to make a performer accept real freedom or responsibility on stage. Actors are

ambivalent. "What am I supposed to feel here?
What's this about? Who am I?" All these things
they can easily hide behind as actors. An actor
can hide behind the old Method approach to performance where the author created a whole structure of personality and then the actor tried to inhabit it in some way. No actor is that clever. My
own view is just to find a way to make people
know who they really are as actors and to experience those things and not be afraid of them or
hide. Hiding is what our whole acting school has
been devoted to for the last ninety years. If an
actor has trouble in knowing where those emotions are in himself, in understanding the buttons
to push in himself, then he doesn't understand
himself. My job is to set up little situations, games,
traps—whatever you want to call it—which will
make the actor respond to himself and the world
honestly.

This impulse for honesty and self-evaluation is embodied
in many of the performance theaters' events. Grotowski's
theater has already defined the new esthetic. "To play a
part does not mean to identify with the character. The actor
neither lives his part nor portrays it from the outside. He
uses the character as the means to grapple with his own self,
the tool to reach secret layers of his personality and strip
himself of what hurts most and lies in his secret heart."[12]
The American events are slowly evolving methods of intro-
spection. In *Tom Paine* the actors stop the play to discuss
it, out of character, with the audience. In *Dionysus in 69,*
an adaptation of *The Bacchae,* they move from primitive
rite to group therapy, where each actor talks about his fears
as honestly as he knows how. Unfortunately, for all these
theaters, the ability to know yourself intellectually is more
highly developed than the physical presence which must still

be attained. But the intention and resource for the theater is intriguing. Yet critics fault it before it has really begun. Walter Kerr concluded his review of *Dionysus in 69* describing this privacy of the new theater without understanding where it wants to go:

> It is only the actors who are liberated in this sort of meeting, and there is something arrogant, condescending, and self-indulgent about that. Clearly they enjoy the unleashing of their own inhibitions. During an impromptu aside on opening night, an actress was asked by another performer how she felt about dancing on the night of Senator Kennedy's death. She thought intensely for a moment, then answered, "I have to. It's my statement."
>
> But it is *her* statement, not ours. She and her colleagues are in control of the master plan. They are free to do what they wish to do. We are only free to do what *they* wish us to do or invite us to do. That is not engagement. It is surrender.
>
> I'm still up tight.[13]

In both painting and theater, anything that challenges conventional form is often branded "self-indulgent" or "arrogant." These are, in a sense, the ingredients which create the climate for discovery. But Mr. Kerr, representative of a theater-wise generation trained in proscenium realism, gets hysterical when theater strikes out toward unstated emotions and nonverbal ideas. By his critical tenets, Galileo's first glance at the heavens would be scientific high jinks; the impressionist's fragmentation of the canvas to experiment with light an infantilism not worth mentioning. In fact, actors have always had control over an audience's impulses; and in *Dionysus in 69,* where the Performance

Group is examining the politics of ecstasy and its potential enslavement of the soul, it is not doctrinaire, but insidiously open to thought. But many Establishment minds are shut tight, not merely up tight.

In their retreat from realism, the performance theaters approach myth and ritual in an attempt to go beyond the perceivable, closer to the rhythms of contemporary life. They are not always successful, but their attempt asks new questions of theater which have been posed by abstract expressionists, who also "looked for authentic experience in primordial symbol and classic myth, seeking a significant rendition of a symbol no matter how archaic," as Dore Ashton has maintained. "Pollock, Gorky, Still, Gottlieb, Stamos, Tomlin, Rothko, Baziotes turned insistently back, deep into the past of civilization, to exercise the thinking that *recalls* rather than *represents*."[14] Pollock's fascination with totemic images was, according to Ashton, indicative of the abstract expressionists' attempt not to "use the unconscious—as did the Surrealists . . . [to] portray themselves as spiritual wholes comprising ethical, conscious man and 'original' man with his primordial unconscious."[15] Writing in *Possibilities,* the avant-garde magazine founded by painter Robert Motherwell and art critic Harold Rosenberg, Mark Rothko emphasized an intention of abstract expressionism which has become increasingly the focus of new performance theater. Speaking of archaic creators' belief in the monsters they created, Rothko maintained:

> But with us, the disguise is complete. The familiar identity of things has to be pulverized in order to destroy the finite association with which our society increasingly enshrouds every aspect of our environment . . . [Shapes must] have no direct association with any particularly visible ex-

perience, but in them one recognizes principles
and passions of organisms.[16]

How closely this emphasis on a mythological imagination
approaches theater. At its best, Jerzy Grotowski's Polish
Lab Theater speaks for similar associations. Grotowski has
written:

> We are especially interested in an aspect of
> acting which has seldom been studied: the asso-
> ciation of the gesture and intonation with a
> definite image. For example, the actor stops in
> the middle of a race and takes the stance of a
> cavalry soldier charging, as in the old popular
> drawings. *This method of acting evokes by associ-
> ation images deeply rooted in the collective
> imagination.*[17]

The stage archetypes, like the visual ones, transcend the
society's strangle-hold on the facts of life. Performance
theater like Grotowski's forces the spectator back to his
primordial past in order to comprehend his present. "Our
culture, our language, our imagination are rooted in this
darkness which science has called by different names," explains Eugenio Barba, a disciple of Grotowski. " 'Savage
thought' (Lévi-Strauss), 'archetype' (Jung), 'collective rep-
resentations' (Durkheim), 'categories of the imagination'
(Mauss and Hubert), 'elementary thoughts' (Bastian). In
the Theater Laboratory, the spectators are made to face the
most secret, the most carefully hidden parts of themselves.
Brutally thrown into the world of myths, they must identify
with them in the light of twentieth-century men. Many
experience the revelation as blasphemy."[18]

The American performance theater is nowhere as accomplished or as certain of its direction as Grotowski is. It has

the energy; but the discipline of a totally committed revolution in theater is still to mature. Yet, mythology and a means of creating an iconography from the past aimed toward the future have dominated the new theater. Rochelle Owens, whose play *Futz* was the La Mama Troupe's first break with stage realism, creates fantasies which draw on Biblical and mythological impulses. Owens' *Istanboul* mixes Saracen and Christian images; her play *Beclch* evokes an African goddess with overtones of Greek mythology. In the same way, the Open Theater's *The Serpent* is a step beyond the somewhat figurative *America Hurrah* toward the evocation of old myths with new. *The Serpent* by Jean-Claude van Itallie improvises on the Book of Genesis and uses these images in counterpoint with the assassination of Kennedy, confusing Adam in order to regain him. The Performance Group, likewise, has not only attempted to refurbish the Dionysian myth, but to extend it to a commentary on the orgiastic impulse in contemporary society, which breeds violence in its liberation. Whatever the content, the instinct is to push on toward the unexpressible and unattainable. This romantic notion (already a tenet of Grotowski's method: "Theatrical magic consists in doing publicly that which is considered impossible") expresses a hunger to get beyond the limitations of the finite world and its values, to confront larger questions with a thrilling dignity in action.

With American society bearing down heavily on the creative imagination, filled with a sense of its shame and horror at where the golden dream has led the nation—an unjust war, colonization at home as well as abroad, a violent self-satisfaction—the theater, like abstract expressionism, retreats into itself, not away from the world, but beyond it. The theater, thus far, has been fairly conservative in its departure from established conventions. The Performance

Group's arena is still a center stage, not ready for Grotowski's total environment, where the audience is shuffled between patches of action, and is part of the artifice of the stage. As one English critic witnessing Grotowski's *Acropolis,* where the audience was surrounded by actors simulating inmates of a concentration camp, observed:

> The actors moved around and behind you; you could smell their sweat. The pile of bronze metal pipes from which they gradually built an incinerator was within kicking distance. Every inch of acting space was precisely circumscribed, no superfluous movement tolerated from anyone. The critic who scribbled notes on his programme was committing an outrage equivalent to daubing paint on a canvas at an exhibition, as my neighbors quickly and rightly made me realize. The collective function of the audience was to sit still and symbolize the "civilized" world, helplessly witnessing gross crimes against humanity.[19]

The search for new sounds and different music, the development of the body to externalize an inner state, the planning of the event to incorporate the audience creatively into the theatrical experience have still to be sufficiently developed in the flamboyant experiments in America. Yet, it is here, where the canker runs so deep, where the vitality and commitment have been so polarized by current events, that performance theater may well flower as abstract expressionism did in reaction to oppressive times. If critics groan that they cannot hear, that they cannot understand, that the word is more important than the gesture, or that the process of improvised creation argues against the vitality of the theater, the performance theater, it must be recalled, is only just beginning. The theatrical equipment needed for effectiveness is only now becoming apparent to actors and directors. The groups need patience, but so do the audiences. In a society where consumers expect art, like detergent, to be new and improved with each package, performance theater will also need luck to accompany their diligence. Richard Schechner, answering Walter Kerr's backhand to *Dionysus in 69* in *The New York Times,* indicated the instinct of all the directors who are trying to move beyond the surface of American life to probe a more difficult and monumental imaginative reality:

> As a director I am not interested in free-for-alls. For every scenic situation there are rules. And if our work is well done it is no more haphazard than the formations of a professional football team.
>
> I readily admit that no American theater has yet achieved the necessary discipline and skills. But to reduce our attempts to the fiddling around of cop-outs, end-of-the-empire decadence, or sex-by-itself is to seriously misread and misunderstand what's going on.[20]

In pure theater, as in abstract expressionism, there exists an aura of transience which upsets minds accustomed to false significance. Performance theater exists differently at each show; and the joy, for the audience, is watching something they know cannot be duplicated, which gives insight in a gesture, only to disappear. This ecstasy in creation is what Pollock understood in his painting:

INTERVIEWER: Well, actually every one of your paintings . . . is an absolute original.

POLLOCK: Well—yes—they're all direct painting. There is only one.[21]

New performance theater will undoubtedly create, in its ferment, an antithesis, sharing its presuppositions but seeking different means. Sam Shepard's cool, silent theatricality is an indication of the first response to performance theater which moves from action to a more passive reflective mode, in the same way that such artists as Ad Reinhardt, Barnett Newman, and Mark Rothko, while sharing with action painting an interest in a uniform pictorial field and a monumentality of pictorial order, moved toward a decelerated kind of painting—cool, illusionistic, minimal. It is too early to tell if performance theater will continue to follow the primitivistic pattern set by abstract expressionists. But in discovering a similar cause and in seeking a way to create it, the performance theater holds the possibility of invigorating American theater with the fresh beauty, commitment, and thought that abstract expressionists bestowed on America's visual arts at an equally treacherous moment in history.

13

John Osborne:
Poor Johnny One-Note

In a rebellion, as in a novel, the most difficult thing to invent is the ending.
—Alexis de Tocqueville

. . . Now I am boring. I am quite certainly the most boring man you have ever met in your lives. I see you're not going to contradict me so I won't let you.
—John Obsorne,
The Hotel in Amsterdam

*O*nce upon a time, John Osborne was interested in the world as well as the private battles of his middle-class soul. He was a fighter whose roundhouse blows had a sinewy wit and hatred-hard logic. His hectoring gave voice to the disenfranchised and aimless younger generation of England in the late fifties and produced a vibrant, uncouth, honest, and abrasive *Look Back in Anger.* The play singlehandedly blasted the smudge and blur of Victorian melodrama off the West End stage and earned him a footnote to theatrical history.

What has become of the destiny of that seething rage, that call to social and emotional honesty? Audiences shattered by Jimmy Porter's outrage have lived to see its heritage— a sad and confusing spectacle. At thirty-eight, twelve years after his initial success, Osborne's latest plays, *Time Present* and *The Hotel in Amsterdam,* show his literary muscle turning to flab, his ruthless self-examination going to sleep amidst his new affluence. Once, Osborne could dedicate a play (*The Entertainer*) this way: "To A. C., who remembers what it was like and will not forget it; who, I hope, will not let me forget it, not while there is still a Paradise Street and Claypit Lane to go back to."[1] But Osborne has forgotten; and there begins the steady decline of his craft.

The Hotel in Amsterdam, for instance, is filled with the bric-a-brac of the affluent life which Osborne has inherited. Where Jimmy Porter and his candy store were outside society, Osborne now finds himself within the Establishment. The people who clutter this newest play are rich, successful, bored, and too tired to fight. Their lives are not a matter of animal survival or even aggressive lust, but one of bourgeois pleasures accompanied by bourgeois civility. Food, accommodations, endless gabble about prices and prestige fill the stage. With Jimmy Porter's snarls at a recalcitrant world which took its toll on the spirit and ambition of the young, Osborne's play helped crash class barriers. He has lived to see a national permissiveness. The world has bent to his whims, and the effect is confusing for someone whose best plays explore the anguish of private disgust. If rage is to be valid it must have a focus. When the targets shift, Osborne must find new ones. "I see treachery everywhere," he told

Kenneth Tynan in an interview in *The Observer*.[2] "In my opinion you should never forgive your enemies because they're probably the only thing you've got." Osborne's disgust, the power which feeds his rhetoric takes on a smaller focus as he moves away from basic concerns. His voice becomes something only partially believed in, an imitation of a former style. Comparing *Inadmissible Evidence* to *The Hotel in Amsterdam* illustrates how the timbre of Osborne's voice diminishes with his recognition of the smaller, more compromised circumference of his world. The invective of Bill Maitland, the obsessed lawyer whose world is falling away from him in *Inadmissible Evidence*, gouges a passion and an irony from experience in prose which tries to corner life and punch it to the floor. It is a hopeless fight, but sometimes awesome to watch. Maitland hurls words at his mod daughter:

> . . . But, and this is the but, I still don't think what you're doing will ever, ever, ever, ever approach the fibbing, mumping, pinched little worm of energy eating away in this me, of mine, I mean. That is: which is that of being slowly munched and then diminished altogether. That worm, thank heaven, is not in your little cherry rose. You are unselfconscious, which I am not. You are without guilt, which I am not. Quite rightly. Of course, you are stuffed full of paltry relief for emergent countries, and marches and boycotts and rallies . . .[3]

The speech spills on, forged with an energy which makes every conjunction seem a necessity, every word an embodiment of the self-defeating rage which is both the subject and object of the play. *Inadmissible Evidence,* in fact, takes on an apocalyptic dimension (not only in staging but in relation to Osborne's entire work) because it is the last flowering, the final vestige of energy before the smothering. In *Hotel in Amsterdam,* Laurie—movie producer, husband, court entertainer—is on the weekend trip he and his friends take to Amsterdam to get away from their movie-mogul boss, K. L. Osborne's rage is directed at second-hand experience: press notices, nannies, the kind of burgher household which has sprung up mysteriously around him. He is too tired, but worse, too successful to expose the nerve ends of his own diminution. Significantly, K. L., the man who feeds his wrath, is present only in his imagination. We never see him. He is not part of the society, but a specter—perhaps villainous, perhaps not. When Osborne's main character, Laurie, speaks, we hear the words; but, without a tension from the world outside, we no longer care.

> . . . But I hope, at least, you will feel alone, alone as I feel it, as we all in our time feel it, without burdening our friends. I hope the G. P. O. telephone system is collapsed, that your chauffeur is dead and the housekeeper drunk and that there isn't one con-man, camp follower, eunuch, pimp, mercenary, or procurer of all things possible or one globe-trotting bum boy at your side to pour you a drink on this dark January night . . .[4]

The rhythms are familiar but the language does not cut through to raw experience. It is merely gratuitous rhetoric; the humor of which is lost in the absence of dramatic tension, making every moment swollen and prolix instead of pertinent.

Osborne's world has closed in around him. He has watched with a writer's clinical interest, charting his soul as it runs aground in shallow waters. Jimmy Porter's inability to do anything about his rage is indicative of Osborne's predicament. The playwright and his character are haters, but too cynical about the world and too ruthlessly absorbed in themselves to consider action. Words are a risk, but in comparison to action, talk is cheap. Sadly, *Hotel in Amsterdam* and *Time Present* seem like they were written by the very "Colonel Blimp" he gave two fingers to in *Look Back in Anger*. Osborne's Colonel Redfern, a military remnant from Imperial India, explains his reaction to England's waning power: "The England I remembered was the one I left in 1914, and I was happy to go on remembering it that way . . ."[5]

Osborne reacts to theatrical change with the same bulldog tenacity, disliking change without really understanding what it represents. Theater must adapt to new worlds, but Osborne has dug himself in for a long siege. "I think these new forms of theater may supplant—are supplanting—what I do. There may be a case for them, but I don't see it, and I *don't want to see it.*" Osborne's desire to widen the circumference of his world is matched only by his instinct for standing still.

TYNAN: Given an unlimited amount of money, what would you buy?

OSBORNE: I long for space. I'd like to live in a place as big as a railway station. But I don't think I'd buy a jet plane or anything like that, because I never want to go anywhere very much.[6]

Like Osborne, Jimmy Porter saw an ugliness and lashed out at it with a curious combination of charm and venom. Osborne has always been certain of his charm, the brute appeal of his verbal momentum. But the resources of his venom have been another, more mysterious matter. It is Porter who ends *Look Back in Anger,* retreating from the world instead of finding strength to meet it:

> We'll be together in our bear's cave, and our squirrel's drey, and we'll live on honey, and nuts . . . There are cruel steel traps lying about everywhere, just waiting for rather mad, slightly satanic and very timid little animals. Right?

Having traded on his rancor, Osborne finds himself in a strange, but perhaps inevitable position. He now has very little basis for his barrage of spleen. His sense of the world becomes a victim to his verbal strength, which acts as radar, bouncing off the ugly, intractable facts of life. It also sets up a barrier between him and the experience. Osborne, whose Jimmy Porter spoke to the restless educated "redbrick" element among England's university graduates, now finds himself talking down students who have surpassed invective and demand justice with action. The man who once gorgeously did battle with British censors now finds himself voting (as a member of the Royal Court Board) against allowing a play to be performed. The world slips away; Osborne dismisses as foolhardy events he has not cared enough to understand completely:

> I don't know any students, and I certainly would not like to see a Negro minority taking over this country. A lot of nice bus conductors running the government isn't my idea of a sensible way out. And student power is a very factitious thing. It always seems to me that "What am I?" is a much more interesting question than "What are we?" but now they're all "we-ing" all over the place. And acting as groups which I find both uninteresting and ugly.[7]

What could be the catalyst for a more flexible, fictive imagination is merely dismissed. Osborne has always been more interested in himself than society, but he has forgotten —or can no longer see—that a man's identity cannot be separated from a country's history or the men with whom he has to deal. He, like his characters, has cut himself off by the ruthless onslaught of his voice—an emotional, lacerating appendage of self which contains both a longing and an impossible demand for empathy. "I've worked in the theater for twelve years, but I've hardly got any close friends," Osborne told Tynan in their printed interview. "In fact, they seem to get fewer and fewer."

Anger can outlive its historical moment. It is an ambiguous passion, criticizing the past but rarely building for the future. Because of England's continuing liberalization, times have changed, and the currency of Osborne's wrath seems spurious. Jimmy Porter raged against the American moment—the sense of imperial destiny, of power, of coherence which had passed to America. England, however, has now adjusted to her role. Even though a loss of power may bring a diminution of dignity, there is still a saving grace in sophistication. It is not unusual for rebels to change voices as they move into a more comfortable middle age. Vituperation numbs the mind; it keeps a man at a constant fever pitch. Osborne has not been able to shake free from the legacy of anger, although in certain theatrical experiments, like *A Patriot for Me,* he has tried. The new plays show him finally coming to grips with his own period of adjustment—one that may prove fatal to his craft. As John Weightman observed in *Encounter:*

> [Osborne] is not so much concerned to find any general significance in his somewhat disabused acceptance of the fact that life is for the most part

a series of disappointments; only he notes almost
casually that he belongs to a generation which
grew up during the war, and that their anger was
largely directed against the conditions and the
society which made that particular war possible.
But the war is over and so are the conditions
which led to it, and Mr. Osborne has the wisdom
to see that there is very little room today for the
particular form of anger which they provoked in
him and his contemporaries. Their anger came
genuinely from looking back, but one cannot go
on looking back forever, at least not if one hopes
to go on creating works of art, or creating anything at all; nor is anger a kind of inexhaustible
fount of inspiration, which can be switched from
one subject to another with the passage of time.[8]

The voices in Osborne's new plays are dyspeptic but not
angry. They are too tired, or in the case of Pamela, the
heroine of *Time Present,* too ordinary to rail against the
world with any precision. Where once Osborne's main
characters created an abrasive liveliness because of their
demand to be heard, the main speakers in Osborne's new
plays are assured of a small, attentive coterie. Laurie has
his friends who let him go on about "El Fag" airlines and
laugh as if he had just uncovered a new social caste; Pamela
has her friend, a successful, strangely masculine woman
M. P., Constance, at whose house Pamela stays after her
father—a famous theatrical actor-manager—dies. Nothing
happens in either play. Each is primarily a monologue in
which Osborne has casually mismanaged structure and the
suspension of disbelief. Everything is tired, verbose, and
bathetic. The canker has been snuffed out.

Osborne's "heroes" had very little glory except their
obsessed voices which crashed into the world. They were

modern figures—failing, unfair, small. But at the core of
their personality was a belief in the validity of their rage.
Says Jimmy Porter in *Look Back in Anger:*

> Was I really wrong to believe that there's a . . .
> a kind of . . . burning virility of mind and spirit
> that looks for something as powerful as itself.
> The heaviest, strongest creatures in this world
> seem to be the loneliest. Like the old bear, fol-
> lowing his own breath in the dark forest. There's
> no warm pack, no herd to comfort him. That
> voice that cries out doesn't *have to* be a weak-
> ling's, does it?

Osborne's plays uncover a heroic voice no longer in
heroic circumstances. This is the tragedy of his characters
up until now, but it is also their dignity. They are chest-
beaters, unable to act but always willing to talk. And talk
they do. Jimmy Porter, Bill Maitland, and Archie Rice
(*The Entertainer*) demand gut reactions from the world.
They settle for a good listener.

In *Look Back in Anger,* Alison, Jimmy's wife who suffers the thrusts of his ruthless barbs, explains the curious
demands of this heroic timbre: "He wants something quite
different from us. What it is exactly I don't know—a kind of
cross between a mother and a Greek courtesan, a hench-
woman, a mixture of Cleopatra and Boswell."

Once, the Osborne hero was seductive, his language
precise, bitter, trenchant in its flights of satire. It was a
voice which isolated everything and yet demanded impossible sympathy. There was a dignity in that stance, which all
of Osborne's characters understood and were all too willing to explain. Archie Rice recollects a moment of beauty
—a singer and a song:

... But if I ever saw any hope or strength in
the human race, it was in the face of that old,
fat Negress getting up to sing about Jesus or
something like that. She was poor and lonely and
oppressed like nobody you've ever known. Or
me for that matter, I never even liked that kind
of music, but to see that old black whore singing
her heart out to the whole world, you knew some-
how in your heart it didn't matter how much you
kick people, the real people, how much you de-
spise them, *if they can stand up and make a pure,
natural noise like that,* there's nothing wrong
with them, only everybody else ... I wish to God
I were that old bag. I'd stand up and shake my
great bosom up and down and lift up my head
and make *the most beautiful fuss* in the world ...

That gorgeous fuss was honest; it acknowledged a jagged
humanity which Osborne can no longer feel. Rebellion is
a gorgeous fuss, as is anger. But Osborne's rage seems
tepid now; the injustices he fought seem a petty scuffle compared to the questions of genocide or colonization which
haunt Western man a decade later. "My instinct," he says,
"is to lower the temperature rather than raise it, because it
seems to me that there's an unreal sort of medium hysteria
going on in this country. If anything, it needs a bromide."
No more muckraking then; Jimmy Porter misjudged the
effect of his choler. It was perhaps a call to change, but
Osborne in 1968 wants to move backward rather than forward: "I'd like to see this whole headlong rush into the
twentieth century halted a bit." Perhaps Jimmy Porter, like
Osborne, was too easily cast in the mold of significance. For
both Osborne's fictional characters and his real personality
are, for all their rantings, politically unreliable, combining
fiery convictions with a dislike of mankind in particular—

a fascination with the self, unable to reach out to society.

Osborne has given up trying to make his words purify the world. His earlier heroes tried; his present ones have forgotten how. Laurie has sold out to the film industry; Pamela is lost between mediocre acting parts and mundane affairs. The hard fear behind the words of earlier Osborne spokesmen has given way to a glibness, as if Osborne knows that people will listen to him and no longer needs the security of that relationship. The great fear, of course, was that no one would listen, that the rage would be vented on deaf ears. Bill Maitland continually barks on the telephone, "Is that you?" "Are you there?" Archie Rice, in his last song and dance, plays to an audience as dead as the sudden click of the receiver at the other end of the phone. "You've been a very *good* audience," he says. "Let me know where you're working tomorrow and I'll come and see you." Even Jimmy Porter's baiting of his wife is a child-like attempt to arouse another voice to counteract the sound of his own words:

> All this time, I have been married to this woman, this monument to non-attachment, and suddenly I discover that there is actually a word that sums her up. Not just an adjective in the English language to describe her with—it's her name! Pusillanimous! It sounds like some fleshy Roman matron, doesn't it? . . . Hi, Pusey . . .

Behind all the voices in Osborne's theatrical rogues' gallery were a style of living and a disguise. Behind the bold, virile braggadocio about women there is a fear of weakness. They protest too much. For Bill Maitland, the sordid, nervous liaisons are sweaty, transient moments of forgetfulness; for Jimmy Porter, burning dissatisfaction. He says:

I've just about had enough of this "expense of
spirit" lark, as far as women are concerned. Honestly, it's enough to make you become a scoutmaster or something, isn't it? Oh, I'm not saying
that it mustn't be hell for them a lot of the time.
But, at least, they do seem to have a cause—not
a particularly good one, it's true. But plenty of
them do seem to have a revolutionary fire about
them which is more than you can say for the rest
of us . . .

Osborne's obsession with invective instead of action has
always taken control of his plays until with *Inadmissible
Evidence* he wrote what is perhaps the longest part (Maitland) in English literature since Marlowe's *Doctor Faustus*.
His next play, *A Patriot for Me,* tried to find a way beyond
rage in spectacle. It was an interesting, bold attempt to get
beyond his obsessional voice. Whatever the limitations of
the piece, Osborne was building—or so one thought—for
the future. However, he has returned to his previous pattern, but with a difference. The characters are no longer
demonic. Before, his plays, as Mary McCarthy pointed
out, resolved themselves in "a kind of running down, the
exhaustion of an impetus, a tire deflating." There is no longer
an impetus; his plays merely trickle past the imagination,
occasionally finding a laugh or a moment of pathos, but,
more often, spilling over into his special kind of verbosity.
Osborne has told Tynan:

I don't know whether my focus is getting
smaller or my England is getting smaller, but if
it is I don't make any apologies. I think it's more
real, and more human.
This is why words are important. They may be
dispensed with but it seems to me they're the last

> link with God . . . When millions of people seem
> unable to communicate with one another, it's
> vitally important that words are made to work. It
> may be very old fashioned, but they're the only
> things we have left. When I turn on that electric
> light, I don't know why it works, and i don't want
> to. It's a mystery I'm delighted to preserve. But the
> verbal breakdown is getting to the point where it's
> dangerous and nonsensical. I have a great alle-
> giance to words.

Although he claims to respect the word, his texts are
loose and strangely undisciplined. He distorts language instead of infusing it with greater clarity. His self-indulgence
stifles the ability of his audience to hear clearly. Words
spill out so blandly and in such quantity that the mind is
numbed. The language of dismissal, the peckishness, which
fills so much of Osborne's prose does not make for communication but only for static. Pamela, returning to an
old Osborne war horse, homosexuality, observes:

> Homosexuals? Well, they've mostly given me
> up. I'm ultimately unrewarding to them. Which
> is just as well . . . If you're a woman or a moll,
> you do have to spend quite a lot of energy flatter-
> ing them with your sympathy and admiration and
> performing like captured prize dogs for them . . .
> Like most sizeable pressure groups, I suppose,
> and not even poor liberal Constance can really
> escape the fact, beyond all her Parliamentary rec-
> ommendations, that as a group they *are* uniformly
> bitchy, envious, self-seeking, fickle, and usually
> without passion.

The language forces every auditor back to the simple
question—so what?

In both new plays, Osborne just lets his people talk. The action, when there is any, is minimal and contrived (K.L., the loathed movie tycoon in *The Hotel in Amsterdam,* kills himself—a fact relayed at the conclusion of the play by a melodramatic telephone call). No one is moved to tears. They raise a glass. The pattern of boredom, momentarily interrupted, will continue in another place at another time. But Osborne forgets that one cannot create a sense of disorder with disorder—that is merely chaos; nor can one find a valid metaphor for middle-class ennui by having a fundamentally *boring* experience served up for the audience.

People revere Osborne's craft, and well they should. For many years he has opened his soul for the kind of public exhibition which is both thrilling and often embarrassing. But, no longer believing in the validity of that anger, cut off from the political radicalism which once fed his wrath (if indeed it did), his theatrical possibilities seem limited. He is not a thinker, but a talker; he is not even an intellectual, merely smart. He has never been able to sustain a fictional world where people interact and grow; there is only that stunning voice, highlighting everything in its radiance. Osborne has come to know his predicament and his people so clearly that there is no place for discovery in himself; now he merely reports. His newest plays have no sense of unconscious insight, no mystery, only contrivance. In order to grow, he must be open to experience. He is not. As a writer, he must trust his own instinct, but he refuses to engage in any meaningful communication with his audience. As a result, his plays become self-indulgent and tedious. He rarely revises his work, an impulse which comes from his one literary strength— spontaneity—and underscores his main weakness—lack of structural discipline.

TYNAN: You never revise your plays once they're finished. Is that your way of opposing democratization?

OSBORNE: I suppose it's just arrogance, but I've always thought that ultimately I know best. That's why George Devine was such a sheet-anchor for me. He would put the case to you for cutting out the things that made people yawn, but ultimately he would stand by your judgment. Your private wound was more important than somebody else's satisfaction.[9]

The wound Osborne speaks of might very well become more evocative, more haunting, with an economy which he will not work toward. Osborne was once an actor, but his impulses indicate he must have been a bad one—with no respect for the audience and an unwillingness to learn from the very humanity with which he would talk. "I'd never seek opinions. They frighten me to death. Those people who come up to you and say, 'Do you want to know what I think?' are the people I want to kick in the crotch. I'd rather not know what they think. Because if I gave anyone's opinion too much emphasis and the next time it changed, I would have to try and . . . refunction. So I avoid it."[10]

Osborne will continue to write and rant. People will straggle to his plays, remembering the embers of an earlier vitality and concern. He has, in his time, given us a theater which adds to the debate of modern consciousness, which fills the mind with surprise and no little awe. But that variety of language dwindles when his world loses its focus. And Osborne, that grand gladiator of private despair, seems certain to write himself into the sticky, soft corner which always betrays his heroes. He is already talking in the past tense. "I think I was rather fortunate to live when I did. That sounds as though I'm talking about myself in the past, and I find myself doing it more and more. I think I lived in the right time for my own talent." But that time has passed, and so too has the talent.

14

Theater
and Propaganda

*I told Lady Bird—she came to
see us—that I wanted the President to see I Do, I Do because
it's not against anything.*
—Mary Martin[1]

A radical theater is not new to America, nor
is the ferment against Broadway's mooning over its middle-
class rainbow. At a time when the President can manipulate
national opinion about the Vietnam war as easily as a television critic can sway his viewers about a play, anti-Establishment sentiments must find other media. Theaters for

social change have emerged in the last few years, traveling the country to tell their side of history. El Teatro Campesino, the San Francisco Mime Troupe, and the Guerrilla Theater are the three most prominent insurgents who are conscious of developing revolutionary propaganda. They differ from their spiritual fathers of the thirties in taking protest off the proscenium and into the streets.

Richard Schechner, former editor of *The Drama Review* and ideologue for the Guerrilla Theater, has provided a manifesto indicative of the movement which, unlike the thirties, seems more political than artistic:

> . . . Theater must not retreat to prepared positions. *It is an art of permeation:* its boundaries are ill-defined and far extended. It can include demonstrations, political rallies, religious festivals, celebrations of daily life. The theater will be more of an art when it becomes less consciously esthetic. Our models should be the civic celebrations of Athens, the processional pageants of the Middle Ages, the tumultuous simultaneity of the Elizabethans, the embracing rituals of many pre-literate peoples . . .[2]

Schechner's historical inadequacies, which overlook the careful control of the mystery plays or even a medieval mass, are not as important as the direction of his argument.

The most moving and successful of these revolutionary theaters has been El Teatro Campesino, a troupe representing the Union of Farm Workers from Southern California which has been instrumental in organizing the grape-pickers and bringing national attention to their cause. Their efforts have earned a $1.75 hourly wage from Schenley Industries and a $1.85 pact with Almaden and Christian Brothers vineyards. The stars of this theater are nameless. When they came on stage at the Village Theater, they wore no make-up except sweat. By the end of the evening, a tired New York audience, beaten by the heat and the tarnished gaiety of an old vaudeville emporium, was rushing to the stage to shake their hands.

Their performance brought the theater back to the spirit of its origins. The primitive devices and blunt intentions illustrated how excitement could still live on stage when the theater stalks reality.

El Teatro sings about its *"Huelga"* (strike), a word which, like "scab," has not been long on Spanish-speaking tongues. El Teatro is stripped of fine phrases and Living Theater pyrotechnics. It confronts its audience with the same immediacy and urgency with which it entertains workers standing in picket lines.

Their union propaganda is mixed with a laughter which acknowledges both the pain and the enormity of their task. This is the fifth time in American history that farm workers have tried to organize. Their hopes and the justness of their cause infect their playing.

Their songs are simple—as propaganda must be—with straightforward, driving rhythms: "Long Live the General Strike," "I'm Not Afraid of Anything," "Picket Signs." In "We Shall Not Be Moved," they turn the lyrics to fit their local ethnic balance—Mexican and Filipino:

> Brown and brown together
> We shall not be moved . . .

El Teatro, like a medieval morality play, seeks to make symbols from the strikers' horizon stand out like a cattle brand. The "Migrant Song" captures the irony of the land-scape—a land of dramatic vistas where men never match Nature's benevolence:

> And see how the land
> Yields up her treasures
> To a man's patient hands . . .

The robustness of their sketches has the social pertinence and resilience of slapstick comedy. It is easy to hiss the villain, and the bumbling comedian who has always borne the brunt of the law and who gropes his way from the precipice of failure toward a vision of a better life.

The skit "Fifth Season" depicts the workers' relationship to Nature—a dramatic problem urban theater has forgotten but which medieval drama incorporated into its spiritual message. The characters wear signs which spell out their roles. "I am Summer," says an actor, as innocently as Snout declares himself in *A Midsummer Night's Dream*. The spirits of the Church, the labor movement, and Pancho Villa repel the winter in a primitive ballet, reducing hunger to its abstract rhythms. In the sketch, Schenley asks for fifty workers. The union contractor, speaking with a new boldness, says, "Schenley, you a big man. What's wrong with you, baby?" They settle for seven hundred men.

Fantasy also enters into the farm workers' drama. The union leader complains with a wink which acknowledges Big Business's beleaguered arguments, "Schenley! The sun is too hot!" As Schenley meekly holds a chair for Don Sottaco, the eternal farm hand, he looks at the chair, and swaggers toward it with a delicious sense of new freedom.

In showing an audience how it teaches the migrants the vocabulary of social protest, El Teatro also teaches its audience. A scab enters wearing a sign describing himself. The union organizer urges the audience: "Tell him to take off his sign!" In the end, he listens, and the audience learns.

The San Francisco Mime Troupe, founded in 1959, utilizes an updated *commedia dell' arte* format which adds a

social significance to Pantalone and his *zanni* they would
never have claimed for themselves. A theater with more
esthetic pretensions than El Teatro, they see themselves as an
anti-toxin for the deadening clichés of contemporary theater.
They play in parks and in streets and maintain their own
indoor theater in San Francisco. The *commedia dell' arte,*
they point out in a program note, is a form which is "popular, free, engaging and adaptable." The energy of their
performances has won them wide underground acclaim,
but the borrowed structure for propaganda limits the ultimate effect of their revolutionary intentions.

"We have embarked upon a guerrilla scheme of living
off the land and traveling, trying to provoke change." The
SFMT wants to unify public sentiment in the same way in
which the radio brought a sense of united effort to the FLN
in Algeria. As sophisticated performers, they know what
political leaders from Napoleon to LBJ understand about
the masses. Inundated with data, the public seeks clarity
in stereotypes, conviction in easy explanation. Napoleon
was the first to probe the dynamics of public opinion.
Ninety-three percent, he found, could be influenced in their
interpretation of events. The percentages have not changed.
For minority propaganda to have the necessary force, its
images must be sharp and evocative, its emotional argument overwhelming. It must appeal to a particularly intense
experience shared by a large segment of the audience. The
art of such propaganda lies in knowing the pulse of the
environment; the difficulty is maintaining the proper balance. To adapt Keats' dictum on poetry, we hate theater
that has designs upon us. The Mime Troupe, more conscious of combining statement with art, faces the same
dilemma which Bertolt Brecht outlined in 1959 in *Theater
der Zeit:*

How can the theater be both instructive and entertaining? How can it be divorced from spiritual dope traffic and turned from a home of illusions to a home of experiences . . . How can the unfree, ignorant man of this century, with his thirst for freedom and his hunger for knowledge . . . obtain his own theater which will help him to master the world and himself?[3]

Certainly, living off the land is a commitment not limited to guerrillas. Harold Clurman, an unlikely Digger, recalls in *The Fervent Years* a similar hand-to-mouth existence among members of the Group Theater:

. . . At least half of the Group had moved into a ten-room flat on West Fifty-Seventh Street near the railroad tracks. The rent was fifty dollars a month . . . Meals were provided through a common fund, marketing done by the two girls, and the cooking was attended to in turn by four or five of the men who had a knack for it . . . On special occasions a friend or a more fortunate Group member sent a chicken or meat for dinner. . . .[4]

In denying the traditions of the American theatrical past, the SFMT has failed to learn from them. "Preferring the risk of amateur status to the showbiz escalator, we will continue to risk our own egos in order to keep the search open for better ways of making theater in content and in style a living, radical force." As an organ of propaganda, they refuse to see where Broadway is demonically effective. A Broadway entertainment differs from the SFMT by inculcating passivity rather than action. Its song and dances are about essentially middle-class myths: abundance, moderation, the benevolence of man. Its opulent extravagance of emotion and set, its "stars," all of this reaffirms the lavish ethic of Success. The appeal is overwhelming; and even in a mediocre production, there is a polish which coats the gold cavity of its premise.

The *commedia dell' arte* of the SFMT wanders from seventeenth-century Italy to modern America and raises important questions about fact and propaganda. El Teatro, with its actor-farmers and clear images of exploitations, appeals not merely as a group diversion, but as a chronicle of a real situation. Conducive propaganda is based not on falsehood, but fact. Brecht's epic theater provided a spectacle of human history to be viewed like a scientific hypothesis. "The essential point of the epic theater," wrote Brecht, "is perhaps that it appeals less to the feelings than to the spectator's reason." Brecht wanted to provoke social change by the logic of his historical arguments:

> The dramatic theater's spectator says: Yes, I have felt like that, too. Just like me—it's only natural—it'll never change—the sufferings of this man appall me, because they are inescapable—that's great art; it all seems the most obvious thing in the world—I weep when they weep, I laugh when they laugh.
>
> The epic theater's spectator says: I'd never have thought it . . . That's not the way . . . That's extraordinary, hardly believable . . . It's got to stop . . . The sufferings of this man appall me, because they are unnecessary . . . That's great art; nothing obvious in it . . . I laugh when they weep, I weep when they laugh.[5]

If propaganda is to shape history it must convince its audience of the certainty of its argument. This takes as impressive a technique as Broadway's veneer. The jagged performances of the grape-pickers need only the justness of their cause. But for a general call to revolution, there must be more than bravado. The SFMT's ad-libbing lacks the concrete situation to provide that impetus.

The *commedia dell' arte,* like American burlesque, was a benevolent entertainment with its eye more on the box office than the heads of state. In the SFMT's adaptation of Goldoni's *L'Amant Militaire,* Pantalone, the Jewish Mayor of Spinachola, is at loggerheads with Garcia, General of the Spanish Armies occupying Italian territory. The parallel to the contemporary scene would be obvious to a hermit. The troupe mistakes fun for facts. "I got a lot in dis vor," says the Jewish Mayor, like a Venetian Buddy Hackett, "I got 51 percent of dis vor. You expose me to recession, depression." The jokes unwind with gratuitous good humor. "As Barnum and Bailey said to General Hershey—there's a sucker born every minute." The SFMT wants action but it rarely allows involvement; when it does, the emotional effect is obvious. The players ask the audience to chant: HELL NO, WE WON'T GO. An actress with pompoms leads the crowd with the joyless smile of a UCLA coed.

Their play rambles between these oases of laughter. Using *commedia dell' arte* masks, their argument seems less emotional, but also more debatable. The last scene is an apocalyptic vision in which the Pope (a girl) looks down on the crowd from the makeshift set ("Like to kiss my ring?"). She hands out her Rx for revolution. "You're empty and your country is empty . . . There will be a guaranteed wage and just a pinch of sabotage and a little bit of revolution." "Fatty Profits" will be dissolved. When an actor balks, the Pope, gazing toward the spheres, yells, "Get 'em, cherubims."

At its funniest, the troupe is destructive to its intention.

There is a thrill to their energy which dwindles like a
magician who cannot produce the rabbit. "My friends,"
says one of the actors at the finale, "do you want something done? Then do it." The performers' confidence
comes from preaching to the converted. An actor runs out
into the audience yelling: "All Bobby Kennedy Democrats
get the hell out of here." No one moves from his seat.
Although the troupe points out that they play in parks and
streets where audiences are less selective, their language
rarely recognizes the *lumpenproletariat*. In the SFMT adaptation of Lope de Rueda's *Los Olivos,* an actor explains:
"If you can't manipulate the dialectic, if you don't know
your place in history—you're lost." Ultimately, the product
of their manifesto seems barren of imposing radical force.
"It's our society and it's our job to change it; and if we
can't change it, then it's our job to destroy it." For the be-
lievers there is no doubt; but for the novitiates in revolution
that leap of faith is a much larger moral hurdle which their
plays never consider. Without a focus for their propaganda,
the troupe become cheerleaders rather than catalysts for
social change.

The SFMT suffers from incipient amateurishness and
naiveté about propaganda. The same question of professionalism faces Schechner's do-it-yourself public events
which produced one day of Guerrilla Theater around New
York. Brecht writes: "In the arts, if nowhere else, the principle that 'if it doesn't do much good at least it can't do
any harm' is quite mistaken. Good art stimulates sensitive
art. Bad art damages it. It doesn't leave it untouched."[6] Bad
propaganda numbs the mind as well; and leaves its audience
insensitive to it.

Schechner's Guerrilla Theater places the responsibility
for action in the hands of amateurs, making radical propaganda more frolic than ferment. His attitude is to antago-

nize rather than reform. A description of a "model event," *The Village*, indicates his vision:

> When the audience is involved and enjoying it, bring from a distance the sound of approaching planes. Four actors enter from each of the corridors, dressed as airplanes, and they bomb the village. Show pictures of napalm and other kinds of bombs. Lots of noise. The actors stomp the village to splinters, rip the puppets apart, throw red paint on everyone. Then the actors and technicians leave.
>
> The audience is alone in the wreckage. Thinking their thoughts.[7]

Propaganda is not a moral spanking, but an attempt to control public opinion. Schechner wants to bludgeon the audience rather than create an environment for consideration and in "Guerrilla Warfare," he transfers the elusive Maoist tactic to a city protest. He wants to move from the theater into the street to create a public disturbance.

> Get six performing groups. Two will always be in reserve. Decide on an appropriate day for action. Do not do any advance publicity except for mimeographed sheets announcing the time and places of the first set of events.[8]

When Schechner's first guerrilla event took place, one of the actresses recalled: "We waited at the Actor's Playhouse for the *New York Times* man to arrive." A surprise attack is never as good as publicity! Schechner, like a good scoutmaster, includes every possibility in his manual for revolution: "All of the group may be arrested. If that happens, the event is over."

What happens when the fever chart of the society goes down? The protest of the thirties lost its momentum to World War II. The current radical theaters have forgotten that propaganda is guilty of committing the same crimes it castigates in the Establishment. Provocations without focus and such obvious contradictions in content must ultimately flounder. Propaganda is only effective for short durations and if its goals are not achieved swiftly, enthusiasm gives way to discouragement and despair.

What will happen to the audience cheering the SFMT and following the Guerrilla Theater through New York in a few years' time? Already El Teatro has left its AFL-CIO affiliation and changed its name to El Centro Campesino Cultural. The rigid discipline of communal life and the uniformity of approach are conspicuously missing in the various radical theaters. The Theater Collective, the Theater of Action, and a handful of other entrenched reformers in the thirties are now musty footnotes. Revolution needs more than images of action, but the American ideologues have not found a theatrical way to incite their society. There is the stomach for revolution, but not the talent. The radical voices taking the stage may be necessary, but they are already hoarse from screaming into a high wind.

15

In Search of
a New Mythology

It may in truth be said, that in no part of the world are the people happier . . . or more independent than the farmers of New England.
—Encyclopedia Britannica, 1797

We do not know how to celebrate because we don't know what to celebrate.
—Peter Brook,
The Empty Space[1]

*A*merica has lost its dream of dynamic youthfulness which nurtured two radical poetic images of itself as a bountiful Eden and a Wilderness to be tamed by action. Technology has eliminated Nature from the urban landscape and reshaped our mythologies. The farmer, once the social ideal, has been forgotten as the frontiers of land

257

give way to those of outer space. The heroes of the past are now fossils of history, deadwood from human battles with a stubborn, virgin America (cowboys, pathfinders, adventurers) or laughable exemplars of an embryonic capitalism (Horatio Alger, etc.). These symbols once charged with meaning are now dormant from misuse. The myths which held the daydreams of a nation are now ossified. Contemporary heroes are either warped by overexposure or assassinated. The national imagination is riveted now on spacemen, crew-cut sons of technology. Their aim is ultimately to claim the moon in the name of a stagnant dream grown inflexible with old age on earth.

What has become of America's destiny? Nothing in the nation—except, perhaps, Chicago or a Wallace rally or a riot—gives us back a sense of what we have become. Chaos spins the country out of control; no faith, no man in power seems able to bring order. The theater, so intimately related to the public imagination, is at a loss for pertinent words and proper images. The old axioms of living are barren; the future is too capricious to guess. How can you play at a world whose disorder is so colossal? As R. D. Laing has maintained:

> We live in a secular world. To adapt to this world, the child abdicates ecstasy . . . Having lost our experience of the spirit, we are expected to have faith. But this faith comes to be a belief in a reality which is not evident. There is a prophecy in Amos that a time will come when there will be a famine in the land, "not a famine for bread, nor a thirst for water, but of *hearing* the words of the Lord." That time has come to pass. It is the present age.[2]

The imaginative search for a new universe and new gods to inhabit it has already begun. In previous decades American drama focused its attention on psychological man (Williams, Inge, Miller), sociological man (Odets, Steinbeck, Kingsley), economic man (Broadway musical comedy). American theater is now turning toward the void—a gesture at once potentially liberating and fearful. There is urgency in the new work, the penchant to grab at any idea as mortar for the construction. There are also many misguided attempts to mold synthetic demigods. But through all of it, American mythology is being reassessed in a struggle to find a destiny worth living and symbols from which to take strength, if not hope.

I

The Living Theater: The Return to Eden

The Living Theater's voyage in *Paradise Now*—a four-hour depiction of man's search for regeneration and psychic unity—is intended to redeem the actors and the audience from the barrenness of modern life. It is the theatrical equivalent of other literary quests—Thoreau's *Walden*, Melville's *Moby Dick*, Twain's *Huckleberry Finn*. The cries of the actors who move out into the audience, their tactic for a successful revolution, is, at its roots, a demand for the nostalgic dream of Eden which has been lost in America.

> We will stop using money.
> We will do only useful work.
> We will plan ways ahead of time to bring apples
> to the city, and you will go to the public
> storehouse and take what you need.
> No money, no barter, no more bullshit.
> And if you don't work you don't have to . . .[3]

Society must return to Eden's benevolence and freedom —a world guiltless and free of barriers. This is a pastoral ideal, once vivid in the American imagination when the land offered a fecundity and freedom that the chaotic, cluttered European continent could not. The pastoral, which reflects a nostalgic yearning for peace and innocence, became especially important before and after the French Revolution, and now is emerging again. At a time when history seems spiraling out of control, when injustice is not met with immediate action, Eden becomes the most seductive and resonant of goals, a state worth fighting for. Eden is safe and lavish. The gifts of Nature are easily bestowed. The energy of the living and the energy of Nature are benevolently balanced, not frustrated. Eden denies "calculated human effort, the trained intellect, and the idea of civilization itself," Leo Marx points out in *The Machine in the Garden*.[4] This mystical primordial state answers to the fear of the destructive intellect and eliminates the idea of history. In a nation now separated from its innocence and wonder, Eden is the continual rebirth, an eternity of beginning, but not decline.

Julian Beck chants his prolegomenon for change in *Paradise Now:* "Freedom to create, to learn for the love of it, to free the energy wasted in financial transaction, to value life and make it irresistible, to seek what we desire. To get to know God in his magnet." In the Living Theater's Eden, technology is banished, life returns to a primordial balance, an America which the first Pilgrims might have envisioned before they met the wilderness. The Living Theater's dream for modern America is Crevecoeur's vision of a pre-Revolutionary America: "no aristocratical families, no courts, no kings, no bishops . . . no great manufacturers employing thousands."

If anarchy is the Living Theater's message, which it literally spells out, the rejection of emotional and social boundaries is not far from the Leatherstocking tales, the

anarchic impulses associated with Daniel Boone as well as
Dany Cohn-Bendit. The troupe moves through the aisles,
the men in loincloths, the women in brief bikinis. They are
symbolic Indians in their pristineness, metaphors of the
new, radical Adam and Eve. Muscular, vulnerable, erotic
—they demand the rights of the bower—a panoply of
sensual and imaginative delight. This vision seemed assured
when Robert Beverly wrote his *History and Present State
of Virginia* (1705). Its description of Indians parallels the
very purity the Living Theater demands when it rails against
the shackles of an industrial state: "I am not allowed to
travel without a passport." "You can't live if you don't
have money." "I am not allowed to take my clothes off."
Beverly had written about the Indians:

> They were not debauched nor corrupted with
> those Pomps and Vanities, which had depraved
> and enslaved the Rest of Mankind; neither were
> their Hands harden'd by Labour, nor their Minds
> corrupted by the Desire of hoarding up Treasure:
> They were without Boundaries to their Land; and
> without Property in Cattle; and seem'd to have
> escaped, or rather not to have been concern'd
> in the first Curse, Of getting their bread by the
> Sweat of their brows. For, by their Pleasure
> alone, they supplied all their Necessities; namely,
> by Fishing, Fowling and Hunting; Skins being
> their only Clothing; and these, too, Five Sixths
> of the Year thrown by: Living without Labour,
> and only gathering the Fruits of the Earth when
> ripe, or fit for use. Neither fearing present Want,
> nor solicitous for the Future, but daily finding
> sufficient afresh for their subsistence.[5]

The Living Theater wants to help bring about the I-Thou
relationship between man and man, aspiring to the unity

which produced Eve from Adam's rib. The actors act out a
return of the mind to the body. The sense must live again,
regenerated by a return to Eden: "We want to feed and to
fuck everyone." The troupe talks about it, moving down
the aisle mumbling, "Holy hand, holy eye, holy hair." This
is the Marxian "humanized nature" in which the "senses
capable of human gratifications, senses confirming themselves as essential powers to man . . . are brought into
being."[5] They try to show this state, creating love-zaps
which soothe hostility with embrace, a group-grope in which
performers and disciples spin together in a bond of touch
and finally collapse in a flesh pile. At another time, they
chant a chorus cribbed from the last lines of R. D. Laing's
Politics of Experience:

> If I could turn you on
> If I could drive you out of your wretched mind
> If I could tell you I would let you know . . .[6]

The Word is locked within their mystical experience.
The Living Theater's tactic is to surround its audience,
creating a carnival of anarchy, so seductive a spectacle that
it smashes middle-class decorum and wins adherents to
the newest (and oldest) of faiths. The theater is nonviolent,
its vision intended to be an evocation of love. Yet, in a
hostile world, challenged by conflicting emotions, things
can get confused and Eden momentarily lost. "Who'll give
me money for Molotov cocktails?" yells an actor to the
audience milling around the theater. Another actor walks
on the tops of the seats to the back of the auditorium. He
steps on a patron's back. The man grabs the actor, pum-
meling him to the ground while his wife screams, "For
God's sake, don't dramatize this." The boy cannot calm

him with love. He keeps yelling: "I love you. I'm sick to death. I'm scared." The moment is thrilling and horrific, the barrenness of the nation's moral geography suddenly and convincingly apparent. The performers try to use this rage, asking the spectator why he would hit another man. The spectator answers in the name of anarchy.

Other moments are harder to handle, illustrating the sad distance between a primordial Eden and sullied mortality. An actress is stopped by a member of the audience; he reaches for her bikini and pulls it to her knees. Exposed, she waits for him to let go, her eyes needles of betrayal, her flesh lusterless. She is not ashamed of nudity, but in her defiant righteousness there is no innocence. "And they were both naked, the man and his wife, and were not ashamed." On the night of their final New York perform- ance, one of the cast was screwed on stage—random, violent, impetuous. More uncontrolled, in fact, than the Utopian dream at the base of the Becks' revolution.

Whatever the appeal of Eden, nothing remains on the American terrain to remind us of it. Even the Living Theater can return to the body and to their revolution only through an elaborate and intellectual series of rationaliza- tions. Their philosophy and their mass of anarchy is com- posed from an eclectic liturgy of Zen, Norman O. Brown, Carl Jung, R. D. Laing, Che Guevara, Herbert Marcuse, and many others. Yet, even Julian Beck tries to maintain the illusion of a spontaneous will at work. "We're not inter- ested in intellectual process because it cuts off feeling. Anyone can verbalize and agree with war." But the Living Theater's eclecticism diminishes its force as theater and attests to the distressed confusion of its search. Looking back to a mythology of Eden with no directives except to "Change Now!" the troupe looks forward to a revolution of anarchy without the ability to control the neophytes in active protest. It incites the audience to a frenzy in the auditorium, only to abandon them when the event leads into the street. This is a call to a formless revolution made with a strong sense of theatrical form. It is a demand for humanity, made in auditoriums so large that nothing human —except the most literal emotion—is possible. The empathy which goes out to the performers' private moral concern is lost to the mass of camp followers, and girls in Gucci shoes who laugh and shout, "Burn money, burn money."

The Living Theater's *Paradise Now* is a morality happening which turns into a carnival of impossibility. America holds no avenues open for a new Eden, as if the discoverers' prophecy of the riches of India had finally come to pass and lavishness of well-being had overshadowed richness of spirit. The revolution did not come that night or the night after, although one actor kept insisting that the revolution was here. "We'll get it over by Monday morning." The conversions shook the minds of some spectators, but the monotone shrillness numbed most to the intensity of feeling. In America in 1968 there is no place to hide from the technological society.

Technology, the appendages of capitalism, the law, now organize an entire continent. If they are repressive, they cannot be shouted down; if they impede living, they cannot be wished away. The theatrical event, intended to go into the streets after the audience had been readied for revolution, stopped at the front door of the New York theater because of previous legal hassles.

Like Icarus, the Living Theater wants to fly toward the sun, the primal source of energy; the plan is bold, their equipment limited. What evolves is a gorgeous and horrendous masturbation, a wet dream in a cold universe.

II
The Great White Hope:
Making it by Faking it

If the Living Theater acknowledges America's chaos and urges a return to simplicity through action, *The Great White Hope* offers its audience the spectacle of a story aspiring to be a popular daydream. Here the search for a coherent present is not the creation of a new community (like the Living Theater), but of a new symbol. The nation longs for an epic hero, a man of towering strength like Bunyan, or of native cunning like Crockett, a figure who can purify our dreams and answer our frustrations. For the liberal conscience in 1968, that hero must be black. In *The Great White Hope,* when James Earl Jones strides onto the stage as Jack Johnson, the first black heavyweight champion of the world, it seems as though America's gargantuan appetite for power and victory has found its physical correlative. Jones is a colossal man: stark, monumental, his body glistening in a voluptuous sweat. His strength has a center of confidence, a dignity beyond the controlled power with which he lacerates a punching bag. The role is tailored to the mythic proportions to which *The Great White Hope* aspires; yet, the final irony of performance is that the character outdistances the play, drawing on a reservoir of anger and joy, resilience and despair, which go beyond the script's moralizing possibilities. The play, which has the sweep of an epic, has an intellectual softness which betrays the deadness of its literary symbol. Where it is illuminating is not in its banal discussions of race relations, but what the play shows us of the imagination of its author, Howard Sackler, obsessed by a black god, but unable to inhabit him.

Johnson, who is renamed Jack Jefferson for the play,
shares much in common with earlier folk heroes. He is not
a preposterous fiction, but a superman—both a physical
and emotional extension of commonplace facts. Like Mike
Fink or Daniel Boone, and more pointedly like Cassius
Clay, Jack Jefferson is both hero and clown—a man capable
of guilt and goodness, of serious conviction and cutting up.
His gentleness underscores the dream of strength and dominance over Nature and authority, which will shape his life
and haunt him. Jefferson quips to reporters who pester him
to pick the KO round:

> If I lets it go too long in there, just sorta block-
> ing, and keepin him offa me, then evvybody say,
> "now ain't that one shif'less nigger, why they
> always so lazy?" And if I chop him down quick
> third or fourth roun, all at once then they holler,
> "no, tain't fair, that poor man up there fightin a
> gorrilla!" *But I gonna work it out.*[7]

Jefferson wants to be a world champion on his own
terms. He wants to live well; he wants to love well. The
woman he wants is white; and for that love society frames
him and forces him to leave the country. He is a boxer, not
a politician; his dignity and his purpose come from his
work. The white man's anger at Jefferson is not merely the
flaunting of color taboos, but worse, the apparent theft of
one of his most treasured myths. Jefferson steals the title
like Jason the fleece. White must pervade symbolically in
strength, in domination; and, as in real boxing history, if
not white then a Negro, but never a black. The society can
tolerate a Joe Louis who fits into the white mold, but not a
Cassius Clay, who took boxing mythology and its con-
notations in the white world and turned it back on that

society with a vengeance.

Cassius Clay is, in a sense, the real counterpart to the fiction of Jack Jefferson, sharing his defiance of injustice with a new political conviction. Still the strongest, still the most outrageous, even when stripped of his symbolic title, he showed the world not the power of America but its weakness. He demonstrated its hypocrisy instead of its imperial hope. And like Jefferson's stoic endurance, Clay's silence left the actual mythology of boxing cracked, the people seething and confused.

In *The Great White Hope,* the man Jefferson beats for the title is a white farmer, the last hurrah for the agrarian ideal. Subsequently, Jefferson is hounded by the law, framed on the Mann Act, and forced to live in exile with his white mistress. He moves from country to country seeking fights but finding the matches and the public interest paltry. The pattern of exile as well as harassment is familiar in America; the talent gradually became flaccid, the energy and sparkle snuffed out. In the play, Jefferson, broke and stripped of the last vestiges of happiness, is forced into a title fight in Havana with the understanding that if he loses, he can return to the country and his sentence will be lifted. The final scene in the play is the strongest; the author allows a stage image to draw its own conclusion. Jefferson loses; we see him coming out of the stadium. He can hardly talk. He is completely defeated, and he knows it. When the White Hope enters, carried in a victory parade on white shoulders like a religious Madonna, his face is crusted in blood, every inch of skin now raw flesh. The Black Man has been defeated, but the price for the White Man is almost total destruction.

Sackler has reworked history, simplifying the race question to make his hero more pristine. In the play, Jefferson is hounded by a viperous and black common-law wife. Her evil nature makes his love seem purer and casts him in an emotional martyrdom which will finally ascend to a political one. In the same way, Sackler simplifies Johnson's character to fit the role of his heroic Jefferson. In fact, Johnson was as cagey as he was affable. For two years after he won the championship, no one could be found to fight him. He refused to fight black opponents like Joe Jeanette and Sam Langford, the "Boston Tar Baby," who had given him difficult fights, preferring white meat which was easier and drew bigger purses. Johnson inaugurated the era of the Big Gate, but Sackler avoids the complexity of this issue, settling for the sainthood of a scapegoat.

While the play is never boring, it rarely taps the wonder and sheer humor of boxing. Sackler, so eager to beat the chest of his liberalism, forgets the man he created. Everything is on the surface except James Earl Jones' anger. Sackler loses his claim to folklore when he forgets the story for a morality tableau, compelled by his own guilt to keep talking to save his soul. There are some embarrassing moments of pathos: Jefferson, his trainer, and mistress are forced to perform *Uncle Tom's Cabin* in a cabaret; Jefferson's mistress throws herself down a well, only to be carried back on stage like a sodden Ophelia. Sackler's language betrays a visceral disgust which is not lived but only imagined. He forces his characters to look out at the audience with poetic hostility (quite a contrast to the Living Theater's Rufus Collins who keeps taunting—"Rage, rage against me you white motherfuckers; rage against me, baby!"):

> I know what most of you sitting there believe in,
> or think you believe in, or try to believe in. But
> I know something else too, and so does every one
> of you, something outlasting all the issues and

> the mottoes and the tears and upheavals: what
> black means, yes, what it is to you truthfully . . .
> how it lives in the words you learn to think with,
> the dark and the fright of it, pitch black, black
> as dirt, the black hole and the black pit . . .

For Broadway dowagers, this has the shock of truth. Mr.
Sackler's script, which moves so smoothly from point to
point and covers such interesting ground, is just bright
enough to make audiences feel they are getting an intellectual experience while leaving their prejudices comfort-
ably intact (after all, Jefferson does lose!). Without James
Earl Jones' performance, the dimension and stature of the
play would dwindle to melodrama.

Sackler's play is Broadway's answer to the dime novel.
He joins a long line of popularizers who have felt the pulse
of a national longing and provided monuments for their
own profit. Bunyan was a northwestern figure created to
sell lumber; Buffalo Bill was fact turned into lucrative
fiction. Despite Sackler's political liberalism, his own lib-
erality of spirit (he is a millionnaire) never extended to the
Washington Arena Stage where *The Great White Hope* was
first mounted. He has made the race question palatable for
Broadway's middle-class white population (if not the blacks
for whom Broadway ticket prices are prohibitive). Despite
a half-million-dollar movie sale, a lucrative publishing contract, Sackler has not donated one cent to the regional
theater where the play began and which needs financial
support.

Jack Jefferson (as well as his real-life counterpart) won
the heavyweight title on Independence Day, 1910—a time
usually set aside for defining the national purpose and
shaking out dusty national symbols. What angered people
then was that the black man could dominate that festival

of patriotism. ("What the hell is this country, Ethiopia?")
Jack Jefferson was a pertinent barometer of change. The
hero must now be black in order for the white liberal to
feel part of America. And more important, where once the
country overlooked the Negro on the way to an alabaster
and manifest destiny, now it is the black race whose defeat
or victory holds with it the moral destiny of the land.

Sackler refashions a story whose roots and dialect are
too far from his experience. His fiction does not spring
from that well of mystical national intuition which makes
for myth. It becomes a disguise of importance, longing for
a redemptive strength.

III

Indians: Myth and Madness

Where the Living Theater forges a new mythology, trying to become its own hero, and Howard Sackler hol-
lows out a black Hercules, Arthur Kopit's *Indians* plumbs
deeper into the American character, intrigued by the
process of mythology and its seductive failure. Buffalo Bill,
the self-styled frontier hero, is the focus of Kopit's brilliant
theater piece which weaves the drama of Indian coloniali-
zation into the spectacle and reverie of a Wild West show.
The play is Buffalo Bill's dream, a search for the glories of
the past, an attempt to solve the riddle of a vanished destiny.
Buffalo Bill's neurotic obsessions, his elaborate evasions
of himself not only have a historic curiosity but a prophetic
one. The winning of the West was our first Vietnam, an
attempt to reclaim the Virgin Land by eliminating any
vestige of hostile forces.

In choosing the West in the late 1800's, Kopit centers
on a moment when the nation looked beyond the hardship
of the plains toward history. Buffalo Bill wants to be a

hero; like Wild Bill Hickok and many others, he dressed himself for his new role. In the play, Buffalo Bill speaks with a special self-consciousness:

> Well. My dream . . . is to help people. (*He laughs embarrassed; General Custer smiles warmly.*) I mean great numbers of them. The nation. Everyone in the nation. And . . . whatever it is I do to help, for it they will name towns after me. Counties. States. I will be as famous as . . . Dan'l Boone. An' somewhere, on top of a beautiful mountain that overlooks more plains an' rivers than any other mountain, there'll be a statue of me sittin' on a great white horse. An' I'll be wavin' my hat to everyone below. Thankin' 'em for thankin' me, for havin' done whatever it is I'm gonna do for 'em all.[8]

In this speech is the voice of Hubert Humphrey as well as the national diplomacy. It speaks of a dumb kindness longing for a Christian divinity, confusing purpose with pride. Like LBJ and "his war," Buffalo Bill considers himself the savior and spokesman of the Indians. He is driven by fears that he may also be their greatest betrayer, freeing them from prison only to perform in his circus, turning the glory of their race into humiliation. Buffalo Bill's myopia is matched by his obsession with historical greatness. He does not employ historians, but pulp fiction writers; he does not have a scientific marketing approach, like Nixon, to his physical image, but a salesman's studied nonchalance. Standing tall in his beaded buckskin, Buffalo Bill is that tottering symbol of the frontiersman, a pathfinder with no more trails to follow. When Buffalo Bill reminisces, he defines the boundaries of his dream: "My life is an open book. I am not ashamed of its bein' looked at . . . I'm sorry; this is rather hard fer me t'say. But, I believe I am a hero! A GODDAM HERO!" In the process of forcing himself into myth, Buffalo Bill (like Sackler and the Living Theater) loses the pristine wonder and innocence which gave the image of America as a Garden of Eden its gorgeous appeal. Our society has lost the pulse of its new world; experience is no longer an ingredient of fame. Suddenly conscious of history as an ambition, we bypass experience on the way to a synthetic eternity. Buffalo Bill's dreams and other new mythologies are shells of the first encounter with America which F. Scott Fitzgerald epitomized in *The Great Gatsby:*

> And as the moon rose higher . . . I became aware of the old island here that flowered once for Dutch sailors' eyes—a fresh, green breast of the new world. Its vanished trees that had made way for Gatsby's house had once pandered in whispers to the last and greatest of all human dreams; for a transitory enchanted moment man must have held his breath in the presence of this continent, compelled into an esthetic contemplation he neither understood nor desired, face to face for the last time in history with something commensurate to his capacity for wonder.[9]

In Kopit's *Indians,* the myth finally rapes America. Barrenness is mistaken for purity; silence becomes an active assent. The claim of innocence exists alongside annihilation and the call for heroism outshouts the social malaise. The American, given the gift of a new life in a new land, is compelled to prove himself not only master of the elements but of its destiny. Kopit, with terrifying documentation, pinpoints the stalemate of clashing territorial imperatives. An

Indian is brought under Senate investigation; Eden is being bargained for:

SENATOR LOGAN: In other words, you thought you could have both cows and the land?

JOHN GRASS: Yes.

SENATOR MORGAN: Even though it was explained that you couldn't?

JOHN GRASS: Yes.

SENATOR DAWES: This is quite hard to follow.

SENATOR LOGAN: Mister Grass, tell me, which would you prefer, cows or land?

JOHN GRASS: We prefer them both.

Buffalo Bill becomes paranoid, confused between the mythical idea of a hero and a mortal replica. In the abstract the hero has always represented the desire for total control of his universe (King Arthur, Paul Bunyan). But when man actually seeks to be a myth, like LBJ, he becomes a force of separation, straddling good and evil, peace and destruction, without the immortality of the gods. In this position, he is compromised, creating confusion by the inhumanity of his false stature.

Kopit's play takes us back to history and not, like the Living Theater, away from it. The Living Theater offers an image of the Indians, a vision of their death and resurrection, which moves from chiseled Indian totem poles to prostrated performers who shout, "Don't step on the Indians." Their symbolic resurrection comes when the cast moves out into aisles in a war chant. The image is loose and literal, neither informing the mind nor impelling the heart. On the other hand, Kopit can use a carefully placed fact as a bludgeon, raising questions deeper than rational concern. When Sitting Bull is Gatling-gunned to death by the military, Buffalo Bill describes "the wonderful grey horse I'd given him for appearing in my Wild West show danced his repertory of tricks in the background, since a gunshot was his cue to perform . . . They also killed the rest of his tribe."

Kopit's play makes the most genuinely American comment on society in this decade. If Buffalo Bill's schizophrenia is chronicled primarily in a mock-heroic vein, parody is a negative energy, and the national myths it skewers are no longer worthy of straightforward seriousness. The play challenges the alluring shibboleths of law and order and the violent inhumanity of the terms; it dramatizes the spectacle of man becoming myth, something advertising has made more feasible in our day. It is also the spectacle of a gaudy deflation of a national soul, a circus with nothing to hold the center ring. This is perhaps America's fate. Kopit has used a resource which few other American playwrights have tapped—the imaginative energy still posited in our frontier myths. "We don't know how to celebrate because we don't know what to celebrate." *Indians* is a genuine celebration, the beginning of a new inquiry. Only by acknowledging the emotional ambiguity of the past, can the nation (as well as the theater) build a vital mythology for a difficult future. We have lost Eden, but there is still a world, waiting.

NOTES

References for plays quoted by the author are given only when the plays have been published. Only the first reference to the specific play in the essay is identified in the *Notes*.

1

The Theater's Voluptuary Itch

1. Nora Sayre in *The New Statesman*, April 5, 1968.

2. William Graham Cole, *Sex in Christianity and Psychoanalysis* (New York: Oxford University Press—A Galaxy Book, 1966), p. 12.

3. Florenz Ziegfeld quoted in Marjorie Farnsworth, *Ziegfeld Follies* (New York: Bonanza Books, 1956), p. 81.

4. Norman O. Brown, *Life Against Death: The Psychoanalytical Meaning of History* (New York: Vintage Books, 1959), p. 321.

5. Robert Anderson, *You Know I Can't Hear You When The Water's Running* (New York: Random House, 1968).

6. Lenny Bruce, *How To Talk Dirty and Influence People* (Chicago: Playboy Press, 1965, and New York: Pocket Books, 1967), p. 159.

7. Norman O. Brown, *op. cit.,* p. 63.

8. Leonard Melfi's play *Jack and Jill* was incorporated into *Oh! Calcutta!* (New York: Grove Press, 1969).

9. Norman O. Brown, *op. cit.,* p. 65.

10. Harold Pinter, *The Homecoming* (New York: Grove Press, 1965).

11. Michael McClure in *The Westside News* [New York City regional newspaper], November 9, 1967.

12. Richard Schechner, *Public Domain* (New York: The Bobbs-Merrill Co., 1969), p. 228.

13. Albert Camus, *The Rebel,* trans. Anthony Bower (New York: Vintage Books, 1954), p. 271.

14. William C. Schutz, *Joy* (New York: Grove Press, 1967).

15. Albert Camus, *op. cit.,* p. 272.

2

The Adaptable
Mr. Albee

1. Edward Albee, "Creativity and Commitment," *Saturday Review,* June 4, 1966.

2. Edward Albee in *The New York Times,* January 6, 1966.

3. Edward Albee, *The Ballad of the Sad Café* (New York: Atheneum Publishers, 1963).

4. Edward Albee, *The New York Times. op. cit.*

5. Edward Albee, Paris Review Interviews, *Writers at Work* (New York: Viking Press, 1967).

6. James Purdy, *Malcolm* (New York: Avon Books, 1959), p. 10.

7. Edward Albee, *Malcolm* (New York: Atheneum Publishers, 1966).

8. Edward Albee, *Saturday Review, op. cit.*

9. Edward Albee, *The New York Times, op. cit.*

10. Giles Cooper, *Everything in the Garden,* New English Dramatists F. (London: Penguin Books, 1963).

11. Edward Albee, *Everything in the Garden* (New York: Atheneum Publishers, 1968).

12. Edward Albee, *Saturday Review, op. cit.*

3

The Street Scene:
Playing for Keeps

1. All of Enrique Vargas's quotes are from conversations with the author.

2. All of Joseph Papp's quotes are from conversations with the author.

3. Denis Diderot, *Deuxième entretien sur le Fils naturel,* quoted in Romain Rolland, *The People's Theatre*, trans. Barrett H. Clark, in *The Theory of the Modern Stage*, ed. Eric Bentley (London: Penguin Books, 1968), p. 460.

4. Joe Walsh in conversation with the author.

5. Albert Camus, *Carnets 1935-1942* (London: Hamish Hamilton, 1963), p. 119.

4

The Language
of Silence

[Author's Note: This essay was provoked by Susan Sontag's reflections on silence.]

1. *The New York Times,* December 25, 1968.

2. Norman O. Brown, *Love's Body* (New York: Vintage Books, 1968), p. 257.

3. *Ibid.*, pp. 258-9.

4. Susan Sontag, *Styles of Radical Will* (New York: Farrar, Straus & Giroux, 1969), p. 21.

5. Karl Jaspers quoted in Susan Sontag, *op. cit.*, p. 19.

6. *Ibid.*, p. 23.

7. Franz Kafka, "The Hunger Artist" in Franz Kafka, *The Penal Colony: Stories and Short Pieces* (New York: Schocken Books, 1967), pp. 255-6.

8. Harold Pinter quoted in John Russell Taylor, "Accident," *Sight and Sound*, Autumn 1966.

9. George Steiner, *Language and Silence* (New York: Atheneum Publishers, 1967), p. 22.

10. Don Judd in *Minimal Art: A Critical Anthology*, ed. Gregory Battcock (New York: E. P. Dutton & Co., 1968), pp. 142-43.

11. Hugh Kenner, *The Stoic Comedians* (London: W. H. Allen, 1964), p. xv.

12. *Loc. cit.*

13. Kevin Brownlow, *The Parade's Gone By* (New York: Alfred A. Knopf, Inc., 1968), p. 338.

14. *Loc. cit.*

15. *Op. cit.*, p. 466.

16. Samuel Beckett, *Cascando and Other Short Dramatic Pieces* (New York: Grove Press, 1968), p. 75.

17. Antonin Artaud, *The Theater and its Double* (New York: Grove Press, 1958), p. 60.

18. *Ibid.,* pp. 117-8.

19. Aeschylus, *The House of Atreus,* ed. John Lewin (Minneapolis: University of Minnesota Press, 1967).

20. Rochelle Owens, *Futz and What Came After* (New York: Random House, 1968).

21. Susan Sontag, *op. cit.,* p. 19-20.

22. Harold Pinter quoted in Ronald Hayman, *Harold Pinter* (London: Heinemann, 1968), p. 79.

23. John Kershaw interview with Harold Pinter; transcript of television program broadcast by ITV, England.

24. Norman O. Brown, *op. cit.,* p. 257.

25. Gregory Battcock (ed.), *op. cit.,* p. 140.

26. Susan Sontag, *op. cit.*

27. Harold Pinter, *Landscape, Evergreen Review,* No. 68, July 1969.

28. Norman O. Brown, *op. cit.,* p. 257.

29. Samuel Beckett, *Endgame* (New York: Grove Press, 1958).

30. Samuel Beckett, *The Unnamable,* in *Three Novels* (New York: Grove Press—Black Cat Books, 1958).

31. Samuel Beckett, *Molloy,* in *Three Novels* (New York: Grove Press—Black Cat Books, 1958).

32. Samuel Beckett, "Three Dialogues," *Transition,* 1949.

33. Samuel Beckett, *All That Fall,* in *Krapp's Last Tape and Other Dramatic Pieces* (New York: Grove Press, 1960), p. 35.

34. Hugh Kenner, *op. cit.,* pp. 96-7.

35. Harold Hobson quoted in Ihab Hassan, *The Literature of Silence* (New York: Alfred A. Knopf, Inc., 1967), p. 137.

36. Hugh Kenner, *op. cit.,* p. 76.

37. *Ibid.,* p. 113.

38. Arthur Adamov quoted in George Steiner, *op. cit.,* p. 71.

5

Jules Feiffer:
Satire as Subversion

1. Jules Feiffer, "Talking to John Lahr," *Transatlantic Review,* No. 32, Summer 1969. All of Feiffer's quotes in this essay originated from this article.

2. Marc Connelly in conversation with the author.

3. S. J. Perelman, *The Beauty Part* (New York: Simon and Schuster, 1963).

4. Neil Simon, *Barefoot in the Park* (New York: Random House, 1964).

5. Jules Feiffer, *Little Murders* (New York: Random House, 1968).

6. John Guare, *Cop-Out, Muzeeka and Home Fires* (New York: Grove Press, 1970).

7. Jules Feiffer, *Dick and Jane,* in *Oh! Calcutta!* (New York: Grove Press, 1969).

6
The End of
the Underground

1. Lorraine Hansberry, *The Sign in Sidney Brustein's Window* (New York: Random House, 1965).

2. Robert Jay Lifton, "Protean Man," *Yale Alumni Magazine,* Vol. XXXII, No. 4, January 1969.

3. Norman Mailer, *Advertisements for Myself* (New York: Signet Books—New American Library, 1959), p. 305.

4. *Ibid.,* p. 336.

5. Jerry Rubin, "Emergency Letter to My Brothers and Sisters in The Movement," *New York Review of Books,* February 13, 1969.

6. Robert Jay Lifton, *op. cit.*

7. Douglas Cooper, "Establishment and the Avant-Garde," *Times Literary Supplement* [London], September 3, 1964.

8. Norman Mailer, "Who is the Enemy?" *New York Free Press*, January 23, 1969.

9. Jerry Rubin, *op. cit.*

10. Free (Abbie Hoffman), *Revolution for the Hell of It* (New York: Dial Press, 1968), p. 133.

11. *Ibid.*, p. 128.

12. Jerry Rubin, *op. cit.*

13. Michael Smith, ed., *The Best of Off-Off-Broadway* (New York: E. P. Dutton & Co., 1969), p. 18.

14. *The New York Times,* January 27, 1969.

15. Norman Mailer, *Advertisements for Myself, op. cit.,* p. 306.

16. Robert Jay Lifton, *op. cit.*

17. *Ibid.*

18. Herbert Marcuse, *One-Dimensional Man* (Boston: Beacon Press, 1964), p. 61.

19. Jerry Rubin, *op. cit.*

20. Robert Brustein, "The Third Theater Revisited," *The New York Review of Books,* February 13, 1969.

21. Slawomir Mrozek, *Tango* (New York: Grove Press, 1968).

7

The American Musical:
The Slavery of Escape

1. John Dewey, *Freedom and Culture* (New York: G. P. Putnam's Sons, 1939), p. 18.

2. Daniel J. Boorstin, *The Americans: The National Experience* (New York: Random House, 1965), p. 296.

3. "Something's Coming" from *West Side Story*. Copyright © 1957 by Leonard Bernstein and Stephen Sondheim. Used by permission.

4. *Ibid.*

5. John Dewey, *op. cit.,* p. 10.

6. Max Beerbohm quoted in George Jean Nathan, *The World of George Jean Nathan* (New York: Alfred A. Knopf, Inc., 1952), p. 435.

7. "The Man I Love." Copyright © 1924 by New World Music Corp. Reprinted by permission of Warner Bros. Music. All rights reserved.

8. "Harlem Serenade." (G. & I. Gershwin-Gus Kahn) Copyright © 1929 by New World Music Corp. Used by permission of Warner Bros. Music. All rights reserved.

9. "When the Idle Poor Become the Idle Rich." Copyright © 1947 by The Players Music Corporation. Used by permission of Chappell & Co., Inc.

10. "Oh, I Got Plenty of Nuttin'" Copyright 1935 by Gershwin Publishing Corp. Copyright renewed. Used by

permission of Gershwin Publishing Corporation and New Dawn Music Corporation.

11. "You'll Never Walk Alone." Copyright © 1945 by Williamson Music, Inc. Used by permission of T. B. Harms Co.

12. John Dewey, *op. cit.,* pp. 123-4.

13. "Can You Use Any Money Today?" Copyright © 1950, 1952 Irving Berlin. Reprinted by permission of Irving Berlin Music Corporation.

14. "Soliloquy." Copyright © 1945 by Williamson Music, Inc. Used by permission of T. B. Harms Co.

15. George Jean Nathan, *op. cit.,* pp. 436-7.

16. George Gershwin quoted in Robert E. Kimball, *The American Musical Show: The Explosive Years,* 1961, unpublished.

17. "Now's the Time." Copyright © 1967 by Betty Comden, Adolph Green and Jule Styne. Used by permission of Chappell & Co., Inc.

18. "I Want to Hear a Yankee Doodle Tune." Copyright © George M. Cohan Music Publishing Co., Inc. Used by permission.

19. "The Brotherhood of Man." Copyright © 1961, 1962 Frank Loesser. Used by permission.

20. Oscar Hammerstein II quoted in Stanley Green, *The Rodgers and Hammerstein Story* (New York: The John Day Company, 1963), p. 108.

21. Alexis de Tocqueville, *Democracy in America* (New York: Vintage Books, 1954), p. 84.

22. *Ibid.*

23. "But in the Morning No." Copyright © 1939 by Chappell & Co., Inc. Copyright renewed. Used by permission of Chappell & Co., Inc.

8

Arthur Kopit's Indians: Dramatizing National Amnesia

1. All of Arthur Kopit's quotes are from conversations with the author.

2. Robert Dykstra, *The Cattle Towns* (New York: Alfred A. Knopf, Inc., 1968), p. 144.

3. Alexis de Tocqueville, *Democracy in America* (New York: Vintage Books, 1954), p. 354.

4. John A. Hawgood, *America's Western Frontiers* (New York: Alfred A. Knopf, Inc., 1967), p. 308.

5. Arthur Kopit, *Indians* (New York: Hill & Wang, 1969).

6. "Ned Buntline" was the *nom de plume* of the New York journalist Edward C. Judson. "Buntline" made William Cody a folk hero in a serial "Buffalo Bill, King of the Border Men." He also wrote the script for Buffalo Bill's first theatrical venture, *The Scouts of the Prairie.*

7. James Rees, an eighteenth-century critic and dramatist, quoted in Frank Rahill, *The World of Melodrama*

(University Place, Pa.: Pennsylvania State University Press, 1967).

8. Joseph Schumpeter, *Capitalism, Socialism, and Democracy* (New York: Harper Torchbooks, 1962), p. 128.

9. George Catlin quoted in William Goetzmann, *Exploration and Empire* (New York: Alfred A. Knopf, Inc., 1966), p. 188.

10. David Grimstead, *Melodrama Unveiled* (Chicago: University of Chicago Press, 1968), p. 199.

11. Alexis de Tocqueville, *op. cit.*, p. 369.

12. Daniel J. Boorstin, *The Americans: The National Experience* (New York: Random House, 1966), p. 274.

13. John Croswell, *A New World Planted; or The Adventures of the Forefathers Who Landed in Plymouth, December 22nd, 1620* (Boston, 1802).

14. Jean-Jacques Rousseau quoted in David Grimstead, *op. cit.*, p. 219.

15. Quoted in Dixon Wecter, *The Hero in America* (Ann Arbor: Ann Arbor Paperbacks, The University of Michigan Press, 1963), p. 355. Erasmus and Irwin Beadle were the publishers of popular dime novels. The novels, filled with violence and melodrama, were the popular pulp fiction of the day. The stories focussed on folk heroes and heroines like Buffalo Bill, Davy Crockett, and Calamity Jane.

16. Richard Hofstadter quoted in Lewis Chester, Godfrey Hodgson, Bruce Page, *An American Melodrama* (New York: Viking Press, 1969), p. 44.

17. *Ibid.,* p. 192.

18. *Ibid.,* p. 44.

9

The Open Theater's
Serpent

1. Jean-Claude van Itallie, *The Serpent* (New York: Atheneum Publishers, 1969).

2. Albert Camus quoted in Martin Esslin, *The Theatre of the Absurd* (London: Penguin Books, 1968), p. 23.

3. Wallace Stevens, *Collected Poems of Wallace Stevens* (New York: Alfred A. Knopf, 1954).

4. Mircea Eliade, "The Yearning for Paradise in Primitive Tradition," *Myth and Mythmaking,* ed. Henry A. Murray (Boston: Beacon Press, 1968), p. 65.

5. *Ibid.,* p. 68.

6. All of Jean-Claude van Itallie's quotes are from conversations with the author.

7. All of Joseph Chaikin's quotes are from conversations with the author.

8. Joseph Campbell, *The Masks of God* (New York: Viking Press, 1968), p. 671.

9. *Ibid.*

10

Pinter the
Spaceman

1. Alain Robbe-Grillet, *For A New Novel* (New York: Grove Press, 1966), p. 111.

2. E. A. Burt, *The Metaphysical Foundation of Modern Science* (Garden City, N. Y.: Doubleday Anchor Books, 1955), pp. 238-9.

3. Floyd W. Matson, *The Broken Image* (Garden City, N. Y.: Doubleday Anchor Books, 1966), p. 127.

4. Floyd W. Matson, *loc. cit.*

5. Werner Heisenberg quoted in Floyd W. Matson, *op. cit.*, pp. 128-9.

6. Harold Pinter, *The Birthday Party* (New York: Grove Press, 1961).

7. Harold Pinter, *Landscape, Evergreen Review,* No. 68, July 1969.

8. Alain Robbe-Grillet, *Jealousy,* in *Two Novels by Robbe-Grillet: "Jealousy" and "In the Labyrinth"* (New York: Grove Press, 1965).

9. W. H. Ittelson and Hadley Cantril, *Perception* (Garden City, N. Y.: Doubleday & Co., 1954), p. 7.

10. Harold Pinter, *The Homecoming* (New York: Grove Press, 1967).

11. Floyd W. Matson, *loc. cit.*

12. Harold Pinter quoted in Laurence Bensky, "The Art of the Theater 3," *Paris Review,* No. 10, Fall 1966.

13. Alain Robbe-Grillet quoted in Gore Vidal, "French Letters," *Encounter,* December 1967.

14. Nathalie Sarraute quoted in Gore Vidal, *op. cit.*

15. Harold Pinter in a letter to the author (February 12, 1968).

16. Bruce Glaser, "Questions to Stella and Judd," *Art News,* September 1966.

17. *Ibid.*

18. *Don Judd* (New York: Whitney Museum of American Art, n.d.), p. 10.

19. *Time,* March 22, 1968.

20. *Don Judd, op. cit.*

21. *Ibid.*

11

The Language
of Laughter

1. George Steiner, *Language and Silence* (New York: Atheneum Publishers, 1967), p. 123.

2. Joe Smith and Charlie Dale, "The Avon Comedy Four," vaudeville act.

3. Joe Laurie, Jr., *Vaudeville* (New York: Henry Holt and Co., 1953), pp. 448-452.

4. Otto Jespersen, *Language: Its Nature, Development, and Origin* (London: George Allen & Unwin Ltd., 1959), p. 436. Jespersen was one of the most eminent scholars of modern comparative philology, the development of which is due mainly to his research.

5. *Ibid.*, p. 437.

6. Quoted in Walter Jackson Bate, *From Classic to Romantic* (New York: Harper Torchbooks, 1961), p. 39.

7. *The New York Times* pyramid style refers to the standardization of articles in which the first paragraph begins with the essential "who, what, why, where, and when" and pyramids out in further elaborative paragraphs.

8. Vaclav Havel, *The Memorandum* (New York: Grove Press, 1968).

9. Lenny Bruce, *How To Talk Dirty and Influence People* (Chicago: Playboy Press, 1965, and New York: Pocket Books, 1967), p. 1.

10. *Ibid.*

11. *Ibid.*, p. 130.

12. S. J. Perelman, *The Beauty Part* (New York: Simon and Schuster, 1963).

13. Mart Crowley, *The Boys in the Band* (New York: Farrar, Straus & Giroux, 1968).

14. Jean-Claude van Itallie, *America Hurrah* (New York: Coward-McCann, 1966).

15. Jules Feiffer, *Little Murders* (New York: Random House, 1968).

16. John Guare, *Muzeeka* (New York: Grove Press, 1970).

12

The New Theater:
A Retreat from Realism

1. All of Tom O'Horgan's quotes are from conversations with the author.

2. R. D. Laing, *The Politics of Experience* (New York: Pantheon Books, 1967), p. 24.

3. Francis V. Connor, *Jackson Pollock* (New York: The Museum of Modern Art, 1967), p. 80.

4. Dore Ashton, *The Unknown Shore: A View of Contemporary Art* (Boston: Atlantic-Little, Brown & Co., 1962), pp. 91-2.

5. Robert Brustein, *The Third Theater* (New York: Alfred A. Knopf, Inc., 1969), p. 72.

6. Konstantin Stanislavski quoted in Michael Kirby, *Happenings* (New York: E. P. Dutton & Co., 1966), p. 42.

7. Francis V. Connor, *op. cit.*, p. 51.

8. *Ibid.*, p. 79.

9. *Ibid.*, p. 73.

10. *Ibid.*, p. 81.

11. Harold Rosenberg, *The Anxious Object* (New York: Horizon Press, 1964), p. 127.

12. Eugenio Barba, "Theatre Laboratory 13 Rzedow," *Tulane Drama Review*, Spring 1965.

13. Walter Kerr in *The New York Times*, June 16, 1969.

14. Dore Ashton, *op. cit.*, p. 42.

15. *Ibid.*, p. 46.

16. *Ibid.*

17. Jerzy Grotowski quoted in Eugenio Barba, *op. cit.*

18. *Ibid.*

19. *New Statesman*, August 30, 1968.

20. Richard Schechner, "Beyond Nude Dancing," *The New York Times*, July 28, 1968.

21. Francis V. Connor, *op. cit.*, p. 81.

13
John Osborne:
Poor Johnny One-Note

1. John Osborne, *The Entertainer* (London: Faber and Faber, 1957).

2. "John Osborne: Interview with Kenneth Tynan," *The Observer* [London], June 30, 1968 and July 7, 1968.

3. John Osborne, *Inadmissible Evidence* (New York: Grove Press, 1965).

4. John Osborne, *The Hotel in Amsterdam* (London: Faber and Faber, 1968).

5. John Osborne, *Look Back in Anger* (New York: Criterion Books, 1957).

6. "John Osborne: Interview with Kenneth Tynan," *op. cit.*

7. *Ibid.*

8. John Weightman, "Grousers, Male and Female," *Encounter,* September 1968.

9. "John Osborne: Interview With Kenneth Tynan," *op. cit.*

10. *Ibid.*

14
Theater and
Propaganda

1. Mary Martin in *The New York Times*, November 21, 1967.

2. Richard Schechner in *The Village Voice* [New York], September 7, 1969. Schechner and his troupe turned from the crude political tactics of their Guerrilla Theater to the Performance Group, where, six months later, a much more interesting and provoking esthetic experiment began and still continues.

3. Bertolt Brecht quoted in *Brecht on Theater,* ed. and trans. John Willett (New York: Hill and Wang Dramabook, 1964), p. 135.

4. Harold Clurman, *The Fervent Years* (New York: Hill & Wang Dramabook, 1957), p. 96.

5. John Willett, *op. cit.,* p. 71.

6. *Ibid.,* p. 150.

7. Richard Schechner, *Public Domain* (New York: The Bobbs-Merrill Co., 1969), p. 204.

8. *Ibid.,* p. 205.

15

In Search of
a New Mythology

1. Peter Brook, *The Empty Space* (New York: Atheneum Publishers, 1969), p. 47.

2. R. D. Laing, *The Politics of Experience* (New York: Pantheon Books, 1967), p. 101.

3. Excerpts from *Paradise Now* published in *Los Angeles Free Press,* 1968.

4. Leo Marx, *The Machine in the Garden* (New York: Oxford University Press, 1964).

5. Quoted in Leo Marx, *op. cit.*

6. R. D. Laing, *op. cit.*, p. 138.

7. Howard Sackler, *The Great White Hope* (New York: Dial Press, 1969).

8. Arthur Kopit, *Indians* (New York: Hill & Wang, 1969).

9. F. Scott Fitzgerald, *The Great Gatsby* (New York: Charles Scribner's Sons, 1925), p. 218.

INDEX

297